The Fortune
On the Rocks with Angel

Martin Popoff

WP
WYMER
PUBLISHING

Bedford, England

First published in Canada, 2019
Wymer Publishing
Bedford, England www.wymerpublishing.co.uk
Tel: 01234 326691
Wymer Publishing is a trading name of Wymer (UK) Ltd

Copyright © 2022 Martin Popoff / Wymer Publishing.
This edition published 2022.

ISBN: 978-1-915246-05-9

The Author hereby asserts his rights to be identified as the
author of this work in accordance with sections 77 to 78
of the Copyright, Designs & Patents Act 1988.

All rights reserved. No part of this publication may be
reproduced or transmitted in any form or by any means,
electronic or mechanical, including photocopying, or any
information storage and retrieval system, without written
permission from the publisher.

This publication is sold subject to the condition that it shall not, by
way of trade or otherwise, be lent, re-sold, hired out or otherwise
circulated without the publisher's prior consent in any form of
binding or cover other than that in which it is published and
without a similar condition including this condition
being imposed on the subsequent purchaser.

Every effort has been made to trace the copyright holders of the
photographs in this book but some were unreachable. We would be
grateful if the photographers concerned would contact us.

A catalogue record for this book is available from the British Library.

Typesetting and over design by Eduardo Rodriguez.
Cover photos © Richard Galbraith.

Contents

Preface

Welcome back folks. Let me tell you, it's gratifying to finally get a nice, long, fresh new book out, and what can be fresher than a book on those cheeky cherubs in white, Angel?! I'm just going to level with you. I wrote this book entirely in virus times, and it's been hard to get any work done at all, even though I've certainly had the time to do it. It's, I suppose, partially a happy story, namely that I've been selling, signing, packing up and mailing a lot of books lately, having minor hits with the Van Halen and the Mercyful Fate, and then major hits with *Anthem: Rush in the '70s* and *Limelight: Rush in the '80s.*

But part of why this book took so long might have to do with the fact that I might be moving slower in my old age. My window of being alert enough to do the heavy lifting to write a book seems to be closing, currently comprising sort of between eight in the morning and noon. But hey, I also console myself with the fact that as I write this, I've got a book on Sweet that is 80% finished that just got bogged down dealing with the last couple of albums as I turned my attention to Angel. But of course, I'm so close to being done, it would be a shame not to get back to that which, barring death, I will.

Okay, enough boring stuff about process. We're here to celebrate Angel, five studio albums in the '70s, an ignored live record in 1980, and then nothing, until a sort of millennial Angel album with *In the Beginning*, and then the gleaming real deal with *Risen* in 2019.

I actually really enjoyed doing this book because of the impressive re-ascendance that is *Risen*. As well, the guys are just too much of a gosh-darn pleasure to talk to. To be sure, there are some interviews I conducted in this book with people who are no longer with us, but I guess what I mean is right near the end of the process, I had the pleasure of talking to Charlie Calv for the first time, keyboardist in today's version of Angel, and once again, Frank and Punky, who were more than helpful, more than gracious, just all-around great guys. And then there was Felix, who I really knew nothing about, but was more than pleased to hear that he was much more than just the new bass player, but a musical genius of sorts, to the point where everybody else was kind of intimidated by the guy. I love that! And then—bonus—Felix turned out to be another extremely gracious interviewee, expounding upon in great detail and with wisdom anything this fan boy might ask him about.

That really put the icing on the cake of making the writing of this book a pleasurable experience. And I've got to say, through Punky's continual and enthusiastic (almost to the point of manic) proselytizing for the power of pop, I've come around to appreciate *White Hot* and *Sinful* much more than I had in the past. See, I was one of those classic headbanging old-school curmudgeons who has worshipped since the day those records came out, *Angel* and *Helluva Band*, but then, at the time, dropped off and wandered off looking for heavier fare, which was about to arrive in the record stores in droves once the New Wave of British Heavy Metal became a thing.

So that was a little bonus to the writing of this white paper as well as, like I say, the happy end to the story with the arrival of *Risen*. And look, I am as surprised about this as anybody, but again, through the power of Punky's persuasion (as well as that of super-fan Alexandre Hebert, who knows a thing or two about Angel and loves these records), the thing I love about *Risen* the most is the softest, most delicate, most '60s-nostalgic songs of love across the whole damn record, and not the occasional technical heavy metal, which is also impressive.

One more thing about this book that I think is somewhat new with me in these biographies 90 books in (and sort of 40 or 50 of those being biographies, I suppose), is that I think there's somewhat of a narrative throughout in terms of an abstract theme revolving around why the band didn't break big. I'm hoping that what you can gather from the times and instances where the topic comes up throughout the following pages, is that it's not just one thing and it's not just the first thing that might come to mind for the casual music fan casting a glance at Angel's lack of success in the marketplace.

After talking to the guys in the band as well as various industry people, I think there was a real jealousy out there about how this baby band was getting so much attention and investment lavished upon them by their record label, Casablanca. And to make matters worse, the guys themselves fuelled that jealousy, sort of scratching that jealous itch that existed in others—be that other bands or industry people that might be able to help them—by being what we might politely call over-confident. Tell me if I'm crazy, but I think you're going to be able to gather from the various interview clips throughout this book that the guys in Angel thought they were pretty great!

And it doesn't stop there. As I immersed myself in thinking about all things Angel for months, I really started to wonder if the melodramatic intro to their concerts, the appearing and disappearing act, along with the white costumes and yes, even their pinup good looks, held them back, exposing them to not a small degree of ridicule. It almost seems sensible that critics could cast all the barbs at Angel that they might level at Kiss, but even more so, because with Angel, it lacked the humour, the obvious and self-aware absurdity of being over the top that you get with Kiss.

Anyway, all these things went through my head, along with the agreement with some of these speakers here that if Angel had stuck around for MTV and the rise of hair metal, they could have broken huge. Again, I say that with a twist: through thinking about the band for so many months, I really think that to see any success, they would have had to ditch the all-whites. Which is a viewpoint that seems to run counter to what Punky believes, although as you'll see, he said as much in the context of 1980—he seems like too smart a guy not to have me think he'd see things a different way if we were talking about 1983. Everything else—great. The guys and their good looks generally, the songs, the obvious quality of the singing, the guitar playing, the keyboards, the bass playing and the drumming. Folks, that is every damn corner of the band as far as performing and noise-making goes, which is quite uncommon, if you think about it.

Alas, I'm too stupid and not enough of a real writer to artfully weave these narratives throughout the book, so here I am bluntly restating them, and telling you that these ideas are parachuted in from time to time, and that I hope that through this sort of chaotic approach, for the first time with one of my books, you can read it on multiple levels, dig? Also the idea is that by framing it here at the outset, I'm hoping you are reminded that when you see this supporting material, it's doubly important to the story, as I see it, in terms of explaining the band's success or lack thereof.

Anyway, let's get on with the magic show, beginning, essentially, with 1975, which is poignant to the point of poetic, because the centrepiece of the *Risen* reunion record that ends this saga is, indeed, a song called "1975."

Martin Popoff

martinp@inforamp.net; martinpopoff.com

Early Days
"I'm quitting. I saw a band called Kiss last night."

Ignominious as is it, Angel were a bit of an assembled act, and then a shtick, what with their white satin regalia setting the band up as the good and virtuous foil to the more dastardly Kiss.

But that is where the undercutting stops—and the superlatives begin.

Honing their chops in other bands and then this one all over the Washington, DC area, Punky Meadows (born Edwin Lionel Meadows, Jr.), Frank DiMino, Gregg Giuffria, Mickie Jones and Barry Brandt soon got it together and proved to those who have ears that there was an incredible depth behind the bright-as-a-bed sheet glam image, fathoms beyond Kiss, really, in parallel with the likes of Sweet over in the UK, once we get to *Sweet Fanny Adams*, *Desolation Boulevard* and especially *Give Us a Wink*. Angel, very quickly from its disparate parts, were on that level for a brief magic couple of years, and that right there is why a book like this got written.

"I've been playing since I was 14, mostly with Barry Brandt," begins Mickie's assessment of those formative years, speaking with Circus magazine back in '77. "We were school chums. Barry and Punky and myself all grew up in Washington, DC. I was in basement groups, groups that never got out of the basement. First time I met Frank was when Barry and I formed a group called Max, several years ago. Then I was with Punky in a group called Daddy Warbucks. The name was shortened to Bux, and we did a job for Capitol. I think we were a tax shelter. Before the album came out, Punky and I got together with Gregg, then Barry, then Frank, and we formed Angel. We were at a club in DC called Bogies. Barry was in a group called The Cherry People, which was Punky's original group for seven years. The Cherry People and Bux were the only groups in Washington that would draw. No matter how much the club owners hated us because we played so loud, they would book us."

Now, my own chat with Mickie 31 years later has the fat-stringer telling the story of Angel's origins this way… "I knew Barry Brandt since seventh grade. When I first heard Barry Brandt, I was walking down the hall, in the seventh grade, and I heard these enormous drums coming from the 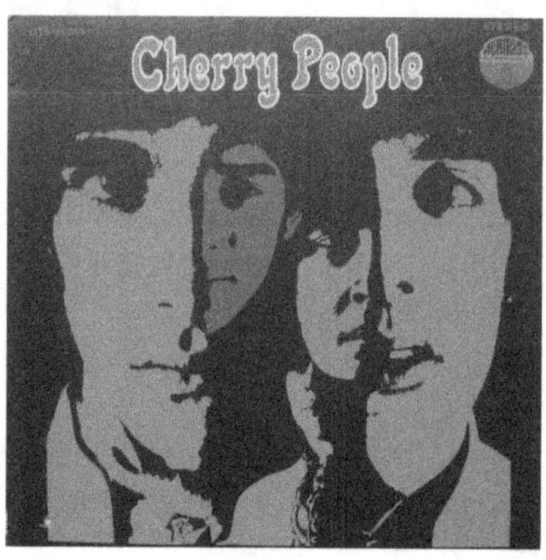 music room. I walked into the music room and there was this kid sitting behind what looked like a huge set of drums, at the time, and there was no 26-inch bass drum then. So what he had done was he had taken a marching bass drum and turned it up on its side, and he had affixed some legs to it. And he was this big mop of curly hair, and he played just like John Bonham."

"I found Frank DiMino in Boston," continues Jones. "I had seen him before I had seen Daddy Warbucks. When I was up in Boston, I'd gone up with Barry Brandt. We'd taken a U-Haul truck and we didn't have driver's licences (laughs), but we went up there during the winter, and we made our way out there, and Steven Tyler told me about Frank DiMino. He was in a band called Autumn Stone, and I went to see him, and I didn't think the band was great. I thought they sounded original but I didn't think the band was great. But I tell you, his voice was amazing. And so that's when I first saw Frank. I first saw Punky when I was around 15, too. Punky was in The Cherry People and I saw him in a club, The Silver Dollar on M Street. And I thought, this has got be the best-looking guy I've ever seen in my life (laughs). And there's not a gay bone in my body. I just thought the guy was like... I mean, girls would walk into this club and see this guy, and they wouldn't be able to talk to him. They would just sit there and stare at him."

Asked about his vision for the band, Mickie explained that, "My influences at the time were Queen, Humble Pie and David Bowie, because I'd seen David Bowie at Radio City Music Hall, for the *Ziggy Stardust* tour, and they lowered David onto the stage in a moving gyroscope, and Frank DiMino, although 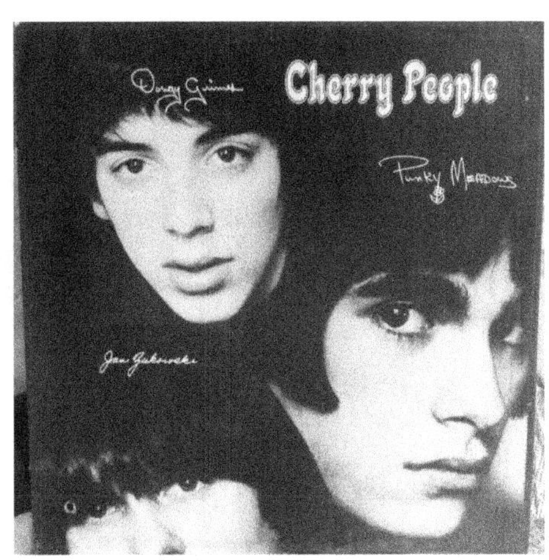

I didn't know him, I think he was at that show too. He had come down from Boston, but I didn't know him at the time. Queen was a heavy influence. Gregg's influence really came in with Rick Wakeman and his influence with Yes. We were also influenced by Yes as well; I mean, everybody in the band loved Yes. But Punky and myself were really more into guitar bands, but with piano players, like the Jeff Beck Group. We also liked Cream, which of course had no keyboard player."

"We played in all the clubs around DC, up and down Virginia," affirms lead singer Frank, asked to run down the band's history. "Barry and myself and Mickie were in a band called Max, and then Punky was in The Cherry People. And then Mickie left Max and was with Punky in Bux. Barry went to The Cherry People. Cherry People had records out, but not Max. I stayed with the guitar player, and then they asked me to come down. Mickie and Punky asked me to come down, to sing. And at that time they had a different drummer, a guy named T.C., who originally, before that, was in The Cherry People." This is T.C. Tolliver, who is sometimes considered part of the early Angel story in place of Barry; Tolliver went on to play with The Plasmatics.

"So you see, it was intertwined at different times, with different people," laughs DiMino. "And we played all the same clubs, like in Georgetown and throughout Virginia. So at the time they asked me to go down and I was going to do it but then I said, 'I've got this other thing happening.' I was happy writing with this guitar player. We were doing some stuff in New York. And I said no, I'm really happy where I'm at. So they went to look for another singer. And when they went to look for another singer, Barry was the drummer. And Punky said to me… I mean, this is what he told me after, when we went to listen to the other singer, the first thing I thought of, 'We've got to get Barry in the band.' So they replaced T.C. with Barry, and then when they did that, Barry called me up and said, 'Man, you've got to come down one more time.' So I went down, and from that point on, that was it."

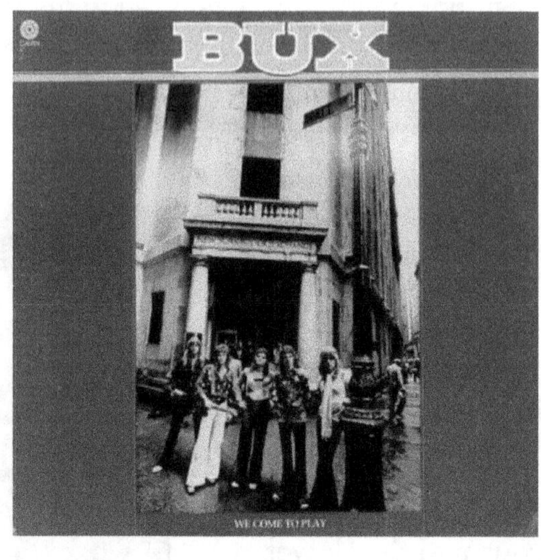

"No, that wasn't until after," answers Frank, asked if they were all dressed in white in the beginning. "What we had was regular clothes when we were in the clubs. That's the thing—we played in all those clubs so we were all very well-known. So when we put this band together, it was from three different bands that had their own followings. So it was pretty nice. And the owner of the club did this whole build-up, because he had owned a couple clubs in Georgetown, and each one of our bands played those clubs. So there was kind of an anticipation. We did two shows a night, which was great. And we were able to do all our stuff and we even had like an opening band. So it was pretty cool. I think everyone pretty much were virtuosos, yeah. And they kind of came together in this band. You know, everyone kind of came from their own band. Gregg came from this other band that he had in Mississippi and stuff; it was one of those things where you think about putting it together and see what happens."

In the same Circus profile piece cited above, Punky Meadows explained that he had "worked bars for six years. When Macy's department store first had a Carnaby Street thing, we had to wear all the crazy clothes and play in makeup… '66, '67, granny glasses. The English Setters was the first group. That group started playing in bars and became The Cherry People. They put an album out on Heritage, which was a subsidiary of MGM. It was bubblegum stuff. I split to go play with Gregg. He gave me a bullshit story."

And then Gregg explains that, "At the time, I was in New Orleans, playing jazz-oriented, technical stuff. When I heard Punky play, I knew the only way to change was to get someone in the group who played differently. I was in DC, in a bar having a drink, and Punky was playing. I was sitting on the side of the stage and he came over and said, 'Hey, what's happening, dude?'"

Giuffria had played the piano since the age of four, with a couple of his early bands including Telstars and then Flower Power, where there was some success through regional opening slots with the likes of Jimi Hendrix, The Who, the Allman Brothers and Vanilla Fudge, this last of which could be argued as an early template for what Angel were going to do. "I guess I was well liked in high school," Gregg told Bill Gupton. "But I've always gone my own way, and the things I did when I was growing up made me kind of an outcast in my hometown. I never did really fit in." One of those things was growing his hair down to his waist which had his school administrators so up in arms, they didn't want him to attend graduation. This was solved by hiding in amongst the girls until his name was called. "That shook up some people," chuckled Gregg. "They all freaked out when I stood up to get my diploma. The principal even refused to shake my hand."

"It was the beginning of a beautiful relationship," continues Punky. "I knew Mickie and Barry, but we were always in different groups. I used to see them hanging around drunk all the time. I decided to leave The Cherry People, and go to New Orleans with Gregg. I liked him, but I couldn't stand the group. They were terrible. Finally I split and we went to play with Mickie in Daddy Warbucks for about two years. We were doing all right at first, but we had an alcoholic singer and a screwed-up manager. We decided to disband Bux. Gregg was hanging around and the three of us decided to put a group together. We auditioned Frank as a singer. We had another drummer. But Frank didn't want to go with us, because we only had about three half-assed songs. We went to see another singer in a bar band, but all we could see was Barry, who was drumming."

Said Brandt in 1977, to Timothy Green Beckley, "It all just seemed to come together of its own accord, as if by some miracle. We were working in different groups, although some of us had played together before in bands, and we had all seen each other perform. We had been hanging out in the nation's capital for quite some time, and nothing was really happening. We did all kinds of original material, some of it pretty good, but it didn't start to click for us until we decided to leave whatever else we were doing and join forces."

Again, in a similar comparison made between Mickie's then-and-now explanations above, here's the way

Punky explained the early days tale to me fully 39 years later, adding a few details versus the above telling.

"What happened was, I was in a band with Mickie Jones called Daddy Warbucks, which became Bux. And we had an album on Capitol Records, and we were the house band at this club called Bogies. Well, backtrack a little bit, about three years earlier, I was playing in a band called The Cherry People, at the Bayou, and we were the house band there. And Gregg Giuffria had come up and saw me play there and was like, 'Man, you were so fucking cool.' So I'd met Gregg, who's a guy that had so much charisma and stuff, and I think he felt the same about me. But he was really cool, with all that hair and everything. When he walked into a room, you knew he had a lot of charisma. And we said, well, we need to start a band together. And so I went down to Biloxi, Mississippi, where Gregg was living at the time and had a band. And I was playing with that band, but I hated the band so much that I couldn't do it. I loved Gregg, but I just didn't like the band. So I left and moved to Boston, and Mickie and I started Daddy Warbucks up in Boston, and then we came down to DC, where we could work. And we played in this nightclub called Bogies for two years, and then Gregg showed up again, and then we knew we had to put a band together. So Gregg and Mickie and I put Angel together."

"And then we found Barry," continues Meadows. "Barry's a talented guy but he's a pretty good guitarist too and actually, he's gotten better over time. Barry loved John Bonham; that was his man. And actually when we got Barry in Angel, we were looking for a singer—we weren't looking for a drummer. But I played in The Cherry People before that, and Barry actually wound up going into The Cherry People, playing with that band. So Gregg and Mickie and myself went down looking for a singer—we went down to look at Doug Grimes, the Cherry People singer. We saw Barry playing and we forgot about the singer. We said, 'He's a motherfucker, man.' From there it was, 'Hey Barry, we got this new band.' And Barry was into it because he knew me from my guitar playing. Barry and Mickie used to come and watch me play all the time when I was playing in The Cherry

People; they would hang out and watch me play. But so we got Barry and Barry was just one of those cats that can play drums; he's a natural at it. He knows how to play big and heavy and he's got that feel. That's hard to find; there's not many drummers you can find like that."

"And then we got Frank, and together we actually rehearsed upstairs at this Bogies, where, again, Daddy Warbucks were the house band. We rehearsed upstairs in this loft there and we showcased ourselves at Bogies. We had the whole glitter thing going on before anybody had ever done that, at least in the DC area. It had happened in New York, but it hadn't happened in DC yet. And so that's when Kiss came down."

Ah yes, legend has it that Angel were discovered by Kiss.

As Punky explains, "We had just put the band together and we were blowing up the nightclub with flash bombs and all kinds of stuff, knocking all the whiskey bottles off the shelves, and we had lines around the block, people coming to see us. And Kiss were playing at the Capital Centre, in DC. They showed up that night. You know, they went out to a nightclub, and they wound up at Bogies, and we were playing. And Gene and Paul and Ace came in. I'll never forget it. Because I'm like 6'1", 6'2", and they had their platform shoes on, and I had to reach up to shake their hands, because they were so tall. I thought it was so cool."

"But Gene looked at me and said, 'You fucking guys are fucking awesome.' I used to do this move where I hold my hand over my head, and play with my other hand. And Gene looked at me and he made that move that I did and said, 'That's classic.' And they just raved about us. They thought we were so great. And so they split and then we started to have different managers come up to see us. And it started a bidding war, at Bogies, between Leber and Krebs, Toby Organization and Sandy Pearlman. Leber and Krebs managed Aerosmith, Nugent, AC/DC, all those guys, and then Toby Organization was out in California—they had managed Gary Glitter, and they had Quiet Riot at one time, before Quiet Riot made it (note, also the Angel-like Legs

Diamond). And Sandy Pearlman had Blue Öyster Cult. Sandy had a partner too. Sandy was saying things about a direction we should go in, and do certain things. He would say, 'Well, the sound is very cohesive' and he always had a really intelligent kind of vibe, like a professor in a way. But we didn't go with him for whatever reason. Anyway, so we kind of had a bidding war with management teams. We wound up going with Toby Organization back in California."

To add a little detail, Frank relates that it was rock scribe Gordon Fletcher who had brought Kiss down to the club; he would often shuttle bands down after their shows at the Capitol Centre in Largo, MD. But again, as we swing back to 1977 and an interview in Creem, Mickie downplayed the idea that Kiss had discovered the band, contradicting Punky's timeline with respect to the band securing management.

"That's a lot of bullshit," scoffed Jones, again, the sticking point here being that Mickie says when Kiss came in to Bogies, Angel already had David Joseph as a manager. "They just happened to stroll in on our last gig at this club after they did a gig at the Capitol Centre. They walked in and saw that the group was really a knockout, so they talk to Neil Bogart a couple of days later, but they didn't know that David Joseph (Angel's new manager, a.k.a. Toby Organization) had already talked to Neil about us. Neil said to David, 'Well, I'll put them on at Long Beach, with Kiss.' David said he'd better check with Kiss about that, because they might not like it. Neil said, 'What do you mean they won't like it? Kiss will play with anybody.' Neil called Gene and Paul and they said not to put us on the show and Neil calls David back five minutes later, and says, 'I'll try 'em. I don't even want to see 'em.' Eventually a couple of days later, Neil did get to see us in a really tiny rehearsal hall in Burbank, and he was knocked out. We were really impressed with him too, and the whole operation. We were talking to other companies at the time who we easily could've made deals with, but we wanted to go to a smaller company."

To back up a bit to the band's management deal, which as Mickie avows, came before the record deal, Jones told me that, "Honestly I blame myself. Because what happened was, in the very beginning, you know, I was good friends with Steven Tyler and Joe Perry, and I knew David Krebs and Steve Leber very well, and actually Punky and I just talked about this like two months ago. We wanted to go with Leber Krebs, for management. They were begging us to go with them for management. And it was Gregg that brought David Joseph into the whole mix, who was Australian and didn't have a hit group, but was very, very wealthy, and had managed Herman's Hermits, and had managed another early English guy."

Gregg had first been approached when he was playing in a different band in Florida. A waitress handed him a note singling him out as a future star. The instruction was to call Laurence Myers in London. Myers had been managing David Bowie and Gary Glitter. Gregg eventually contacted Myers, whose management group by this point, Gem-Toby Organization, included former TV producer David Joseph.

"Now, what actually happened," continues Jones, "was that Punky Meadows and I were signed to Capitol Records. We were already signed to them, and they thought that they had Angel locked up. You know, we were Capitol artists, Punky and I, with Bux, and we were not out of our contract. And Rupert Perry, who was the president of Capitol, they had already seen Angel. Not to jump ahead, but it came down to a vote between Leber Krebs and David Joseph and Warren Entner, who later managed Quiet Riot, and Billy Sammeth, who later managed Cher and a bunch of people years later."

"But anyway, it came down to a vote, and three of the guys wanted California—swimming pools, beach houses— and me and Punky Meadows wanted to go to New York. We didn't want to go into debt. They wanted to get us flats in Manhattan and they didn't want to give us an exorbitant amount of money, because, you know, we were young guys. But common sense dictated to Punky and I, because we had been through the business, the real business, since we were young, that anything someone puts in your hands, they're going to take out of your hands, you know, immediately. When the first money is in, they are going to take it back.

That's the way the contract reads and that's the way it's just done. That's the way it's always been done. But you know, a lot of young guys, they are short-sighted, they don't care. They want the instant gratification, they want swimming pools, they want California."

"And California was attractive and all that stuff, but anyway, long story short, we wanted to go to New York but we ended up going with David Joseph. We came out here, and Capitol thought they had us. And we were going to sign with Capitol, but their legal department went on holiday, during Christmas—as you know, it's warm out here during Christmas. And David Joseph had already paid for the first album to be done; I think it cost like $75,000. Which at the time was a lot of money. So David Joseph paid for the first album to be done, paid for Derek Lawrence and Big Jim Sullivan to come out here, leased them a house in Beverly Hills, leased them cars, and the money this fucking guy put out was just... and he lived in a mansion on Bedford Drive, himself; the money was just staggering."

"So anyway," continues Mickie, "he was driving down Sunset Boulevard from the Columbia film lot where we were rehearsing, but not where we ended up rehearsing later on. I'm really giving you all the information. Because later on we ended up recording on the Columbia film lot but not on the same soundstage. We were rehearsing at S.I.R. at that time, Studio Instrument Rentals, which still exists out here in California. And he passed by Casablanca Records, which already had Kiss, that had already done the first two albums, which weren't hits. And they had the Hudson Brothers, which weren't a big hit—they had a hit TV show. Kiss were selling a couple hundred thousand units, I think, at that time, based on live performance only. And that was just a gruelling touring schedule. I mean, those guys just got on the road and didn't come off the road. For like seven years straight they were on the road and never came off. So anyway, he stopped at Casablanca Records and he knew Neil Bogart, and he played the album for him."

"Now, you remember that scene in *Annie Hall* by Woody Allen, and Paul Simon played a record executive in that movie, and there was a big mansion in that movie where Paul Simon lived? Well, the guy who owned that mansion, okay, is the guy that actually put the money into Kiss, and Casablanca Records. He put the money into all that black leather and all the hydraulic lifts that lifted Peter's drums. I can't remember his name, some Italian guy. Anyway, to finish this portion of the story—because I could go on forever—Neil Bogart heard the Angel album, and he asked David Joseph how much he wanted up front. And David Joseph got really cocky and said I want $1 million up front. And Bogart, the following week, got $1 million, from that guy, from that same guy, and he put it into an account. The Italian guy loaned it to Neil Bogart who gave it to David Joseph, to sign Angel. To Casablanca Records. So we were on the front cover of Billboard magazine, 'Angel signs to Casablanca Records, $1 million advance.' So it was a big deal."

Frank's recollection of Neil hearing the album includes a bit more colour.

"The manager said, 'I'll tell you what, let's go to Neil. Because Neil said he wanted the band.' And everybody was saying, 'Don't go with Neil, because the company is going to fold. Casablanca's going to fold' (laughs). 'They're having problems with the company, it's probably going to go down, it's going to go bankrupt. And at that time Kiss was on *Dressed to Kill*, the third album. And so David Joseph said, you know, let's get in the studio. So we got the producers, Derek Lawrence and Big Jim Sullivan, to produce the album, and David said, 'Well, we're going to get a record deal, so let's just go ahead and do it ourselves and I'll work on a record deal. You guys work on the material, work on the production, and I'll get us a record deal.'"

"The thing is, when we finished the album, we were supposed to do it with Capitol," continues DiMino. "And we brought the finished product to Capitol before we signed the deal, played it for them, and the first thing that came out of their mouth was, 'We like that, but you know, how about we do a little bit different mix, this song needs a little more guitar here, put in a bit of this…' And immediately, as that started to progress, you thought, 'This is the last place we really want to be.' It's the last thing they really should be saying to us, when we bring them the finished album. I think they were trying to shape us into something that maybe they wanted, as opposed to who we were. But they hadn't even sat with it and listened to it. They were listening to it as we brought it to them, and they were already making comments of what they wanted to do, and change things. We're going, 'Wait a second, this is the finished product—we're done.' And so we started having second thoughts about it."

"And David said, 'Listen, I don't want you guys to worry about it, but let's go bring it to Neil. Let's see what Neil thinks.' We said okay, we'll go along with that. So we went and brought it to Neil, and Neil just knows how to talk to everybody. He knew how to talk to the guys. He knew how to talk to every one of us. And he made us feel so comfortable and so welcome. I remember when we first brought the album—the finished product—to Neil, he said, 'Let's do this right.' So we sat down in his office, and he had big JBLs in there. And he rolled this big, big fat joint, and called some people down, and Neil lit the joint up and passed it all around. It went around like a couple of times, and he said, 'Okay, let's listen to it now.' And that in itself… I thought, this is cool. At least the guy is settling down and listening to the shit. It's not like one of these things where someone is going to say, 'Well, you know, I think…'"

"So I felt good about that. And then he said, 'I'd love you to sign with Casablanca. I love the album and I'd love to be able to promote it.' You know, you can't ask for something more than that. And we said absolutely. But there was quite a bit of wild stuff going on at Casablanca other than just smoking pot (laughs). But Casablanca was always a fun place to visit, and the main thing about that label, was that Neil was always a guy you could go and talk to at any time. He was someone that we really felt kind of got what we were doing."

As well, if in the beginning, Casablanca's offer was the least attractive, in the end, says Frank, Neil matched the deal that Capitol had put on the table. Oddly, for his part, Gregg still swears the album got made *after* the deal was struck with Casablanca, going so far as to say that it was Neil that suggested that they use Wally Heider in which to record.

Ironically, Giuffria had his own murky ties to Capitol, having once been signed to the label with a Laurel, Mississippi act called David and the Giants, which featured another budding star in the guise of hotshot drummer Tommy Aldridge—this was Gregg's band after Flower Power. The band has a strange recording history, doing a few singles from 1963 through 1970, and then nothing until 1977, when they changed to a Christian format, issuing a slew of albums. But Gregg was indeed a member of the band in 1971 and '72, and Aldridge was there with him, in '72. Giuffria also maintains there's a shelved album that got recorded. As well, the 1970 single just before Gregg's joining was indeed on Capitol. One final note, now that we're giving a bit of history on the long-maned synthesizer wizard of the band, his first name is spelled "Greg" on the entirety of the Angel catalogue, but since the '80s, there's been a pretty wide standardization on "Gregg" as the accepted spelling, which I've adopted here. As well, Mickie started as Mickey, but similarly, I'm going with the later-days, more widely accepted spelling.

Now, you will note that Mickie's modern-day recollection doesn't state outright that Bogart's interest in Angel was based on Kiss being afraid to have Angel open for them, which is what he said back in 1977. Importantly though, it doesn't contradict the early telling either. It looks like this phone call about Kiss supporting came first, and that Neil later heard the album—a pair of events. It's even possible that Neil had heard demos just with David Joseph, and that Frank's story is about hearing, as he specifies, "the finished album." Furthermore, Punky, again, speaking with me in 2016, re-affirms the story about Kiss being hesitant to have Angel open Kiss shows, underscoring the importance of the call.

"We were sitting in our manager's office," explains Meadows, "and we were thinking about showcasing ourselves to record companies. Ahmet Ertegun wanted to hear us, and so we were talking, and our manager David

Joseph said, 'You know, Neil Bogart has this new label called Casablanca, and Kiss is on the label.' And so we told our manager that Gene and Paul and Ace came out and saw us and raved about us and this and that. And he says, 'I'll tell you what, let me call Neil Bogart and see what he says.' And so David calls Neil Bogart up at Casablanca, 'Say, I've got this band, they're called Angel, they're from Washington, DC, and they're out here, and we're shopping a record deal. Gene and Paul and Ace had come up. They had come to see them when they were back in DC and said that they were great. Why don't you check the band out?'"

"So Neil Bogart said to our manager, 'I'll tell you what. Kiss are playing out in Anaheim this next week. I'll have Angel open up for them, and that way I can see them play.' So we said that would be great. And he says, 'Let me call you back. I'm going to call Gene and talk to Gene about it.' So David hangs up, Neil Bogart hangs up, we hang up, and then Neil Bogart calls back about 15 minutes later and says, 'I'll tell you what. I'll sign the band sight unseen. Because Gene Simmons said, "Under no way will Angel ever open up for Kiss."' So that was great."

"He was going to sign us right away to a seven-album deal, but we actually did play for him a couple weeks later. He came down to the rehearsal hall and we played for him and he just loved it. So he was behind us 100% then. And so that's how we actually got that record deal, and got signed, more or less."

The dalliance with Leber Krebs had David Krebs suggesting Punky and Mickie join the New York Dolls! Open-minded about it, the guys went and took a listen to the band's second album *Too Much Too Soon* and subsequently "laughed their balls off," deciding to stick with this new, still malleable venture of theirs.

"Yes, now Leber and Krebs, they were friends of mine," explains Punky. "David Krebs asked Mickie and I to play with the New York Dolls because they'd lost Johnny Thunders and stuff. David was a friend of mine; I knew him through Daddy Warbucks. Jack Douglas had produced all of the Aerosmith stuff back in the day, and he produced my

Daddy Warbucks album, now called Bux—it was a Bux album. And so I met David Krebs through Jack Douglas and we became friends. And he always loved Mickie and I a lot. And so he wanted Mickie and I to play with the New York

Dolls, but we said, 'Listen David, we have this band called Angel, and we would like you to hear Angel.' And of course he came out and saw us and he was just blown away. And I'll never forget. We had a three-way conference call with him on the phone between Mickie, Gregg and myself, and David Krebs. And he was saying, 'If you guys don't sign with us, it's mental masturbation. We'll blow you guys up.' And I wanted to go with Leber and Krebs, because I already had a relationship with David Krebs. I liked him a lot and I knew what he could do. The other guys kind of wanted to move to California, so we wound up going with Toby Organization out in California. They wanted to go see palm trees."

"But, I always stayed friends with David Krebs. There a lot of stories that go along with that too. He asked me to play with Michael Bolton at one time, when he first came out. He was dressed in leather and was kind of doing a hard rock thing. He thought that I could give Michael Bolton another dimension of some sort. So David, yeah, I love David. He was great guy."

So there's really no contradiction other that the one small wrinkle there on the securing of management. On the subject of whether the band were discovered by Kiss, it's more like the lynchpin was the fact that Kiss had happened to witness the power of Angel live and didn't want them on the same bill as them. Still, Mickie shows an indebtedness to Kiss in an even more profound way, through the magic of inspiration.

"Right, well, I was the only one who had ever seen Kiss," explains Jones. "And I'd only seen Kiss at the Bayou Club in front of 40 people, in Washington, DC, when I was in Daddy Warbucks. And that was by accident. And honest to God, that was the last straw that got me to quit Daddy Warbucks. The next night I went in to Punky Meadows, because the singer from Daddy Warbucks was Ralph Morman, who is a great singer, but he was getting drunk every night and I wasn't having it. So I went to Punky and I said, 'I'm quitting. I saw a band called Kiss last night. They are musically…' I didn't care for the songs, but the presentation, they just threw everything at you but the kitchen sink. And I said, 'I'm going to form a band—I'm doing the same motherfuckin' thing. But it's going to be musically better, and I'm doing it. And if you're smart, you're going to come with me.'"

So both presumably—and if so, amusingly—when Kiss saw Angel, they were already seeing a band at least a little bit influenced by Kiss. Originally the first post-Bux incarnation had been called Sweet Mama from Heaven (note the pun), but soon it was changed to Angel, based on the Jimi Hendrix song of that name plus the fact that Punky had named his white Stratocaster Angel. At this point Gregg puts up his hand to say that Sweet Mama from Heaven was never the name of the band, nor was it ever Foxy, which is also brought up. As well, he says that Angel came up because it was the name of his first wife's pet poodle.

The band's connection to Jimi Hendrix includes another tale, this one happening to Punky. "Yes, what happened was, I was in The Cherry People and I went to New York one week, one weekend with the gang, and we happened to go into Steve Paul's The Scene. That was the big nightclub back then, and Rick Derringer was the house band there and he was tinkering around with his Echoplex and stuff up there trying to get his guitar working. And we were sitting at a table and in walked Jimi Hendrix. We all just about shit ourselves. And Hendrix walked over to our table because he knew we were in a band and Mitch Mitchell and Noel Redding had just called off somewhere and he needed some musicians and he knew we were musicians. So he invited us up to the Record Plant."

"Billy Cox was playing bass, but my drummer Rocky, from The Cherry People, actually played on a couple of Hendrix songs up there. But it was a funny thing. He'd put us in the studio for three days and would come to the hotel with us and the whole bit. But I remember being stoned out of my fucking mind. This is when The Record Plant had black lighting and had shag carpeting, and I was laying under this baby grand piano and Hendrix was in there recording. And that's when he hit with doing his Band of Gypsies kind of thing. He had the bandanas and all that and I remember he was under this black light and he had his white fur pants on and he was singing. And so his white fur pants were just glowing and he was singing and playing guitar at the same time and recording."

"Eddie Kramer must've been there, but I was so young, I can't remember. But Jimi was playing and singing and it just freaked me out. And I remember the thing about Hendrix was, you know, when I first met him, I thought he was going to be like (deep voice) 'Foxy Lady,' you know, this really cool guy. But he was so soft-spoken and so intelligent and articulate and he had a really good sense of humour. And that kind of threw me back because I thought he'd be this braggadocio kind of guy and he wasn't—he was exactly the opposite and very nice and funny."

"And then he would get behind the desk in the control room and when he would play the playback back, he would be panning the guitar in stereo left and right and it was just amazing. Watching him play and do all that kind of stuff, and he would make plenty of jokes about different people out there and stuff. It was just a wonderful thing to be part of and to see—and as a kid, because to me Hendrix was a god."

"And he still is to this day. What a lot of people don't realise about Jimi Hendrix was it wasn't just his soloing. It was how he could play that beautiful chordal stuff, like 'Wind Cries Mary' and 'Angel,' those songs, all that beautiful chord-y stuff. It would take me to another planet or another universe while I was listening to him with the earphones. The heavy stuff of course I love 'cause they're blistering and they're bluesy and that sort of thing, but when he plays that beautiful choral stuff, that's where the beauty of the guitar lies. Him and Stevie Ray Vaughan, they just channel music. I don't know what it is. They're one-of-a-kind guitar players. A lot of guitar players play great, but Hendrix and Stevie had something else going on and it's hard to explain. If you're a guitar player, you know it when you hear it because it's just as right as rain."

"But no, I just sat there quietly, laying under the piano on the shag carpet and just staring, watching in awe. And when I went back home after that… because I was still playing in a night club, the next night we played, it was almost like what had happened was a dream, because it was so surreal seeing Hendrix like that. And of course he was  up all night long, doing whatever drugs he was doing, you know what I mean? Up all night and all day in the studio. So I would fall asleep at certain times, and then wake back up and he'd be there doing his thing. And I was just a kid, 18, 19 or something like that, just into my thing, you know?"

Back on earth, Angel's soon-to-bleach image aside, the guys' individual resumes thus far didn't reveal the dramatic and Deep Purple-hued direction for Angel that was to come. But there was quite a collective past, so there was a level of craftsmanship at the ready. To recap, most experienced, Punky had put out three singles with The Intruders, more singles with Cherry People plus the full album in 1968, even if he didn't do any of the writing. The Cherry People even landed a slot on *American Bandstand*, plus toured the country, one highlight being a date at Caesars Palace in Las Vegas. Then, of course, Punky and Mickie had made the Bux record, which was recorded at the Record Plant in New York, again, with Jack Douglas producing. On the Bux record Punky only had the one writing credit, for "White Lightning," which Angel would rework for their third album, and Mickie didn't figure in the writing at all. On vocals for Bux was the aforementioned Ralph Morman, who would go on to sing for The Joe Perry Project and Savoy Brown. Morman passed away after a long illness in 2014 at the age of 65, but his legacy is assured due to the classic first record he recorded with Joe, 1980's *Let the Music Do the Talking* (also produced by Jack Douglas).

Still, from modest roots, particularly when it came to recording experience, Angel would soon craft an album that would be lauded as one of the most well-regarded debut hard rock records of all time.

Angel
"Led Zeppelin meets Yes"

Just in time to see their first album hit the shops, things were suddenly looking good for Angel. On September 10th, 1975, their new label—new to Angel and barely two years runnin' as a business—issued a two-LP Kiss live album called *Alive!* and Casablanca was a happening place all of a sudden. *Angel* followed on October 27th, and all eyes were on this new "baby," band about to compete with the likes of Blue Öyster Cult, Black Sabbath, Led Zeppelin, Uriah Heep and Deep Purple, along with Ted Nugent, just breaking in the fall of 1975 with his self-titled solo album and Aerosmith, shifting units of their *Toys in the Attic* record, issued April 8th of that year. Like *Ted Nugent* and *Alive!*, also issued in September was the third Montrose album, *Warner Bros. Presents*, which, unlike *Montrose* and *Paper Money*, fits the wheelhouse of what Angel were doing, namely the crafting of a hard rock sound by an American band that possesses some of the characteristics of the British masters, most pointedly Deep Purple.

"The first album, where our heads were at, we wanted to do a mixture of guitar and keyboards," explains Frank, on the band's mission. "Barry, myself and Punky were more guitar-oriented. But we wanted to do kind of a fusion between guitar and keyboards—and still keep it heavy. So that was the philosophy going into it. Our influences back then were probably what they are now: Zeppelin, Purple, Queen, the normal stuff. But like I said, we were trying to do something, trying to make like a heavier sound with synthesizer and guitar."

Production duties for the project fell to Derek Lawrence, working with session guitar legend Big Jim Sullivan, both veterans from across the pond—Lawrence died in May 2020, age 78 and Sullivan died in October 2012, age 71. In fact, Sullivan's demise was a month before the death from heart attack of Angel manager David Joseph. Engineering on *Angel* was Peter Granet, with the team working at Wally Heider in Hollywood.

Says DiMino, "Derek Lawrence did, I think, the first three Deep Purple albums (note: his only other quite notable credit was his work on a few key early Wishbone Ash records). Big Jim Sullivan was… well, he was Tom Jones' guitar player. But Big Jim Sullivan was one of these big session guys. He and Jimmy Page were like the two hottest session guitar players in England, at the same time. The question is, whether he or Jimmy Page played on like, 'It's All Over Now' and the two Kinks songs and stuff like that (laughs). No one else is willing to say that anyone but Keith Richards or Dave Davies played on them. I don't know. He's the guy who plays in the James Bond movies, that guitar part."

"We did that first album in about ten days, because we were so polished; that was the stuff we we're doing in the clubs. That was the easiest record we did, because we were playing it every night, two shows a night. Five and five, whatever we were doing… five or six nights a week. And when we got to Los Angeles, we kept rehearsing, so that was an easy one to do. Still, it was a bit odd, those first two albums, because we were in Wally Heider, which was at that time kind of a strange place, kind of ending and stuff, and there were different studios. We were in the big studio there, but it was a little bit different."

"They were real characters," continues Frank, asked for a profile of the team. "Partying, yeah, but, you know, Angel, even though we had a lot of fun, I don't think we ever did anything that got in the way of what we were working on. We drank pretty good, but none of us ever did anything before a show. And it wasn't like anybody said, 'Okay, no drinking before the show.' It was just a conscious thing we could do. Because all of us had come from playing clubs and all of us really liked playing. That's what we enjoyed doing. I mean, to this day I do. I go out and sing in clubs. I just like doing it. But yeah, Derek was the guy who made the final decisions. And when we were talking about sounds he was important; he was the engineer at the time, while Jim was more the musician guy. Musically he was always there to help us round out certain things. If we ever hit a snag, 'What about this; what about that?' He was a great guy; both of them were great guys. But Jim was a really, really nice guy."

"I really liked working with them," adds Mickie, "and I really loved working with Big Jim Sullivan. Big Jim Sullivan, during the early years, before Led Zeppelin, Jimmy Page and Big Jim Sullivan, they played on all the stuff, Gerry & the Pacemakers, Herman's Hermits, some of the Beatles stuff; I mean, just everything, The Searchers, you name it. All the English beat stuff. So the stories he had… and Derek

Lawrence had worked with Deep Purple. You know, basically I'm a very honest person. I'll give you the honest stuff. I liked working with them, and I really liked working with Big Jim Sullivan. Derek Lawrence was soused most of the time. But he had worked with Deep Purple, and Frank was more familiar with him, actually, than anybody else."

"They were funny guys," recalled Lawrence, speaking with the author back in 2009. "I took Big Jim Sullivan over to work with me just because he was my mate, and I was going to go work seriously in America for the first time and I needed a shoulder to lean on. I thought they were a really good band. I thought they were better than Kiss, but didn't have the aura of Kiss. Punky Meadows, I mean, they would pick us up from the house we were renting to go to the studio, in the morning, and Punky had already drunk six beers. Gregg Giuffria, to me, was a pain in the ass. Because he had these big bloody keyboard things that took up three-quarters of the studio—and Jim loved all that, so that was great, because he would just get on with it—but you know, Moogs or whatever they were called, I hated all that. Plus I do remember, once in the studio, that Barry Brandt said to me over the intercom, 'Make me sound like John Bonham.' So I gave him John's number and I said, 'Phone him and have him come down and play it.'"

For his part, Jim Sullivan was impressed with the guys, saying they had everything pretty much sorted, and that the most substantial thing he did was instruct Punky on a few things. He considered the band to be smartly together as a unit and even ahead of their time and thought the production job he and Derek applied to the band was appropriately "futuristic," matching what the band was doing.

But whoever deserves the credit, be it Derek, Jim or any one of the band members, the resulting album sounds epic and expensive, panoramic and plush, well beyond what Derek ever accomplished with the psychedelic Deep Purple of the '60s and indeed better than classic Purple or Led Zeppelin. The sounds dialled in here were somewhat in the realm of Uriah Heep at their very best, which of course means *Look at Yourself!*

Not eager to take the compliment, Derek told me, "You know, I sat with someone about two years ago, and they went, 'Oh, you are brilliant.' And I said, 'Look, it's all down to the band.' And he said, 'Have you ever sat down and listened to all the albums you've produced?' And I said, 'No, why would I do that? If I was a bus driver, I wouldn't come home and drive a bus.' And they said, 'They have your sound! There is you in them.' So what I thought, I guess that all comes from Joe Meek: get the bass and drums right, and then get everything to sit and fit with that. And I think that's true of Angel, I think that was true of… I did the Quiet Riot album (note: the debut only, issued March 21st, 1978) and hated the lead singer, DuBrow, but that album became collectible because it had Randy Rhoads on it. But once again, they all had songs. And hey, listen, every producer is great—if he has good players. You can't make a good player sound bad."

"And Frank was great," continues Derek. "He was really, really easy and nice. I mean, they were a nice bunch of guys! As I say, Gregg was just a pain in the ass, because of his synthesizers, and we spent seven hours working out what sounds could come from a synthesizer. And the  only thing good about it is that we did it at Wally Heider in LA, and next door was Tony's, my favourite bar. And so we would go in there and drink pretty heavy. Don't forget, they all moved out from Boston, to get away from the Aerosmith thing, I think (ed. more accurately Washington). And they had walked into the Kiss thing. And it's like the day they signed to Casablanca… I think there was a whole political thing going on. I maintain to this day that Casablanca signed Angel to bury them, because they were a serious threat to Kiss."

"But no, the first album was cool, and was what we saw of them," continues Derek. "That's how I saw them. Hey, the truth is, for the first album, basically, we flew in from London to LA and four days later they were in the studio. So it was taking what they were and doing with it what it was. Because otherwise it would have been three months doing an album, which you don't do for a first album. Listen, I never took more than two weeks to do any album. If it took longer than that, I was bored. That was one of the things that a guy once said—I forget which band he was in—'Derek's great for the first four tracks, then he's bored.'"

As for Angel sounding like Deep Purple, "The managers never said, 'Make them sound like…' They always said, 'Make them as big as…' On the other hand, I'm talking about three years ago, I get a call, 'Hey, listen, we've got this young rock band, and this label, and we need them to sound like the new Deep Purple.' And I would say, 'Well, there ain't no new Deep Purple, thank you.' But David phoned me and said, 'Do you want to produce it?' And I thought no, not really, but my mate Big Jim Sullivan needed some money and I said, 'Come over, we'll go and produce an album.' He went 'Yeah, all right.' We both needed some money at the time, to be honest, and they were there."

Very soon Lawrence would be producing Legs Diamond, another new act based in California that sounded like the second coming of Deep Purple. Same management too, but Legs Diamond didn't get the attention Angel did, according to the band's keyboardist Michael Prince.

"We always tried to have—when it was allowed—flash pots or smoke pots," chuckles Prince. "But we never had the stuff that Angel had. We used to just go and ogle at their stuff and go wild. But they were with Casablanca and Neil Bogart really liked them. He was taking a lot of the money he made from Kiss and spending it on Angel. He really expected them to be his next big, big moneymaking band. It just didn't happen. And I still don't know why. Angel probably had ten times, if not 20 times the money spent on them as we did. Every time they went on tour they had brand-new cases, brand new equipment, and we would just look at them and go, 'You guys… you are just so lucky.'"

"And they went really poppy eventually, right?" continues Prince. "I think at some point somebody really put some pressure on them to write some singles. I mean, they were a good band. My story about them is the time that we were opening for them in New York, and we were getting a much better audience response, and their guitar player kept going backstage and kicking the power out. I think it was Punky, and I think he did it three or four times, and we didn't know about it until a couple of weeks later. Because we were just… our roadie would go back there and he would find the cable and plug it back in. And they would come back out on the stage, and then five minutes later the power would go off again. And then once we found out it was him we wanted to kill the guy. And he was just… he thought it was funny. He was showing off for some girl. But we got along great with them. I think there was just the sort of New York attitude about a couple of them; if the band was really good, they wanted to figure out a way to hurt you. And that really hurt us, having the power pulled out four times. And our live show, even though we had no props, generally speaking, it was just a better response we were getting."

"Complete bullshit," defends Mickie. "No, Punky Meadows, he never had that kind of energy to do that kind of thing. And he was way too confident in everything that he ever did. In his self-image and everything, he could have cared less. He pretty much thought he was like… I wouldn't say that he thought he was better than everybody, but let's put it this way, there was a time where he and I were walking around like our shit didn't stink. We weren't assholes, but maybe our shit didn't stink, I don't know."

But it wasn't all bad, being part of the David Joseph stable, says Prince. "No, we definitely had good budgets for the first two records. Our management company managed Angel at the time that they also managed Quiet Riot. So they had… well, not much clout, because none of those bands did that well back then. We actually got signed before Quiet Riot back then. Their first record deal was actually a Japanese deal; then years later of course they became the biggest band of all those bands. But it was a fun time in LA; it really was. It really felt like if you wrote some songs and worked at your craft, you could get a record deal."

Another similarity between the two acts is that both bands worked with Derek Lawrence first and then later Eddie Leonetti. "I think he's doing hair now; he's a hair stylist," chuckles Legs Diamond guitarist Roger Romeo. "I ran into some people who were friends of him—yeah, he was doing hair. But he was pretty good. It was fun working with him because he would go, 'Hey, you know, this is great, let's put a little bridge here' or something like that. So he helped us fine-tune the songs, doing more or less pre-production. He was just a really good person to work with. I mean, he was solid, he was focused every day, quite unlike our first album."

Eddie produced Legs Diamond's second album, 1977's *A Diamond Is a Hard Rock*, and then Angel's *White Hot* record in 1978 and *Sinful* the following year. Not kind words for Derek though, from Michael Prince.

"Derek Lawrence actually did one or two Deep Purple records," states Michael. "Of course Deep Purple was one of our favourite bands, and we put out a call to several people and he was one of the people who said, 'Sure, I'll do it.' And I don't really want to say anything bad about him, but by the time we worked with him, I would say he was in the middle stages of his career. There were a lot of things we wanted to try on the first album that he didn't want to let us do, because he had already done them before. It was one of those things. I was talking to Roger about this the other day; we'd have an idea like, 'Well, we want this echo on the vocal' or something like that, and he would go, 'No, no, I did that on the blah blah blah album in 1970-something.'"

"And I was thinking, why didn't we come back with, 'Well, this is our first album. We want to do this.?' But we're thinking, well, he's done a bunch of albums and we haven't done anything, so I guess he's right. And then I thought, we can't make that mistake anymore. If

you've got an idea, you've got to run with it. Also it was funny because when he came down to pick out the songs for our album, we literally had probably 30 songs ready to go. So we start playing songs and he'd go, 'Yeah, like that one, like that one.' He basically picked the first ten songs. We said, 'Well, we've got a lot more.' 'Nope, no, that's it. Great songs. I don't want to hear any more.' And you just felt like he was trying to get his money and get out of there as fast as possible. Looking back, we should've hit him over the head with a big hammer. But it was our first chance, our first time, so you try to play along and make everybody happy."

"They were funny, because they were all really good drinkers as well," recalls Derek, asked about Legs Diamond. "And I seem to remember bailing out one of them from the police station because he'd been sitting in the lounge of the Holiday Inn in Hollywood, and they found out he hadn't paid for like 30 parking tickets. That band should have been bigger than they were, but you know, I think that's true of Angel as well. But I also think that within America, at that time, if you'd come from California, you couldn't be a rock band."

Not sure what Derek is getting at there, but it might be that California was rife with singer/songwriters and country rock at the time, through the likes of The Eagles, Poco, Linda Ronstadt, Jackson Browne and a transplanted Fleetwood Mac. Indeed it's kind of odd. California would be ground zero for heavy metal from about 1983 through to 1991, but at the time, yeah, in 1976, the big heavy bands were from elsewhere—anywhere else, out East, Detroit, Houston, Chicago, England, even Canada.

Punky, for his part, seemed pleased with Derek and Jim. "Sure, they were great," recalls Meadows. "I mean, Jim Sullivan was a legendary guitar player, and a great guitar player in his own right. He played with Tom Jones and he used to always tell me that Tom Jones is really a blues singer and all this kind of stuff. He was always disappointed in Tom Jones, that he went that route. Jim could play everything and anything. He was kind of like my friends from DC, Danny Gatton and Roy Buchanan. They were two of the best guitar players in the whole world ever. But he was a great guy, and he was very inspirational with me. He loved the way I played and stuff. He would always say, 'You and me, we're the best' (laughs), kind of thing, just trying to get me pumped-up and stuff.

"But yeah, I love that guy. And he was an amazing guitar player. You know, he's the one that taught me how to play 'Rudolph the Red Nosed Reindeer,' which I eventually played for Dick Clark when we did *American Bandstand*. Because I would watch Jim Sullivan play. But like I say, when I would go in and play a solo, he'd come back out and go, 'Punky, you and me are the best guitar players there are.' And to be honest, I was high on my horse back then. I just came out of there and I thought I was a hot-shot guitar play. And he just solidified that and made me feel so good. So he would help me get my guitars where they should be."

"And Derek Lawrence was a great guy too. I was disappointed though, in how it was produced. I don't like the production. I don't think it stood up to a lot of other records. The guitars got lost a lot of times in the rhythm section. I felt that the first album was pretty good, but I was always a little disappointed in the production on those two albums. That's just me, personally."

Punky's got a point. Although the record sounds great in summation, powerful even, from a guitarist's point of view specifically, the cut isn't there. Again, like Heep at their finest, or, say, Deep Purple specifically with *Machine Head*, everything conspires in the mix like a hearty stew, against other records that might demonstrate more separation between the keyboardist and a guitarist—a Man in Black or a Man in White—who might be on his high horse.

"Yeah, and you know what happened was, I think Gregg spoke louder, I guess, than anybody else, and wanted to be heard," agrees Punky, expressing the truism that certain keyboard sounds from Gregg did indeed cut through (although not all of them—like I say, just like with Purple and Heep, keys also crowd the space of rhythm guitar). "And they kind of went that route. There are a lot of fans that knew

Angel before we did that album, and they kept saying… they'd write in, and they would say, 'Where are the guitars?' You know what I mean? 'What's going on? Is Punky playing? Where are the guitars?' 'Cause we actually had a meeting in the office with our manager because the fans were actually writing in and saying, 'Hey, we can't hear Punky's guitar on the first two albums.' And so we had a meeting about that, and had to get the guitars up and stuff. You know, I loved Gregg. He was a great keyboard player and he and I always got along and we were very friendly. But he just had a way of manipulating people and getting things to go his way or whatever. That's just the way it went."

"So that's why… that's when the guitar started coming out of the pocket there, because they wanted to hear guitars. And Gregg is a great keyboard player; don't get me wrong. I love all the keyboard stuff he did. And when we worked together, when we first put Angel together, the thing was, we were going to be like Led Zeppelin meets Yes, that kind of thing. We were definitely a progressive hard rock band. And that was cool back then, because that was when Queen was coming up. If you listen to the first Queen album, they were very progressive too. That was the sound that was going around and a sound we were influenced by as well. That's what we took into that record."

"But it was a thing where everybody wanted to be dominant," continues Meadows, "and Gregg especially. But he did have a lot of good ideas too at the same time. I mean, the intro to 'The Fortune,' to me, it's just genius—it's beautiful. So I guess what I'm trying to say is, even though Gregg was a loudmouth and stuff back then and got his way in the beginning, he was a great keyboard player that inspired a lot of keyboard players too. I'm not gonna say that it was a love/hate thing, but it was a give-and-take thing and he kind of got his way. But later on, when Eddie Leonetti came in, the guitars came up bigger."

Punky admits to being old enough to have incorporated the same influences that the likes of Deep Purple had.

"Sure, all those guys, we all grew up on the same thing. They were doing the same thing that I was growing up on, like the blues. So my natural evolution was from playing in clubs. I was basically just like Blackmore, basically a blues guitar player, but then he just took it further. Like Clapton did and Beck did and like Hendrix did. They're all blues guitar players, and they just took it further, made it heavier and of course could play a lot more, more riffs and so on and so forth. So my growing up playing in bars was playing Deep Purple, Zeppelin, Hendrix, Clapton and Cream, and that's how I got my chops together, playing and copying those songs as a kid. And so it just evolved from there into the Angel sound."

"And then Brian May was coming out, and we were all coming out at the same time—Joe Perry, those kind of cats. We were all coming out in the same era, having all the same influences. And we interpreted those influences our own way, so we all came out having our own sound, just like Blackmore and Clapton evolved from the old blues guys. Same thing. Listen to Keith Richards play all that great stuff—he wrote all those great tunes that he wrote. The Stones were another great band that could write songs that were commercial and singable at the same time. It was fun to do the Stones."

"It was just a really good relationship," sums up Frank. "That's how I feel it works best. Once you start working with each other, that's where it becomes something more—or something less. Because it's the relationship you start to build there. And with Derek and Big Jim, Big Jim was great and he was great with Punky. You know, Punky, I think, even asked Jim to play on some of the stuff, and Jim goes, 'No, no. You're going to play on this. I want you to play all the stuff on this. You know what you want to do. You know what you want to hear.' He made us feel comfortable. He didn't say, 'Yeah, you don't know what you're doing. Let me show you the way to do it.' He was always encouraging. When that happens, you start to grow with each other and the relationship starts to build. So I think that's why those first two albums sounded so great."

It can't be overstated how important it was in 1975 seeing this band on that magical Casablanca label, to this point, associated with three Kiss studio albums. It was a stamp of approval to a kid "in the know."

I asked Larry Harris, Executive Vice-President and co-founder of the label with the aforementioned Neil Bogart, back in 2009—he is since deceased, December 18th, 2017 at the age of 70—for a bit of background on Casablanca.

"The previous company was controlled by a very conservative, educational company called Viewlex. To be honest with you, my partner and cousin Neil Bogart didn't like being controlled very much. I mean, things were happening like they couldn't… Buddha Records was supposed to have the soundtrack to Woodstock but Viewlex got in the way. Founding Casablanca was really for freedom."

And it was touch-and-go until Kiss *Alive!*, says Larry, so when Angel came out, it wasn't like things were on solid ground yet. "Right. Neil believed that Kiss had to come out with an album every six months, to keep everything alive and going. But at that time we had no money to do another album with them. But we did have a bunch of stuff in the can, live stuff, and it was cheaper to record it live. So that's what we did; we came out with a double live album, because we had no money to come out with a studio album. It took a lot of balls because they hadn't had a hit yet. If you look at all these groups that followed our double live album, they all had hits before they came out with them and those songs were on those albums."

"Plus we did certain things that became standard pretty much in the industry. Radio stations in those days, when they put an album in their library, the only thing you could see was the spine of the album. We made sure that our spine was bigger than the average spine. Whether it'd be a double album or a single album, it didn't matter. This was so it would be easier for the disc jockey, who was sometimes in a rush to find the album, to find it. We also put in a whole bunch of paraphernalia. You know, Kiss had started their fan club by then and we were selling merchandise. So the double live album offered more than just an album."

"We were struggling for money," Ace Frehley told me recently, asked about the band at this juncture. "Everybody thinks Kiss made it overnight, but we put out three albums prior to Kiss *Alive!*, and the albums did okay, but they weren't blockbuster records. And if the live record would've bombed, Kiss may have gone under. But according to Bill Aucoin, we were in debt. But the live album just broke records. It was on the charts for, I don't know how many years and it went multi-platinum. What was great about that package was, it was like a souvenir of a Kiss concert. And up until the Kiss *Alive!* record, Kiss was known for the visual show more than our music, in a lot of ways. And the first three records never really translated to that, but the live record did, and that's why I think it had such great success."

But, of course, other than adding excitement around the offices, *Alive!* didn't directly involved Angel. As we've heard, for whatever reason, Kiss and Angel never toured together. "No, we tried to get Kiss to take Angel on tour with them," says Larry, "because Gene Simmons is the person who called us to tell us about Angel to start with. So we thought it would be a no-brainer. But then we were in a contractual dispute with Kiss at the time of Angel, when their first album coming out. They refused to take any of our bands with them, and that's how Rush got on their first tour with Kiss, which helped break Rush."

And on their own Angel was a hard sell, being hard rock and coming from California. "That's right, because LA had the whole Laurel Canyon scene. Most of the musicians were these folkies. You know, whether it'd be Crosby, Stills and Nash or... I mean, all of those guys lived in LA and Frank Zappa was there. It was a whole different genre. The Beach Boys were in LA. It was a whole different genre of music coming out of LA and a lot of it was very successful. You also had Elektra and Asylum with the Eagles and Linda Rondstadt, and Geffen didn't sign any hard rock acts in those days. That was the LA sound; that's what everybody was into and they were selling a lot of records."

But there was a plan, as Larry told Sam Dunn. "Yes, Angel was kind of the antithesis of Kiss. Angel wore all white and they all had this long, flowing, gorgeous hair—incredible; everybody was jealous of their hair including women.

All good-looking guys, really good musicians and some great names. Punky Meadows—I love that name. And Punky was a really, really good guitar player. Gregg Giuffria was the keyboard player. They were kind of a cross between maybe, I don't know, Emerson, Lake & Palmer and Kiss or something, because of the keyboard situation. And we tried to focus on having Angel have a great stage show, too, because it was working for us with Kiss."

Once *Alive!* hit, Casablanca was "drug heaven," says Derek Lawrence. "I don't think I ever went into the building, but they would come back and tell me stories. They would walk in, and as they walked through the door there were like two cookie bowls full of coke, and you just helped yourself."

"Larry Harris was kind of a dweeb, actually," cautions Punky, clearly not a fan of who he called the label's "A&R man." "I mean, Larry Harris was an okay guy, but he was kind of a dweeb, really, compared to Neil. Larry didn't really have any foresight, and he was the kind of guy who would say, 'You know, hair spray gives you lung cancer.' You know what I mean? So he wasn't really a rock 'n' roll kind of guy. But what happened with Casablanca, Neil Bogart started Casablanca, and he was broke. He had a Johnny Carson record out, and he was pretty much going to go under, and he wound up starting disco, with Donna Summer and he started making some money with that. Also, he was into Kiss for three or four albums before they broke. And so when Kiss *Alive!* broke, they became huge, of course, and Neil stuck beside them all the time."

"I mean, he had stuck behind them in the beginning too, when they weren't selling many records. And of course they were a live act—you had to see them live. And that's really what broke Kiss. It wasn't their records as much as it was just word of mouth. And then when they did the *Alive!* album, they blew up, because it was a great, great live album. We were always friends with them, with Gene and Paul. We would cross paths when we were on the road  sometimes, touring. They would come to the same hotel and we would hang out and party and stuff, so yeah, we were really good friends with them."

Frank, for his part, maintains that the label spent a lot of money on Angel, and again, money that wasn't there until *Alive!* broke Kiss, exactly when Angel was coming on stream. "Yes, they did, but the only thing that was wrong with it, was that we were on the label that has Kiss and Donna Summer—that made for a difficult situation." Frank is good friends with Richie Ranno from Starz and the two rock veterans have compared notes, with Frank realizing that what Richie went through with being second banana to Kiss on the management side with Bill Aucoin, Angel were having the same issues on the label side. And yes, besides Kiss, Casablanca were busy at the cash registers with Donna Summer. But the end of 1977, Summer had done six albums in four years, with the last five of them being on Casablanca. Each of them is RIAA-certified as gold, with 1979's *Bad Girls*, also on the label, certified as double platinum. Still, as Punky has mentioned, things didn't get off to the greatest of starts, with the label, in November 1974, issuing a double album from Johnny Carson, called *Here's Johnny… Magic Moments from The Tonight Show.*

Back to Angel and their first record, first we see the album cover, and that big Angel talisman, known as the "Gabriel" logo. Warren Entner, ex-Grass Roots, now "junior" manager for Angel and soon to become a major music business executive, was later filmed to create the talking version of the logo that the band would use as a stage prop up into 1977. Not a true hologram, the talking and facial motion was rear-projected through frosted glass, with Entner quipping, upon other things, "I smell the aroma of the gods."

"When we put the band together, Barry bought this trinket," explains Frank. "Or more like a necklace. He got it in Georgetown. It was a necklace where it was kind of like a boxed 'A.' And it had what looked like a sphinx face on it. And he kept saying, 'Look at this; it's cool.' And after a while we kind of said, 'Oh yeah; it is kind of cool. Maybe if we change it a little…' So once we got to Los Angeles, we found a guy who could put some drawings together. We said, 'Take it from this thing here,' and he just embellished from that and we chose one of the drawings that he did."

And so filling the cover was this "A," designed by Jeremy Railton, with the name of the band rendered simply between the wings at the top—again, it's a talisman, as opposed to a logo, which Angel would famously have in spades a couple albums later. Railton worked for Toby Organization and was also credited with designing stage wear for The Osmonds. Flip the jacket over, and indeed the talisman is incorporated into a logo of sorts, but this would not stick. Still, with no pictures of the band (that would have to wait until the buyer cracked the cellophane and discovered the inner sleeve), the sum total of the packaging was both mysterious and powerful.

Angel opens in intense and dramatic fashion, indeed with a song that would become the most beloved epic as far as the deep fans are concerned. "The Tower" (as stated on the record and as accepted, although it's just "Tower" on the back) is announced with piercing and innovative synthesizer tones from the wizard behind the machines, Gregg Giuffria. What sounds like a barrage of video game laser gun fire is interrupted by a muscular snare drum fill from Barry before the whole band (sans Frank) come crashing in like heavy Styx or Kansas or Uriah Heep. A minute of this swirly maelstrom blows until all goes quiet for simple electric guitar, classic Mellotron and the introduction to the world of Frank DiMino as consummate hard rock vocalist.

DiMino's power and diversity of voicing is legendary across this track, but then again, "I took vocal lessons when I was very young," says Frank. "I started at nine years old, ten years old, and I did everything—I did opera stuff, I did musicals, I did all kinds of songs. And so it opened me up to do all kinds of different music. And then when I went to Berklee College of Music in Boston, it opened up a little bit more. Because I was really kind of honing in on rock 'n' roll, because of the Beatles and everything else, although when I got to Berklee it was jazz. So I thought, what's this (laughs)? And they were adamant about it. One of my classes was called The History of Jazz. It wasn't music—it was history of jazz. So I've always been open to doing any kind of music, no matter what it is. And I think the stuff I did with Angel was what I thought needed to be done for that kind of material as well. But my major was composition and arranging, so I had to have an instrument, so I had piano. And that's how I teach."

"On the first Angel album, of course, 'The Tower' is my favourite song," continues Frank. "It's the first song that we wrote together, the first song that kinda drew us all together. It is the only song, I think, that we've opened up every show with. No matter whether it was headlining or supporting or special guesting, we've opened up every show with 'The Tower.' But it's always been a stalwart and a favourite of mine anyway."

"But yes, 'The Tower' was the first song that the three of us worked up together and that was the first song that we played. We didn't even have any lyrics. So ideas were just kind of worked up and listen to it and we added stuff. And then we played it in rehearsal together. Most of that stuff that, we rehearsed it and we played it at Bogies. We played 'The Tower,' 'Long Time' and there were a few others that we had at Bogies. And then we went to LA and we rehearsed out in LA until we got a record deal. So we were writing and rehearsing at the same time."

"The Tower" actually even precedes DiMino. As Punky explains (going over a few points made earlier), "Mickie and I were playing in Daddy Warbucks—well, Bux, I guess you'd call it—at Bogies. And then Gregg came; I had met Gregg a couple years before, and we were going to put together a band but it didn't work out. He lived in New Orleans at the time and I went down there but I didn't like his band. So I left and went back up to Boston and put together Daddy Warbucks with Mickie and Ralph Morman and Jimmy and those guys. We were playing in Bogies, Daddy Warbucks, and Gregg came back up and we started talking, me and Mickie and Gregg. We said we should probably form a band together 'cause I was getting tired of the Daddy Warbucks thing. Bogies had a loft upstairs and that's where the three of us wrote 'The Tower.' That was the first song that we wrote together up there. I had the little verse thing that plays along, and the intro, and then Gregg did the other part. After that, we wrote 'Rock & Rollers.' I had that beginning, Gregg and I put that together and then Mickie of course joined in. But really, Gregg and I were writing all that stuff. Then we finally got Frank and Barry in the band, we showed that to Frank and he put the lyrics and the vocals to 'The Tower' and 'Rock & Rollers.'"

DiMino's lyric on "The Tower" is classic progressive rock, with a knight or warrior or simply an assassin sent from the village at dusk to a tower presumably to slay the wealthy inhabitant or inhabitants and bring the gold back to the town. But there's a humanity to the would-be killer, as he

expresses both fear and indeed doubt as to his mission, calling the village "greedy" and wondering if the reasons he's been given are valid. There's no resolution—we don't find out what happens. At the conclusion, we see that the victor, with his gold, stands in the light of the tower, but it's unclear whether that figure is indeed our protagonist or in fact the original keeper of the tower.

"A lot of the lyrics were finished at the band house up in the Studio City Hills," continues DiMino. "We used

to rehearse and then we'd get back to the house and I'd
sit out in the backyard. It was a great backyard, had like,
strawberries, avocados, huge yard. And I used to sit out there
with this cat that we had—we had a cat that went along with
the house (laughs). One night I was writing and I'm sitting
there—it must have been like three in the morning—and
all of a sudden the cat started spitting, and I'm like what is
wrong with the cat? And I'm looking around, I didn't see
anything, and I look up and there was this possum hanging
from a tree. It scared the shit out of me. I had never seen a
possum upside-down like that (laughs). But yeah, most of
that stuff was written in that house as we rehearsed them."

It must be stressed that "The Tower" is essentially
a very early example of progressive metal, a genre tag that
can be attached only elliptically to the aforementioned
Styx, Kansas and Uriah Heep, but more squarely to Rush.
Interesting to hear that Rush were swept on their way to
fame, with help from Angel label mates Kiss and those early
tour dates, but that Angel were left to fend on their own. And
where were Rush temporally with this idea of being deemed
the prime inventors of progressive metal? Well, *Angel* was
hitting the shops in April 1975 and Rush's second album—
and importantly, first with Neil Peart, who could write songs
like "The Tower" in his sleep—*Fly by Night*, had come out
February 15th 1975. The win, it would appear, goes to Rush,
underscored dramatically by where Rush would go on their
next bunch of albums compared to Angel—basically way
more prog, while Angel would write increasingly
conventional. Still, in the beginning, both Frank and Neil
Peart picked up a lot of ideas from the many books both of
them read, much of it science fiction and fantasy.

But yes, back on Angel, we most definitely were in
the presence of some kind of progressive metal band. "The
Tower" was seven minutes long, as was the album's second
track, "Long Time," necessitating that the album's first side
on original vinyl contained only three songs. "The Tower"
was issued as a picture sleeve single by VIP Records in
France, backed with "Angel (Theme)," but only after *White
Hot* had come out (the back of the sleeve lists all the albums

plus their individual songs). Otherwise, the majesty of this song went pretty much unrecognised.

"Long Time" begins as a type of dark and mysterious King Crimson-esque ballad, dominated by Mellotron and the thespian power of Frank's vocals. But at the two-and-a-half-minute mark, things turn heavy, in fact downright Black Sabbath-esque. This section gives way to an also Sabbath-esque bluesy solo section where Punky plays like—and is recorded like—Tony Iommi. Harpsichord takes us out into a new mellow section, without drums. Once Barry enters, we're into a new theme, buttressed by more Mellotron.

Lyrically, like good prog rock, our despairing protagonist is rendered in timeless terms, "writing letters by candlelight," to a love that has gone, leaving him utterly alone in the world to wander streets "raked with rain." Intriguingly and deftly, the tale is left vague enough for the listener to wonder if the woman pined over has just left or is indeed dead.

All told, "Long Time," especially following upon "The Tower," establishes Angel as an imposing force aeons beyond their baby band status. Not that the world would notice, and indeed, not that the guys would stick with making this kind of music for much longer. Plus there would be the matter of the soon-arriving all-white stage wear, which would help distract from taking the band as seriously as these two strident and theatrical compositions should have warranted.

Side one of *Angel* ends with "Rock & Rollers," and if you think Punky sounded like Tony Iommi on "Long Time," check out the intro to this one, albeit how brief it is, before the band settle into the song's glammy—and yummy—hard rock verse. In fact even Gregg's eerie, angelic keyboard parts in the intro sound like what Rick Wakeman or Jezz Woodruffe might do on a Sabbath track structured this way. Additionally, even as Barry hammers the band through these sublime chord sequences, Punky is throwing in fiery, aggressive licks which again, remind one of Tony. Soon we learn that the intro was in fact an instrumental version of the song's chorus and the pendulum has swung back to Angel as a substantially heavy rocking new act.

And yet, surprisingly, Punky emphatically avows that Tony Iommi was not an influence. "No, he wasn't. You know, I hate to say this, and you're probably going to hate me for this, but I don't know where that comes from because I never listened to Black Sabbath. I remember when Frank and I first got together, somehow Black Sabbath came up and I said, 'I can't stand them.' He goes, 'You're kidding.' I said, 'They just slog along really well and Ozzy can't sing a melody.' When Ozzy sounded great is when Randy Rhoads came in. It's a funny thing. I remember reading an article about Randy and Randy said the same thing—he said he never liked Black

Sabbath. He was into Mick Ronson from David Bowie and that sort of thing. And me too. And I was big into Jimmy Page, so that's the Led Zeppelin in the Led Zeppelin-meets-Yes thing on the first album. That's how we kinda designed that thing. Gregg had all the keyboard stuff from Yes and Emerson, Lake & Palmer and the two fused together. If anything, I had my own style back then, but I was still learning at the same time, to tell you the truth. It's not 'til now 40 years later that I know who I am when I'm playing."

Also key to Punky's aggressive and biting style is a technique he picked up from country music. "Yes, I used to use what are called steel finger picks. I don't use those anymore. I now have three acrylic nails put on my nails at a nail salon. Like a girl (laughs). I get my nails done every so often, you know, so they stay on. But when I started off, when I was a kid, back then you didn't have the internet and you couldn't watch somebody play or have an instructional video. They didn't have that kind of stuff. You would touch your ear to the turntable and figure it out yourself. Or you'd watch TV. I started playing theme songs from TV, from *Beverly Hillbillies* and *Bonanza*."

"So I wanted to play those kinds of songs, TV theme songs like 'Peter Gunn,' and that stuff required finger-picking. So just by chance I saw some National steel finger picks in this little music store and I grabbed them up and I started using them. And I liked them a lot because the attack on the strings was stronger, as opposed to using your fingertips where it would be muted more. So I just got used to using those. Plus you can make some really cool sounds with those by scraping it across the magnet. You could make like bird sounds, all kinds of things."

"So yeah, I would hold a flat pick between my first finger and my thumb. And then I had two of these National finger picks—on my ring finger and my middle finger. They were great. And I used those for forever, until I actually kinda retired from the music scene. And then I really got into country music and stuff like that. And that's how I started getting the nails done. It was from a guitar player that I grew up with named Danny Gatton, one of the greatest guitar players ever, and Roy Buchanan, and they were friends of mine. Danny used to always say that he would get his wife to put on some of these fake fingernails, you know, back in the day, to play with. So I thought about that and I went to a nail salon and got these acrylic ones. And they're just great because they're strong, they don't break and I can feel the strings. Whereas with the finger picks, you don't really feel the strings. You're hitting it with the pick and it's metal, so you don't feel the string. With my acrylic nails, now I can get the same attack 'cause my nails are long, but I can still feel the strings, which I really like."

Back to Angel's profoundly non-country music record, notes Frank, "'Rock & Rollers,' as well as 'Broken Dreams,' were always fun to do because they're just straight-ahead. They were great songs live. And as far as how rocking 'Rock & Rollers' is, it was a nice touch to have Gregg doing that whole beginning section with the choir on the Mellotron, which was a lot of fun. But it's nice having some keyboards, or sort of adding keyboards to the rocking—those elements just kind of married with each other."

What's also cool about this song is that Frank sings the lyric in the first person as a fan going to a show, not as the lead singer of a band up on that raised stage. And given his passion and his skills, the listener is sold that Frank has been in this position many times, going to see his favourite "Rock & Rollers." This track was issued as a single, with picture sleeve in Europe and Japan, backed with "Mariner."

Opening side two of the original vinyl is "Broken Dreams," a crushing rocker like doomy Deep Purple, given the guitar and Hammond mind-meld along with the punchy rhythms coming from Mickie and a biting Barry, who plays tight and halting. Once again, beyond Purple, there's an element of Sabbath here, or at least Atomic Rooster. But also Styx at their heaviest, oddly enough, given, again, the actorly and regal nature of the playing, along with the gratuitous synths. Fitting the leaden crunch of the song is the tragic lyric, where it appears a little boy is watching his mother head off to work turning tricks, with one of them possibly taking her away for good, leaving the child to grow old too soon.

Asked about "Broken Dreams," Punky says, "All those songs, we were under the gun. We had to come up with an album because we had just gotten together for maybe a month or so and we started inviting these managers down to see us and we started a bidding war and they all fell in love with the band. We were doing some cover stuff. We did 'Father to Son' from Queen and we had 'The Tower,' of course, and 'Rock & Rollers.' So we eventually signed with

Toby, we went out to California and we had to get some songs together quickly."

"We just went into a rehearsal studio and started writing. I would go home and come up with an idea and Gregg would do the same thing and we would throw these ideas together. It was done pretty quickly, so it's hard to remember. I would say, 'Hey guys, I got this idea for a song; let's try it.' Everybody was really acceptable at that time too 'cause we were all so hot on each other. We knew we had something special and we all really appreciated each other's talents. Nobody ever said, 'Man, that's not any good.' It was always like, 'Yeah, let's work on that. That sounds cool.' We were all very inspired at the time. But those songs—'Broken Dreams,' 'Mariner'—were written quickly in the studio."

With "Mariner" we're back to the torrid emotional zone that Angel had proven thus far they could take us, through the crafting of these mellow, almost theatrical set-pieces. Here an old man waits for the sea to take him, an inevitable eventuality (or maybe not). This one feels like Procol Harum en route to Queen en route to piano-dominated Savatage from the latter period, maybe even all the way to Trans-Siberian Orchestra. As Frank remarks, "One of the songs that was most fun to do for me was 'Mariner,' because I was able to explore and do a lot of different vocal parts on that. That was the beginning of doing sort of 'answering' and kind of background stuff underneath; it's a lot of fun to do that. 'Mariner' was something where I sat down with Big Jim Sullivan and Derek and asked them about a lot of different English terms for sailors and stuff like that. You know, my idea was to write in that vein. So they gave me a lot of that. Jack Tar was an English sailor, and they gave me a lot of terms like 'around the cape' which was going down around the southern tip of South Africa and stuff. They gave me a lot of those terms that I worked into the song."

File this one with Mountain's "Nantucket Sleighride" and Montrose's "Whaler" as sort of melancholic modern-day sea shanties.

With "Sunday Morning" we're back to the up-tempo progressive rock but again with a Black Sabbath-heavy introductory segment, which, like "Rock & Rollers," recurs later, after a pile of Styx-like pomp. Once more, as with, particularly, "Broken Dreams," Barry attacks his drum part, infusing an uncommon energy into a musical melange up top that's as sober and as regal as the ornate lyric concerning a royal wedding. In this respect, i.e. from the rhythm end, there's more of a similarity with Lee Kerslake and Uriah Heep and to a lesser extent Phi Ehart and Kansas. Mick Tucker and Sweet come to mind as well. In any event, the collaboration between production team and players here far surpasses what one expects from a band's first album, and on a small to medium-sized label no less—case in point, witness the roiling tornado of sounds that closes this one, as the band gradually grind to a halt, followed by a quick speeding-up of the tape effect.

Next is "On & On," which deftly reinforces this band's singular sound as it persists across the record, namely dramatic, melodic music that is heavy at the bottom and tarted up enthusiastically by an array of cutting-edge keyboard sounds and a singer pouring his heart out, this time about miscommunication in relationships. Dovetailed into the plush environs is Punky riffing hard but also firing off licks perfectly placed in the mix.

"I wrote 'On & On' and had no idea that I was never going to get credit for it," Mickie told me back in 2008, intimating that the bad blood with him started early (as we'll see, Mickie would be gone after the third album). "And I was demanding that it was the first single, instead of 'Rock & Rollers.' So song credits are a bit of a sore subject with me— and that had to do with Gregg Giuffria. And Frank DiMino went along with it and Barry Brandt went along with it, and I have to say that Punky Meadows didn't want to go along with it, but he took a backseat to it. And he apologised to me recently, in the last year, for his part in this."

"'On & On' was a quick song that we wrote," notes Frank. "It was actually written in the rehearsal place that we had. We started screwing around with it and then it kinda like fell out, you know, one of those songs where you go, 'Oh yeah, we'll just do it.' Boom, boom, boom. So it was done really quick; I don't remember a whole lot of a labouring with that song. It was very, very simple, an easy song to do."

Mickie does in fact get a credit on the song, albeit sharing it with Gregg, Frank and Punky. However it is indeed his only credit on the entire album. Barry appears on only one as well, and Derek Lawrence and Big Jim Sullivan also get credited, on "Mariner." Frank, for his part, says that "On & On" was written to be commercially saleable, likening it to the creative process and radio-aimed motivations utilised on the later albums. "On & On" was issued as a non-picture sleeve promo-only single, backed with "Angel (Theme)," but only in the UK.

Closing the record is the aforementioned "Angel (Theme)," 1:38 of creepy funereal rock that sounds very much like Don Airey's synthesizer intro to Ozzy Osbourne's "Mr. Crowley," not to be heard for another five years. So that's two links with *Blizzard of Ozz*, given how much Barry Brandt sounds like that album's drummer Lee Kerslake, although really, the quite remarkably close comparison is more with the Lee of golden-era Heep, sort of 1972 through 1974.

It's apt that the credit on "Angel (Theme)" goes to Gregg and Barry—Gregg dominates the melodic structure but like all the songs before it, the drummer really stands out, with Brandt placed high in the mix and then summarily beating the song up more than it deserves or at least more roughly that most drummers would do when presented with a musical track like this. And who else would be so fancy as to do something like this at the end of their album? Why, that would be Queen, of course, who, a month after the Angel album emerged, would issue *A Night at the Opera*, featuring "God Save the Queen" as the album's 1:11 closer. As well, Kiss, a year previous, stuck on their own debut Casablanca album an instrumental called "Love Theme from Kiss."

There's a point about this record that I'd like to bring up, and that's a bit of misgiving with respect to the titling of the songs. There are three titles here—"Long Time," "Sunday Morning" and "On & On"—which literally evoke thoughts of boredom, let alone being boring titles. "Broken Dreams" is similarly both negative and soft as well, while "Angel

(Theme)" is just annoying. The music behind these songs is too grandly dramatic to be sold short by forgettable titles. Bottom line, flashier names—"Sunday Morning" could just as easily been called "Kings and Queens" or "The Baroness"— might have helped boost Angel's claim to the regal status the band deserved. And the problem would persist: three of Angel's most unforgettable songs would be forgettably named "Feelin' Right," "Feelings" and "Can You Feel It," with no question mark on the last one, just to exacerbate the sense of irritation.

"The first one did really well," assesses Frank, summing up the band's admirable debut. "If I'm not mistaken, it was like 100,000, 120,000, 150,000 units. Which was pretty good for the first album. It had a great debut. At that time Circus, in their poll, had chosen us for the best new act (laughs). It was us, Heart and Boston." In fact, Casablanca took out an ad saying as much (and sampling the Circus layout from the poll issue). Only there's a bit of a miscue there with the timeline: *Helluva Band* had already been issued at the time of the poll, and the ad was in fact for the band's third album, *On Earth as It Is in Heaven* and that record's attendant first single, "Magic Touch."

But Frank is dead-on with the result of the poll, out February 14th 1977: Best New Group or Artist: Angel, followed by Heart and then Boston, with the byline reading "Angel's *Helluva Band* aced out Boston's "More Than a Feeling" and Heart's singular attempts for number one." Little did we know that Boston's album would go on to certify at diamond in the States en route to 17 million copies in the US along and 25 million worldwide. Heart wouldn't do too badly either. Creem's 1976 poll results came out in March 1977, and Angel would make a showing as fifth best new group, behind (in order) Boston, Heart, the Ramones and the Runaways. Filling out the ten slots, following Angel were Derringer, Thin Lizzy, Orleans, Dwight Twilley Band and Southside Johnny & the Asbury Dukes.

"When it comes to that stuff, I'm much better dealing with the band than with going to the record companies," continued Frank, on his tendency to stay away from the business side of things. "It was always kind of challenging for me. My thought process was, let us write the material and record it and you guys sell it for us. You know, that's what we want you to do. I want you to take the material, take the album, and make everybody out there believe this is the best thing you've got. Don't come to us and start saying, 'You know what? If you change this, it'll be a little bit better for us to do that.' I don't want to do that."

Industry magazine Record World jumped on board early and reviewed Angel's debut record, suggesting, "Multiply heavy metal exponentially and you have the driving factor behind the newly-formed Angel. 'Broken Dreams' and 'Mariner' are the most defined tracks with interesting solo guitar work and lead vocals from Punky Meadows and Frank DiMino, respectively. A little Mott, a little Mountain—this is the real stuff." Interesting to see a reference to heavy metal so early, and again, it's salient to see the band getting press—Neil was a mover and shaker known for his rock-solid confidence in what he was pushing.

Angel looked like regular rock 'n' rollers in the studio pictures on the inner sleeve of the *Angel* album—Gregg in a Queen shirt, Barry touting John Lennon on his—but that was sure gonna change once touring kicked off in support of the record. With Angel all in white, and the band on Casablanca, fast and furious came the comparisons with Kiss.

"That was when we got to Hollywood," says Mickie, of the change. "Because it was mostly reds and stuff like that, but dark. The background was like black and then red. It was sort of the antithesis to the name Angel, so it was more of a natural to me—in the beginning. And then we got to Hollywood and Neil Bogart came into it, and it was like Kiss was black and we were white—Hollywood, you know? And Kiss liked it. And there was the timing with this music. Ted Nugent was managed by Leber Krebs and I don't know who managed Blue Öyster Cult, but they had a hit single, '(Don't Fear) The Reaper,' and those first few singles were—for that moment in time—genuine hit singles."

Frank recalls that Freddie Mercury from Queen had been ticked off when he saw Angel, because the dressing in white had been his thing, also with the single leotard no less. Frank's bare-chested look, he says, began in the bars back in DC, where he came up with the suspenders with no shirt look, mostly out of necessity, because of how hot it was in the clubs. But now they could develop things further, given a bit of cash to spend.

"Casablanca were great to us," continues Mickie, "and American Talent International were great to us. Broadcast Music Inc.—BMI—were great to us. We got advances from ATI, which was Kiss' agency, who booked them, and they gave us $25,000, which was unheard of, you know, up front. BMI gave us $50,000 on our publishing, on the publishing end of our royalties, in advance before we sold album one, and that was unheard of! I mean, all these deals were being worked, and it was like every other day I was hearing about this going on."

Scoffed Gregg in Creem at the time, asked about Kiss, "Well, I don't know. If you look at it technically, everything from the way we look to what we wear, we're just the opposite. They wear lots of makeup. We rely on the guys in the group to look good naturally. In Japan, they're always playing up that stuff, like we're all pure and white and fly around on our angel wings; Kiss is mean and farts around trying to look like devils. Bye."

"First impressions are killers," continued Gregg. "That's what gets me. If you give it a second thought, and give someone the benefit of the doubt for just a second, the music is there and it is a sincere thing. We didn't just base it on theatrics. Our next tour is going to be a very ultra-original tour for a new group to undertake, using illusions and magic, where we disappear on stage and reappear right in front of people. We're using our time now to build the props so it'll be something out of the ordinary. When it comes to putting on a good show for people, Angel is sincere."

In the same piece, Mickie also remarked on the comparisons of the band with Kiss, musing that, "I think it's kinda silly. But it doesn't piss me off. As long as people dig it, they can associate us with anything they want. We get all this fan mail from Japan and I got this one letter that had a drawing of Kiss on top of us, beating us up. We were little angels with wings on our backs and Kiss had all their monster costumes on. Printed on the outside of the letter was, 'Eternally Kiss in Japan!' They looked at it that way too. But I think it's kinda silly. Our music is different; there's no comparison at all. I suppose we are trying to create the same feeling with the kids when we get out there live, but other than that, I see no bridge between our music and their music. Both groups are basically out to do the same thing: get the kids off and give them the best possible show for what they're paying."

Noted Gregg in a small feature in Circus in March '76, addressing the transition to live performance from having finished the first album, "The pressure on us is so great. Especially in front of 10,000 people when you've never played for that many ever before. So our moves are still awkward; we're still a bit uncomfortable up there. Another thing that hurt us in Detroit was that Roxy Music didn't give us time to do a sound check. In Chicago, where we opened for Sparks, we weren't able to do a sound check either. We're really getting a face-full of what opening acts have to put up with."

But, said Gregg, the way the band put the record together had prepared them for the challenge. "We recorded the album flat-out, like we play live. What you see is what you get. That's why we're confident about our music. Because we did it in the studio, we know we can play it, and we know it affects people."

Mused Punky, "We would like to be an American group that influences English groups. You know, at one time, Britain was influenced by people like Elvis and Chuck Berry. Then came the Beatles, and now we're bombarded by English bands all the time. There's not too many American groups that are successful over there. I wish for once a band from the States would show England a thing or two. And not a Suzi Quatro who stays there all the time. We're gonna hang out here and say we're from here, but we want to be monstrous in both countries!"

Cautioned Giuffria, "It's gonna take time, and that's okay with me. I mean, if we suddenly woke up as headliners, who would I invite on my new yacht or take for a ride in my new car? I don't even know enough people yet. So we don't want to be famous tomorrow." To which Punky replied with a laugh, "That is a lie."

Helluva Band
"We were always trying to fuse synthesizer and guitar together."

If *Angel* is the band's *Dressed to Kill*, all perfect but ignored, *Helluva Band* is their *Destroyer*. Or that's how it should have worked, with Angel rising in stature and sophistication and heaviness with a classic record issued in the same year as Kiss' major studio statement.

Recording once more at Wally Heider, Derek Lawrence says that, "The second album, we talked, and a lot of it had to do with Jim, because Jim was one of the great musicians of all time, *is* one of the great musicians of all time. But together, we would go in and they would say, 'Look, these are three of the songs we want to do.' And we would go, 'Listen, the second one, let's take the chorus out of it and put it in the first one.'"

However it was done, Angel turned in somewhat the same superbly crafted maelstrom of Deep Purple-grooved progressive hard rock, only this time with more conventional songs. *Helluva Band* was every bit as textured, as visionary, as passion-filled as the stellar debut. The pacing, the sequencing, the ethereal synthesizers, Frank's soaring vocals… it's a tour de force, and one of a handful of the greatest hard rock albums the '70s had to offer.

"Derek came up with that idea," says Frank, on the subject of calling the album *Helluva Band*. "We were tossing around ideas, and he thought, well, everyone is looking at the band as so angelic and this and that, if you can let them know that you aren't so angelic… So we were tossing some ideas around, and he said, 'What if you use *Helluva Band*?' 'You know what, I don't know.' And finally we said, 'Okay, maybe we'll go with that.' And then we thought maybe we can make the horns red on the logo, just for the album cover, and Barry Levine (storied photographer, instrumental in the visual image of both Kiss and later Mötley Crüe) was already talking about this idea of having us in chains and stuff. And we thought,

okay, I guess it kind of all works together. And then we got caught up in the whole thing. So yeah, we were all dressed in white, and people were thinking we were angelic and now we are caught in this hell. And actually, originally the back cover was supposed to be the front cover. It ended up working opposite and I'm not sure why."

Indeed on the front cover, Angel's original talisman occurs unchanged but for two matching feathers of the internal wings turned red to look like devil horns. The chains don't leap off the surface as anything particularly associated with Hell, and the same simple sans-serif font is used for the name of the band. Not particularly hellish. Nor is the back cover, where we get, couched amongst the credits, a standard shot of the band and a small thumbnail of the front cover… except the guys have disappeared from their previous perch atop a woman's hand, presumably whisked off to Hell. Front and back, significantly, this is the first time we see the band dressed in their whites. The album saw issue in most Western territories and was essentially standard around the world, one notable exception being Japan, where there's an Obi strip of course but also a red flexi-disc 7" called "Angel Message" which features greetings from the band.

And so to the record at hand. *Helluva Band* cracks
open with a scorching rocker called "Feelin' Right."
Synthesizers battle in jam land with Heep-steeped guitar and
bass and a mood of importance is achieved. Barry turns in a
gorgeous, finessed drum performance and the production is
heavenly and heavy. There's no articulation to the bass, just
the idea and concept of bass, as Mickie melts into the low
tones of Punky on guitar and Gregg on monstrous keys as
metal as they get.

"'Feelin' Right'
was a song that we kind of
wrote live, actually," notes
Frank. "Because what we
did was, we had stuff that
we used to do in clubs when
we first started, and that
was trading off between
the synthesizer and guitar.
And we wanted to keep
that game together, because
there was no one else
doing that at that time. So
we were always trying to
fuse synthesizer and guitar
together, working together,
in harmony and stuff. So
that's how we came up with
the riff, and the idea of both
of them playing off of each
other in harmony."

Indeed that's the
case but there is also a solo
section where Gregg and
Punky trade off licks, Gregg sounding like Rick Wakeman
and Punky, again like Tony Iommi, but a little more stadium
rock this record out.

The textures—fat and bludgeoning—make the song,
as do little details like Barry's high-hat work. Again, come

solo time, Punky and Gregg carry out the ultimate synth and guitar battle, over a throbbing rhythm bed again, blessed and abetted by the Ian Paice-touched drumming of Barry Brandt.

"'Feelin' Right' I co-wrote," groused Mickie, "and there were other bits that I wrote." To clarify, this is in response to the author asking where he might have deserved more credit and didn't get it. He most certainly isn't credited on this one, but he's there on "Pressure Point," his lone credit on the record.

"The Fortune" is placed second, brave move at almost nine minutes long and fully challenging of musical might. This one is an ELP-proud prog opus, or more accurately, something akin to Pink Floyd meets Uriah Heep in their wizardly prime. The crashing close of this one is one of the most powerful and passion-filled conclusions in classic rock. If it sounds adjacent on sound and philosophy to "The Tower," it's because, as Gregg says, it was a continuation of that debut album classic, and in fact a holdover track from the first record.

"'The Fortune' is very epic," notes Punky. "That was my acoustic guitar; that whole thing started with that little acoustic guitar thing I play in the beginning, with Frank singing to that. I had that riff and we made a song around that and then we just got in the rehearsals and I said, 'Hey, this would make a cool song.' We would do that often."

"'The Fortune' was probably one of the most intense recordings that we did," recalls Frank. "Because of all of the synthesizer stuff in the front end of it, and all the time it took to get the right sounds we were looking for—and to program the whole thing. At that time we had someone coming down to help set the sounds we were looking for. Because I think that's when we first got it. We didn't have it on the first album, I don't think. Lyrically it was an idea that I had from this book I had read. I'm trying to think of the name of the book, and it escapes me at this point. But it was just someone who was condemned. It's like a typical 15th century story of someone who is condemned to hang, and finally seeing the light of what life was about, and what he should have been looking at, and then coming to terms with what was going to happen to him."

Indeed the album has a credit for Moog programming that goes to Dan Wyman and Jim Cypherd from Sound Arts. The beginning of the song is all elegant and churchy, but the programmed sort of looping stuff starts at about two-and-a-half minutes, with the band not crashing in until the three-minute mark. Getting Gregg's parts down here was the biggest cause of tension on the album, with Jim Sullivan figuring that the "Special thanks to Big Jim Sullivan and Peter Granet for their infinite patience" note on the back was because of the difficulty Gregg knew he had caused the two engineers constructing the intro to "The Fortune."

"Gregg did take a long time," admits Frank. "The thing about Gregg was he had these two guys that came over, who we saw when we first got the big Moog. He had a lot of guys that came over to try and set it up to get the different sounds, because he was still just learning. When we did the first album, he was still using an ARP. But when we got the big Moog and did 'The Fortune,' it took so long to do that song because of all the different sounds. So Derek might've been talking about that situation. I mean, I talked about that in interviews on the road, how we took so long to get that song done because we wanted to do it right. We knew what we all wanted, but it just took so long to program the synthesizer to get that front part, to the point where I think some of the other songs suffered for it. But it was important to get that song right—and we did."

Indeed the lyric to "The Fortune" charts the musings of a condemned man, famously reprised by Iron Maiden come "Hallowed Be Thy Name." But on the subject of influence, it is said that the song was inspired in part by "Marie Antoinette" by Curved Air, and there are indeed lyrical and musical similarities. Frank sings the song torridly, almost operatic of thespian skill. And true to the Angel ethic, the dark and simple melodies are turned aggressive by the rhythm section. Eventually Punky fires off a riff, overtop of which Gregg does a synthesizer solo.

The credit on "The Fortune," like so many Angel songs, goes to Frank, Punky and Gregg, with Frank explaining that each of these three guys had come from different musical backgrounds to meld together into the Angel sound, writing collaboratively, mostly at rehearsals. This contrasts with the later records where writing would occur more individually, resulting in less of a core sound, which again, originally was this synth-heavy take on Deep Purple at the riffy end and Uriah Heep on the songs that seem like "voyages," like "The Fortune." Still, although

DiMino acknowledges the earlier material as more "interesting," he equally likes the third and fourth records for the growth in songwriting prowess, only disparaging *Sinful* as ill-conceived.

Wrote Kerrang!'s Dave Reynolds, in a large retrospective piece he did on the band, "While the LP was certainly heavier and more rock-oriented than the debut, it lacked the cohesiveness that made the first record so special. There are still some great moments captured, again, by the Laurence/Sullivan production team, one track, even outclassing *anything* on *Angel* all on its lonesome. Put simply, 'The Fortune' is Angel's finest ever moment on record. Giuffria cracks open the bottle with one of the most haunting, spine-tingling keyboard/synth arrangements ever put to tape. It's always baffled me why utter donkeys like Jon Lord or David Bryan are hailed as brilliant keyboard players when a man like Gregg Giuffria gets completely ignored. 'The Fortune' also features a consummate performance from Frank DiMino, who plays the part of a condemned man awaiting the gallows so brilliantly. He may have had a talking voice like The Godfather, but his singing voice was truly celestial."

Things take a quantum leap in cheerfulness (and superficiality?) for "Anyway You Want It," which is actually quite a rocker, even like Zeppelin on an optimistic and sunny day, circa *Presence* perhaps, an album also issued in 1976. It's really only the chorus that crosses that boundary of taste into glam.

Funky like Aerosmith, but still so steeped in unarguable band chemistry, this one seems like a dead ringer for a hit single, yet strangely, it was never launched as one.

Relates Frank, "With the second album, Casablanca asked us to go back and write something a little bit more accessible to be put on the album, and that was 'Anyway You

Want It.' We were about to finish the album, and this came up and from that point on, it was like a struggle back and forth. Us wanting to do things a certain way and the record company wanting you to do it another way. And you get different influences going back and forth, even within the record company, which is crazy as well. You've got one guy saying, 'I think you should do this,' and another guy saying something else, and then the band was a third party, 'Well, we want to do this!' This is always the problem with record companies. You sign the band to the record label because you feel there is potential there. And then they don't let the band do what they want to do. I mean, I can understand guiding things in certain ways, but their end of the deal is to sell it. It's not to write it. The band's job is to write it, record it and deliver it. Their job is to take it from that point and get it on the radio, and sell it to the public. The line gets very fuzzy (laughs)."

Of note, the Dave Clark Five wrote and recorded a hit song back in 1964 called "Any Way You Want It," which was covered by Kiss in 1978, for the studio side of the band's otherwise live album *Alive II*. Frank's song (at 2:52, pretty much the same length as the other two), is not a boy/girl thing, but more about getting out to see a band, like "Rock & Rollers." Through the sparse and banal sentiments however, you can

just feel DiMino trying to write a Kiss song—not to put down Kiss, but it was pretty obvious that Frank's passions and skills lied elsewhere. The track was issued as a picture sleeve single, however only in Japan, backed with "Mirrors."

Side one of the original vinyl closed with "Dr. Ice," another funky hard rocker, yet again, unavoidably bent toward the prog with so much synth bubbling and chirping away in arch-'70s fashion.

"Well, Dr. Ice was a friend that we nicknamed," laughs DiMino. "His name was Barney and he was a poker player. We played a lot of poker back then, and he was the Iceman. He was just cleaning up everywhere. He was a friend of Derek's and Jim's. And finally we said, 'Who is this guy? Did you bring this guy as a shill? He's taking everyone's money' (laughs). So we came up with the idea for 'Dr. Ice.' And again, that's one where the three of us

already had the idea, intact, talking about what we wanted to talk about lyrically, and then screwing around with it together, and then me just taking it home and fine-tuning it."

Derek Lawrence garners a credit on this one, telling me, "Jim did more writing than I did. I did a few lyrics, one being 'Dr. Ice,' which was about my driver who I took out, who was a gambler. And we used to play poker up in the office, and he would end up with everyone's money. Saved me paying him." Indeed, like the previous track not being about sex, it's a bit surprising that this one's not about cocaine—if Angel had a song called "Snowblind," it would be about the band in their whites rendered invisible in a snowball fight.

And same with side two opener "Mirrors," although by this point, with all the white stage wear, one wonders if the guys are making inside jokes. This one's a sword and sorcery number. And how do we know? Well, the first two words are "Magic swords." "Mirrors" peals and squeals out of the gate with a modern, almost futuristic heavy metal thunder—proto-power metal to the core, in fact. Frank's vocal melodies are legion, and Punky lashes out like Sweet's Andy Scott, dive-bombing solos into the fray, a pounding percussion rhythm section as oppressive support.

"Actually, Punky and I wrote that very quickly," says DiMino. "We were at a rehearsal somewhere and we were screwing around with it. He had that lick and we thought, let's see if we can do something with that riff. Because I thought it was a cool riff. So we started coming up with ideas and melodies and stuff, and we were still locked into that kind of sci-fi thing, so I thought, you know what? Maybe we could do something like we did with 'Tower.' So lyrically I just took it to that area."

Frank has noted that this one was influenced by sci-fi author Michael Moorcock, and that the sci-fi direction was partially motivated by the dark classical-styled music the band were regularly crafting, although not always.

Aligning with the curious narrative that is the Angel story, the band's chief writer Punky Meadows is less inclined to like these hard rock classics that the majority of Angel fans worship. "Like I said before, those first two Angel albums, I was never happy about how they sounded. Eddie Leonetti came in and I liked it better then because he kind of captured

it better. But the first two albums, the productions weren't good.
I didn't think that my guitar sounded good and I was never
really happy with my playing. I know people hate that.
Whenever I say that to Danny Anniello, my partner (on Punky's
solo album plus current Angel member, on rhythm guitar),
'cause he's the biggest Angel fan ever, he goes, 'Dude, your
playing's so fucking great on there! Are you kidding me?!'"

"Like,
they wanted to
do 'Mirrors' and
I said, 'I hate that
fucking song!'
Danny would
go, 'No, you're
crazy! That's the
best fucking song
ever! Your guitar
solo is amazing!'
I'm like, 'Shut up.
I hate that song.'
Anyway, we
actually worked
it up because I was outvoted. Frank said, 'No, we gotta do
that song.' So we did that and I actually love playing that
song now (laughs). It's a fucking great song to play. It's a
funny thing how you hear yourself. 'Cause you're your own
worst critic, especially when somebody else is producing
you and telling you how you should do it. You're not doing
it really the way you want to do it. So when you hear it back,
you're not pleased. That's what I know because now that I'm
producing—you know my solo album and the *Risen* album—
I'm doing it and then hearing myself back and I really like
the way the guitar sounds. But yeah, 'Mirrors' is one of
those songs I put together where I said I could sit down and
write a million riffs. Everybody loved that progression at the
beginning, so I put that in there like that. But that was one
of those songs done fast because we had to put *Helluva Band*
together really quickly. We did our first album and had a little
bit of time, but then we went on the tour to promote that and

had to have another album out six months later or whatever. I had a couple of weeks off at my house and instead of going to the beach or hanging around at the Rainbow and shit, I sat home every day and tried to write riffs. So that album has a lot of riffing stuff going on."

"Feelings" finds the band writing in full ballad mode, but smartly and authoritatively like Queen. Frank's vocals are near operatic, and the band responds in kind with a full court press for a loud protracted ending jam reminiscent of Black Sabbath's "Dirty Women," given the carnal, Iommi-like soloing from Punky through this lush sequence. "Feelings" is one of the only tracks Giuffria felt stood up to the quality of "The Fortune" across the expanse of the album, along with "Mirrors." Otherwise, he felt the record was a bit of a let-down because the band felt rushed, writing mostly on the road, and indeed jumping into the studio right off the road, even playing a couple shows with Journey amidst the recording of it.

"'Feelings,' let's see, lyrically I was trying to communicate the difference between being in love with someone and loving someone," explains Frank. "And I had this conversation before with people, friends and stuff, and the point that I was trying to make was that being in love with someone is a little bit more about yourself than it is about the person that you say that you are in love with. Because it's more of a possessive kind of thing. Whereas loving someone means you want nothing but the best for that person, no matter what it is, whether it be with you or someone else. Which is kind of a hard thing to swallow and understand. But in the overall vibe of things, when you take things apart, being in love is more like possession, and loving someone is more about giving."

Next, the guys turn it up for a technical speed rocker called "Pressure Point," an onslaught of bravado and the chops to back it up that is every bit as worthy as the best riff you'll ever get out of The Man in Black. In fact, is that a "Burn" influence detectable in Punky's central riff?

"Yeah, probably, because we were all fans of Blackmore," admits DiMino. "Everyone liked Blackmore. In fact we did a lot of dates with Rainbow, after that stuff. But oddly enough, I think from the third album on, Deep Purple used to rehearse next door to us (laughs), down at the old Gower lot. So yeah, there were ties going on there. But that whole 'Pressure Point' vocal, I was looking for something different to come out, to make it kind of strange sounding, and what we ended up doing was putting a toothpick on one of the capstans, so it gets that warbly sound. And we could put it up whenever we wanted to, whenever that line came up: 'Pressure point is building higher and higher.' At that point, we moved it in."

"We actually taped it to it," answers Frank, when asked if they manually were pressing on the black capstan with the toothpick. "That was the fun part of all that stuff, recording with tape. There was all that unique stuff that you really don't get that much anymore. There was so much more experimenting going on back then, this idea of taking things to the limit. But 'Pressure Point,' like 'Feelin' Right,' was a very early song for us. Actually, with 'Pressure Point,' I had been listening to that David Bowie *The Man Who Sold the World* album. I loved that album when it first came out, and I used to play that album and people would go, 'Who is this?!' No one knew who it was (laughs), and I would say David Bowie. But no one knew who he was, out here anyway, until the *Spiders from Mars* album, but I loved that album when it first came out and I used to like that song 'All The Madmen,' so I kind of took that idea about getting caught in this whole trap of being looked at as crazy, and everything around you was more crazy than it was inside, as if being institutionalised may be the safest place. You know, the craziest people are on the outside, not here on the inside (laughs)."

Frank intimates that the heavier material on the album usually originated with him and Punky—amusingly, the only one who doesn't get a credit on "Pressure Point" is the keyboardist. I asked Frank for a bit of a psychological profile of his vastly under-rated axe man, again, someone who plays quite Sabbath-like yet across arrangements that point to two of the other big four original heavy British bands instead, namely Purple and Heep.

"Punky is pretty easygoing. He's like me. I mean, when we are on stage, it's like we're shot out of a cannon, but when we're not on stage, he's easygoing and easy to come to terms with. Whereas Mickie—and I've known Mickie for a long time—he's the kind of guy who would always do whatever he had to do to get things done. And you know, a good guy to have in the beginning stages, but after we got to a certain point, it started to be detrimental a little bit. Because you've really got to watch what you're doing. You have to make sure you're not saying the wrong thing to the wrong person. You've just got to be a bit more wary. And he was always kind of on a collision course. But I don't think we actually argued that much at all. Sure, there were arguments, but there was no one in the band who was a hothead. I think everyone pretty much had one thing in mind. We all wanted the same thing; we were focused on what we were doing."

Mickie plays one of his busier bass lines on this track, although it must be noted that he's not matching Punky note for note. As for the Barry Brandt writing credit, "Pressure Point" is a bit of a drum showcase, just like "Burn." As for the absence of Gregg, that's rectified when we get to the first solo section, which is taken by Giuffria and is substantially high in the mix. Later Punky takes a solo, and almost like a deliberate nod, this time he sounds more like Blackmore than Iommi. Then Gregg takes another solo and then Punky takes a second one, but now he's back in his carnal but still bluesy Tony Iommi frame of mind.

With respect to his own motivations on this heavy metal barnstormer, Punky explains that "'Pressure Point' was something that I kind of stole from Queen—they were my inspiration for that. I never really cared about any other bands—I just didn't. I just liked Angel, but there was one band that I really loved and that was Queen. To me, they were the benchmark, the ones that really delivered the goods. I mean, all those cats were amazing players, and in terms of the songwriting, they were another band that was not a one-trick pony. They would come out with an album every time that sounded different and they could write anything. When you hear 'Tie Your Mother Down,' that's just your basic rock song, and then you hear 'Bohemian Rhapsody' and it's epic.

And then you hear 'You're My Best Friend,' which is just a pop song that Barry Manilow could do. But when I first heard 'Killer Queen' on the radio, I went, 'What the fuck is that?!' And that was just before we put Angel together. That's why we actually did 'Father to Son' in Angel at one time, because I thought these guys are the best ever. They legitimised everything in rock 'n' roll, you know? So Queen had 'Stone Cold Crazy' and that song in particular was my inspiration for 'Pressure Point.'"

"That's how you get inspiration," continues Punky. "I read a thing about Billy Gibbons in Guitar magazine. They asked him about his songs and he goes, 'Every one of my songs I wrote, I stole from somebody else.' And he proceeded to go down the list, naming every song: 'This song is from that song over there. That song is from this song over here.' He had no bones about it. And I said, why not? I mean, that's rock 'n' roll. I always said I'm gonna write a song called 'Lovers, Muggers and Thieves,' because your inspiration comes from things like that. Why have somebody say, 'Well, that sounds like that' and then feel bad? In the end, you're going to do it your own way and it'll become something completely different. But your inspiration comes from somewhere; there's nothing wrong with that. It's wonderful to be inspired by something and then create your own thing from it. You can be inspired from watching a plant grow. So you don't want anybody to step on your inspiration—just let me do it and see how it comes out and then you can criticise it. But chances are when you do it, it comes out different. But yes, the inspiration came from 'Stone Cold Crazy.'"

As Punky explains, parallels between Queen and Angel run deeper than the songwriting. "Yes, when I first heard Brian May's guitars, all the orchestrated stuff… nobody can deny that, you know? And he still plays with a lot of soul and feeling. Those little lead things at the end of 'Bohemian Rhapsody'—it makes you cry. And not only that, but the production is just amazing, with Roy Thomas Baker in there. Funny thing, I don't know what it is with Queen's background vocals, but they have like this white noise thing in the background or something and I wanted to get that same white noise, that airy sound. It's like a 'shhhh' and it tightens everything up."

"And that was the thing with Angel at the time too: we never had the right producers. Back then a lot of hit songs, that came from the producer. There was Mutt Lange, Aerosmith had Jack Douglas, but Roy Thomas Baker did The Cars, and so he got that sound for The Cars that he was getting for Queen, with the backgrounds. We could never get the producers that we wanted. We wanted to get a Roy Thomas Baker or somebody like that but we could never qualify for that. So we wound up… well, we got Jim and Derek and they were great guys, but the production was terrible and of course Eddie was much, much better."

Second to last, "Chicken Soup" is a bit of a dated funk rocker like bad Aerosmith. Still, if anybody can pull it off, it is these players and this production team. So it's greasy and layered with piercing axes and soaring vocals, not to mention tricky little transitions and a surprisingly moody break or two late in the sequence of events.

"The 'Chicken Soup' song… I looked at it as, there must be a simple cure for everything," says Frank. "It was one of those things like when you have your first love, and you're having a breakdown or something, there's got to be a cure for that whole thing. And I thought, okay, you've got your mother's chicken soup, and that's usually the cure-all for everything. And I guess at that point we had been away from home for such a long time, it was one of those references that hit home."

"Chicken Soup," given its murky and malevolent close (again, oddly Aerosmith-like), transitions nicely into the album's last number, instrumental "Angel Theme," a continuation of an idea from the first album, there formally called "Angel (Theme)."

"The 'Angel Theme' was something that Gregg and Barry screwed around with," recalls DiMino. "A lot of times they would get down to a rehearsal, to the instruments, before anyone else did. So they would play through things when we were setting up and still changing stuff around. And Punky and I thought, you know, you should consolidate some of that stuff and see whether we could do some of it live. The band was basically a live band. I mean, we came from playing clubs. So we were always thinking towards a live audience. So we thought maybe we can do a highlight of both of you guys. So they started working on this thing. And then they came up with this whole idea, that had patterns to it and stuff. And we figured, why don't we just do an instrumental, just the two of you, to highlight the two of you on the album? So that's what we did on the first album, and then it became such a staple that we thought, you know what? Let's do it on the second album as well, and we'll do an updated or different version, and that's when we added guitar to it."

But… "You know what? It actually never was played live!" laughs Frank. "What we used to do was, when we did the keyboard solo, we would just start the keyboard solo off with Gregg and Barry playing things. And sometimes they would interject the 'Angel Theme' into it, and sometimes just a little piece of it, and move it around and stuff, but we never actually did the whole thing. But when we got the full show together, we actually played the recording of the 'Angel Theme' through the PA, when we went off stage. To signify the end of the show. After the logo came down, we used to go into the record sleeve. The sleeve would rise and explode, and we were gone. And the logo, the 'A' angel, would come up, talk to the audience, come back down, and then go into the 'Angel Theme.'"

The *Helluva Band* version was much punchier, with huge molten licks from Punky added. What's more, where the old one sort of lurched to a close, this time the guys end the piece proper but then fly off into a heavy metal jam that fades just before it gets cooking.

All told, *Helluva Band* was a fantastic record, and as alluded to, it looked from the outside—at least to us young pups reading Circus and Creem and Hit Parader—like Angel were big rock 'n' roll stars, already shining bright, glinting, gleaming, killin' it live, basically Casablanca's new Kiss just a step behind the masters.

"That album was just an extension from the first one," reflects Frank. "That's where we were heading. And I think it did a little better than the debut. I know that each of them did a little bit better than the last. I think the best-selling album was the fourth album— *White Hot* was the album that came closest to going gold. I wish that we had had a bit more time for the second album. We did a whole lot of concentrating on 'The Fortune,' putting that thing together and playing it right. Like I say, I feel like the other ones suffered because of that. Not that we neglected them all, but

we spent a lot of time on 'The Fortune.' There are certain things we wanted right on that song and we spent a lot of time on it and the album suffered because of the timeframe we had."

Wrote industry standard Billboard, in their review of the album, "Heavy metal quintet with a twist—synthesizers, Mellotrons, string ensemble and keyboards join bass, drums and guitar in a wall of sound format. Some straight-ahead rock, some spacey material, some raw vocals, punctuating the instrumental work. Instrument material is a step ahead of most bands in this genre, thanks primarily to Gregg Giuffria on synthesizers, etc. Group getting strong FM play around the country. Best cuts: 'The Fortune,' 'Dr. Ice,' 'Mirrors.'"

And then it was time to hit the road, once more dressed angelic, Angel looking as much as the antithesis to punk as they were the opposite of Kiss, not that punk had reared its ugly head in the States as of yet, outside of CBGB. I asked Frank if out on the tour trail, the guys ever got hassled because people thought they were gay.

"You know, not really. I know that the first couple of dates that we did (laughs), a couple of gay guys did knock on Barry's and my room, and I was very confused. 'What?! What's that?' It was the last thing on my mind, that I thought we would be confronted with. And then there was at some point, where we did a lot of dates with Ted Nugent, and he said, 'Before we did any dates with you guys, I wasn't sure about it. I thought you guys are kind of like…' and I'm saying, 'What you're talking about?!' And he said, 'Well I didn't know! I thought your music was going to be kind of like the Moody Blues.' And I said, 'The Moody Blues?!' 'But no, you guys really rock out there.' So he was comfortable with it. After the first date we did with each other, he was okay with it."

The tour for *Helluva Band* was again an exclusively American affair, conducted as part of no regular package in the typical '70s manner, crossing paths with all of our '70s favourites across the rock nation. The highest number of shows seemed to be logged in support of Rush and Blue Öyster Cult in September '76 in the North and Northeast. Angel also shared stages with the likes of Aerosmith, Slade, Status Quo, Bob Seger, Head East, Foghat, Gentle Giant, Rainbow, Nektar, James Cotton Blues Band, Ian Gillan Band, L.A. Jets, Spirit, Starcastle, Piper, Point Blank, Robin Trower, Renaissance, Mother's Finest, Sammy Hagar, Mahogany Rush, Black Oak Arkansas, Manfred Mann's Earth Band, Be Bop Deluxe and Montrose—in other words, everybody but Kiss.

ANGEL MESSAGE

Watashi wa Greg Giuffria
Watashiwa Punky Meadows
  Konichiwa
Watashi wa Frank Dimino
Konichiwa Mickey Jones
Hi this is Greg we're really
  glad for the fan club and
  looking forward to coming
  to your country club
  We hear Japan really likes
  rockin' roll a lot
Konichiwa Punky Meadows hi
  fans and lovers in Japan
  can't wait to get there and
  play in your beautiful country

Konichiwa this is Mickey
  we have a lot of affection
  for our fans in Japan
  and we can't wait to
  come over
Konichiwa this is Frank
  can't wait to come to
  play for you hope to see
  you real soon.
Konichiwa watashi wa
  Barry Brandt the kid
  looking forward to seeing
  you and your beautiful
  country thank you.

Analyzing the band on record, in advance of a Johnson City, Tennessee show featuring Angel, Starz, Hydra and Blackfoot, staff writer for the Kingsport Times-News Mike Clark made some salient points about the band, writing, "They list their influences as the Beatles and Jimi Hendrix, but little of either of these extremes shine through. Lead vocalist DiMino's vocals are expressive in the style of Queen's Freddie Mercury (though he doesn't camp things up nearly as much). They soar over the band, and his overdubbed harmonies are layered for a chorale effect on occasion. He seems a bit shrill at times, but this could be laid at the feet of production."

"The dominant presence on record is keyboardist Giuffria," continues Clark, astutely. "Led by his synthesized 'wall of sound,' some of Angel's instrumental passages remind one of that obscure Welsh band, Barclay James Harvest, but not nearly as 'light.' In fact, in places they give the appearance of deliberately 'heavying' it up to make their sound more palatable to current tastes."

"Angel is a new band with some new approaches to rock 'n' roll, but unfortunately the production is entrenched in a middle '60s heavy metal sound that could cause not a few problems when transferring the material from album to stage; there's the many overdubs of Meadows' guitars and DiMino's vocals that will be hard to duplicate. Unlike many bands, Angel depends solely on DiMino and Meadows for two of the most important instruments in rock 'n' roll. The overdependence could be costly, but perhaps the presence of Giuffria will take up the slack. There is no disputing Angel as high energy rock 'n' roll. They have a solid stage show, complete with an easily identifiable logo. They are not Kiss. But they are better, thank goodness."

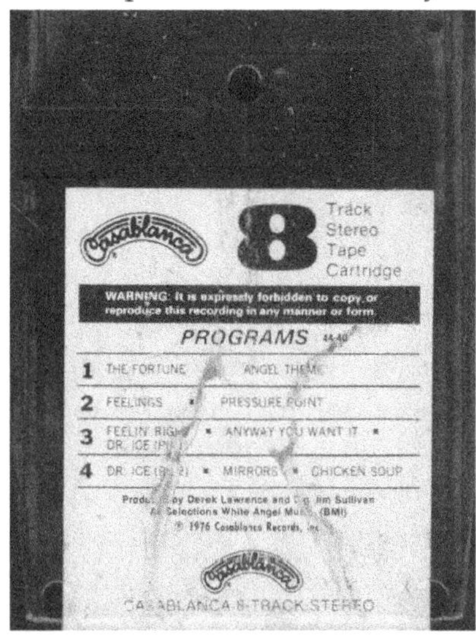

Not sure what he's on about with respect to '60s production, but Clark is right that on the negative, the album is so well-appointed it couldn't possibly sound that way live. But wait. With a technical wizard like Giuffria on board, gaps will be filled, which Clark anticipates as well. When he notes shrillness out of Frank, that, to these ears, is just strong presence. At no point on this meticulously executed album does Frank annoy; he merely steps closer to the lip of the Broadway stage sometimes and sometimes not, and wherever he is in the drama is greatly appreciated. Finally, with respect to influences, the guys in the band are old enough that they are speaking the truth, but one suspects this is also a case of not wanting to puff up your contemporaries or near contemporaries too much. One can step in it, lauding Queen or Heep or, God forbid, Kiss.

After executing a show on July 22nd in St. Louis, Angel didn't win over John Cullinane from the St. Louis Post-Dispatch, who wrote, "Rock group Angel set out to titillate the audience at the Fox Theatre last night. They succeeded in creating about as much excitement as a backyard fireworks display. Even some fine solos— the band is rich in instrumental talent— succumbed to electronic gimmickry and heavy theatricality. For the concert, Angel was hitched to the opening act of Renaissance, which played its usual refined brand of music. The contrast was a bit much for some in the crowd who left before Angel finished its set."

"'Tower,' the first tune of Angel's set, was the best piece of the evening—which made things difficult the rest of the way. It was a Punky Meadows guitar special and had the advantage of effective dynamics, so obviously lacking in most of the band's material. The best and the worst moments of the set were provided by keyboard player Gregg Giuffria, who was surrounded by stacks of equipment. He went from some truly noble sounds on the synthesizer to noise in the time it takes to twist a dial. Singer Frank DiMino spent a lot of time looking over Meadows' shoulder when it wasn't his turn to sing. DiMino's voice sounded a bit shrill, partly due to the sound system. What he called a 'mood' piece turned out to be a little longer, a little more complex, and a lot louder than the piece before. Smoke from dry ice didn't help."

There was a spot of drama that was to take place associated with this show, however, with that same paper, the St. Louis Post-Dispatch running a news piece three days later, on July 26th, 1976 with the headline: "Instruments Stolen from Rock Group." The story reads: "The Angel rock band will continue its concert tour without more than $44,000 in equipment stolen over the weekend in downtown St. Louis. Charles Batton, a spokesman for the band, said a rented truck and $44,265 in band equipment were stolen from a parking lot in the 400 block of South Fourth Street between noon Friday and yesterday noon. The Angel group played a concert Thursday at the Fox Theater. The band planned to spend the weekend here and rented rooms at the Holiday Inn Riverfront. The theft was discovered yesterday when one of the band members went to check the van and found it gone. The rock group had been scheduled to make an appearance in Easton, PA., but its plans now are indefinite."

Recalls Frank, "It was crazy. We got there, I think maybe a day or two early to do some interviews stuff and St. Louis has always been a really good city for us. And somehow we were at the hotel and all our gear was stolen—they took the truck. They stole the truck with all our equipment in it. And we had done a show. It was on the 11 o'clock news and they interviewed us, and we said that we couldn't do the next few shows. We had two shows that were coming up and we couldn't do the shows because our equipment was stolen. So they ran this thing on the news and everything, and somehow someone had seen… they recovered the truck, but none of the equipment. So that was the update on the next news, the next 11 o'clock

news. And then somehow—because I guess it was on the 11 o'clock news—somehow someone saw a piece of equipment, because they ran the logo on the news. Somehow someone saw a piece of equipment and all these cases in a basement, and they called the news and the news called the police and the police went down there and found all the equipment in the basement of this abandoned house. It was pretty crazy. I mean, it's amazing to me that we found all of our stuff."

"I can't remember exactly," continues Frank, "but I think it was a few days later before we had to do the next couple of shows. We must have got the equipment back in and did the shows. I can't imagine that we stayed there in the hotel and then we booked the show. I believe we must have been there like two days before the next two shows and finally got the stuff back in time to do both."

Back on track, there's definitely a pomposity to what Angel got up to on stage that could rub people the wrong way, from the gimmicky white wear (in the beginning, satin, which wouldn't stay clean, soon to be replaced by something brand-new called spandex) to, indeed, the band's intro music. Billy Squier's girlfriend Fleur Thiemeyer was responsible for the early costumes, although Punky tended to design his own and have his seamstress girlfriend put them together. Few examples exist outside of pictures because they'd be worn to rags by the end of the tours.

As for the intro tape, Gregg and Frank had gone down to the library one day and picked up the *Ben Hur* soundtrack album, and that's what they went with, to underscore the epic scope of what they were trying to achieve.

Perfectly happy with Angel's live presentation was Jonna Bartages from Allentown's The Morning Call, who wrote, "Hard rock was the menu last night as the Allentown Fairgrounds grandstand and nearly 4000 fans sampled the smorgasbord. From Angel's white satin to Ritchie Blackmore's Rainbow's 30-foot neon arch, five bands catered to every rock taste. The six-hour marathon was the first outdoor grandstand concert sponsored by the Council of Youth for the 1976 summer season."

"Judging from enthusiastic crowd reaction, Angel was the band many came to see. The five-man band from Washington was discovered by Kiss, another top group, which has played the Lehigh Valley. Garbed in flowing and feathered white costumes, Angel members immediately took command of their audience with their classic rock sound and their stage theatrics. Gregg Giuffra was outstanding on the keyboard and Frank DiMino was a powerful lead vocalist. When Angel lit into hard rock 'n' roll, dozens of fans danced on the track in front of the grandstand stage. Guitarist Punky Meadows was spotlighted during a jam. At the close of the hour-long performance, the crowd applauded Angel back for a lively rock 'n' roll encore climaxed by a wild percussion solo featuring Barry Brandt. Mickie Jones was on electric bass."

But not for much longer, of course.

A couple of early Japanese-issue seven-inch singles:
"Rock & Rollers"/"Mariner" and "Feelin' Right"/"Feelings."

March 14, 1977, Oklahoma City, OK. © Richard Galbraith.

Early magazine advertisements; note the amusingly enthusiastic ad copy
at the hand of Casablanca, great promoters from the start.

Punky wants you. © Richard Galbraith.

Frank and Mickie. © Richard Galbraith.

A synthesizer-surrounded Gregg, plus Mickie in impossible platforms.
All pictures on this page, March 14, 1977, Oklahoma City, OK. © Richard Galbraith.

Pounder of the sound, Barry Brandt. © Richard Galbraith.

Great news turned into a Casablanca ad.

German-issue picture sleeve single for "That Magic Touch"/"Big Boy (Let's Do It Again)."

Gregg, Punky, Frank, Mickie. © Richard Galbraith.

This poster was included in the Japanese issue of the *On Earth as It Is in Heaven* album.

Tour book for Angel's one and only Japanese campaign.

One last goodbye from the guys, March 14, 1977 in Oklahoma City. © Richard Galbraith.

On the left is the French issue of "The Winter Song"/"Can You Feel It." Note the use of an old picture that includes Mickie as the band's bassist. On the right is the Japanese issue with Felix correctly included in the lineup, to Punky's right.

Full page advert for the "scorching" new Angel album.

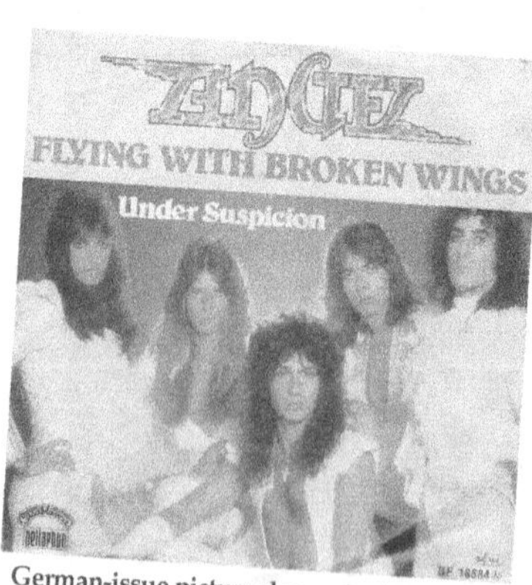

German-issue picture sleeve single featuring "Flying with Broken Wings (Without You)" paired with "Under Suspicion."

On Earth as It Is in Heaven

"We put all the amps in the Wizard of Oz castle."

Angel were to deliver a very different record third time out, recorded under different circumstances and with a controversial production icon manning the board. To recap, Angel had been the talk of the town through '76 and '77, that town being the regular triumvirate of Circus, Hit Parader and to a lesser extent Creem. Still, sales did not bounce in kind, even though the band was now in earnest attempting to make singles, much to the chagrin of the hard rock and prog and hard rockin' prog fan base spoiled by two fantastic records in a row.

"When it comes to the third album, we made a turn," begins Frank. "And what happened was, again, some things that you regret doing. But yes, I'd call it a turn toward less progressive and more kind of rock 'n' roll."

Indeed *On Earth as It Is in Heaven*, issued in early March 1977, contained fully ten songs and no real epics, and even though the pop popped out, a tempering of those accessible instincts took place—mostly unintentional—through the brash, noisy, even muddy production values of the album.

Angel's third record and subsequent tour would represent the last straw for Mickie Jones in the band. More on that next chapter, but at this juncture, it's important to introduce his replacement, Felix Robinson, who enters the story long before his debut recording with the band, *White Hot*.

Felix first met the band in his native St. Louis. "I had, prior to leaving the Midwest, been in a very heavy duty rock band," explains Robinson, "meaning loud, powerful, great players, multiple capabilities with really good equipment, road crew, you know, the whole thing. That was Sky High, amongst several other bands. I was in so many different bands back in the Midwest. But I was on a quest to get back to California, get back to the music business during my last, three, four years in the Midwest, because in 1973 I had joined a group that was signed to A&M Records shortly after I joined and I went to LA and did an album there. So I had already been through the recording industry record signing, destined for glory (laughs). That was The Word, in LA, and so when I was in the Midwest and playing in bands, I was on a track to get back out of the Midwest and get back to Los Angeles."

"But I met the guys in St. Louis while I was still living there and playing with that band Sky High. They came through town and were playing at the Fox Theater, great old music venue, still there. And they were headlining; Starz was opening for them and it was what they called the limo tour because Angel at that point really couldn't afford tour buses. So Bill Schereck, their tour manager, long-term friend of mine and still in touch, came up with a brilliant idea. Well, we'll just get a couple of limousines and a U-haul truck and we'll cut our expenses down. That's the way we'll get around— we'll travel from town to town in limousines. You might wonder how's that gonna work when you have to do three shows in a row and you don't have time to stay in a hotel. And that's exactly what made it so miserable for them was that they had to all pile in these limousines and the stories go on and on. But I was around the band just briefly at that point in time."

"Bill Schereck was someone I knew from the Midwest," continues Felix. "And here he was the tour manager for Angel. So there were roadies that were working for Angel at the time that were from my home area. The guy who was doing the sound system for that show at the Fox was a very close friend of mine for many years. And he had called me and said, 'Come on down to the Fox.' He said, 'I'm doing sound for this band called Angel; they're from California. They really need a bass player.' And he said, 'You know, you'd be great in this band,' he said. 'But they're on tour right now. I think you should come in here.' And so I did. I went down to the show. I sat at the mixing desk. The Fox is about 8000 seats. Roughly the size of Santa Monica Civic auditorium, big traditional movie theatre converted into concerts at that point. I'm being brief here; there's more to the story."

Yes, another piece of the puzzle that Felix and I didn't discuss, was explained to Devorah Ostrov and Billy Rowe in American Music Press. Robinson had just spent $150 on a rare 1969 Precision bass, and the opportunity arose to flip it. "I was told if I went down there and negotiated through Bill Schereck, I could sell them this bass for heck, $300 or $400! After the show, I went to the Holiday Inn where they were staying. I said to Bill, 'I've got a bass that I think your bass player might be interested in.' I opened the case. Bill said, 'We'll buy it.' They all came by, looked at me and said, 'Who the hell are you?'"

As for what Felix thought of the band's show, "I thought it was a pretty lame band! I thought, 'The guitar player looks good, but he's not playing music he's comfortable with. The drummer's too frantic. The singer...' Nothing was right. Of course, I realised they were playing to 3000 screaming 16- and 17-year-old fans, and so who am I to criticise this?"

Back to my interview with Robinson, Felix next is around the band during the recording of *On Earth as It Is in Heaven*. "Yes, they were recording that at what we called The Witch's Castle, which was a building in the Hollywood Hills that had been used for scenery in *The Wizard of Oz*. The wicked witch had this castle where she kept her beautiful globe and the monkeys and all that stuff. And some of those scenes were actually shot in this particular castle-designed building home up in the Hollywood Hills. And that's where Angel recorded the basic tracks for *On Earth as It Is in Heaven*, using a remote truck, which was a custom-built remote truck that was built by Todd Fisher, Debbie Reynolds' son, plus Arthur Kelm, who is to this day still someone I see—I haven't been in touch with Todd; I sent him a note when his mother died—and a fellow named Richard Landers. Just for conversation's sake, Richard went on to become a very well-known live sound engineer, and he was working for Glen Campbell for many years up until the time Glen died. So those three guys had built a remote truck. They were doing the Angel album. They invited me to come down and to be around as Eddie Kramer was recording *On Earth as It Is in Heaven*."

"And this kind of ties in because Eddie was very unhappy with what was going on with Mickie," continues Felix. "And I was there. I was in the remote truck when Eddie flipped out and was like really viciously angry about the way Mickie was incapable of getting a track finished. Plus it was hard for him to keep a bass in tune and Eddie was very particular about instruments being in tune as a musician. He was not going to put up with the difficulties presented by Mickie. I don't want to put too many words to this. He was just difficult. And it was hard for him to take direction regarding the musical changes that I think he was sensing that needed to happen within the record. You know, 'Take the track and play it this way. Don't play it that way, do this better,' whatever. Barry was always right there. Mickie was always a few steps behind, and a little overly arrogant about what he would or would not do. So Eddie was sort of losing it. I was standing behind the console in the truck with Eddie in front of me at the console."

"And I don't know if someone had said to him, 'Let Felix go in and play it.' This is a very vague memory, so I'm not going to put too many exact words to this, but it was kind of a joke and I laughed at it and it wasn't going to happen and I didn't do it. They did float the idea past me at some point, not too far after that, for me to come in and fix some of those tracks, which I agreed to do. Now, this may have been one of the earlier stages where my name was brought up, and I'm not aware of whether Frank or Punky or Gregg would even remember that. Although I remember having it mentioned to me. But there was a circulation going on about the problems with Mickie and what to do about it. I'm sure there were other bass players that might've been considered too."

But to clarify, Felix didn't play on the album. "No, I don't recall doing it. Someone told me once that I had done that, but I don't recall. I don't think so. I don't think so."

Specifically, as stated in the liner notes of the album, the recording location was called "The Emerald Castle." But of course, recording in a "castle," usually doesn't end well, and the results here are indeed open for debate. On the subject of these exotic locales, just ask Rainbow and myriad others who set up shop in France's Chateau d'Herouville. Castles rarely make for adequate sound, which is a reason bands tend to write, for example, at Clearwell Castle but not record there.

"It's Rudolph Valentino's old home here in Hollywood," is how Gregg explained the place to Hit Parader's Richard Robinson, "He had it built for his wife and she didn't like it. It's an actual house, but it's been outfitted as a recording studio. Eddie did a really good job. We were more excited about it, because a recording studio is just four walls, a ceiling and a floor. But this castle was so big that there is every kind of room you can imagine in it. There were like ten studios in it, in that sense. Everybody had their own room, had their own studio. Very expensive, but it was worth every penny of it. We put the truck next to the place and used monitors and video cameras on everybody. Monitors and video cameras were all over the entire house so we could see each other the whole time."

"It was one of those things where it was going to work or it wasn't going to work," continues Frank. "Some things worked out great, like the vocal on 'Telephone Exchange.' That was done in this room that was like a cylinder room, a small round room with a very, very high ceiling. And the nice thing about it was we got a good kind of phasing effect. And that happened naturally because we hung a microphone way up top. That was one of those experimental fun things we were doing. We had Eddie Kramer, and Eddie was responsible for a lot of great drum sounds with Led Zeppelin and stuff like that. And we thought this is going to be great, because we had two separate drum sets in two different rooms that we used on different songs, which was pretty wild. It was fun, but I don't know if we really captured what we were trying to do."

Indeed, the production on the record turned out to be radically harsh, quite the shock compared to the first two albums, and a sound not to be repeated on the last two. But Eddie Kramer was the hot hand at the time, having just done *Rock and Roll Over* for Kiss in New York and soon to head back to New York to do *Love Gun*, which in total, in terms of the stylistic mix of songs, sounds very much like *On Earth as It Is in Heaven*. Although to be fair, Angel's record sounds pretty darn similar in its heft-versus-melody balance to *Rock and Roll Over*.

"Yeah, but we were mostly in rooms with wood floors," offers Frank in defence of Eddie's production job, "and one set of drums was downstairs in a cement room. So there was all kinds of different stuff going on. The castle was great fun, but at the time, Gary Kellgren

had died, who owned The Record Plant (started with Gary's engineering partner Chris Stone). He owned the castle, so he set it all up for us, and it was an idea that we were throwing around to record somewhere else. We had done stuff at Wally Heider in Hollywood for the first two albums, and we were set to go into The Record Plant, with Eddie, and then Eddie said, well, maybe we can go somewhere else. I can't remember why, but anyway, Gary got involved with us and said, 'Listen, if you want to use the castle, take a look at the castle.' Because at that time Eddie was looking for something different to use, and in fact after that, he bought a church in upstate New York and converted it into a studio."

"We wanted to use Studio City," continues Frank, "and I think Studio City was booked or something, so Gary came up with the idea of the castle, so we opted to take a look at it. And he said, 'What I'll do is bring the Record Plant mobile up here.' But then what happened was that all the mobiles were in use; they were all booked. So we ended up getting Todd Fisher, Debbie Reynolds' son. He was just starting up his company, Toddio; Toddio does all the audio and stuff for most of the movies, but he was breaking off from there, I believe, and he was starting his own mobile recording studio. So we negotiated. Gary negotiated with him, with us, and we got the castle, and we got the mobile truck, and we used one of the engineers from The Record Plant. Eddie mostly engineered everything, but he always wanted an engineer there, so he could sit back and have them set everything up, and then he would have a guy there."

"What happened was, when we went into the castle, Eddie had these ideas on the drum sound, and him and Barry would talk about what they were looking for. And we had a drum kit downstairs, kind of like in the cellar, dungeon room, where it was very steely sounding. And we had a drum kit upstairs in another room, where it was a bit smaller with a big sound, but a little more controlled, not so harsh. And then we just went around to different rooms. And whenever we were looking for a sound or doing guitars or vocals, we just kind of screwed around with it and had fun."

"But yes, Gary Kellgren had died in the middle of that whole album," continues Frank. "He drowned in his pool. So everything got kind of sombre there for a while, going in to do the album with that whole thing hanging over us. And Eddie had some problems with Todd Fisher (laughs), and Debbie Reynolds came down to straighten it out with Eddie. There was always drama where we were. But always in the background, you know?" There's no mention of a "Toddio" in the credits, but Frank confirms that Raymax Recorders was Todd's business, the company receiving "recorded by" credit, with Eddie receiving both production and engineering credit, and a host of other guys listed as part of the process.

Circus had reported on the previously discussed heist in St. Louis, getting some of the facts muddled. They had said that the band had had $160,000 worth of equipment swiped from their truck in St. Louis mid-tour. Fortunately, as the report goes, their key instruments (including Greg's $14,000 synthesizer) had been carted up to their hotel rooms, so those weren't lost. The main diversion point from Frank's story is an implication in the piece that everything else was not recovered. In any event, at that point, the band was scheduled to record their third album from mid-October to late November and release it in January. The piece also talked about spiffy new stage props being designed by Disneyland experts for the '77 tour, including a talking logo backdrop with moving eyes, hologram projections, and Plexiglas cylinders to be used in the band's "appearing" act.

Notwithstanding the album's muddy recording, bassist Mickie Jones figures that *On Earth* is his favourite album of the catalogue creatively speaking. "Yes, and working with Eddie Kramer, those production values… he co-produced Led Zeppelin *II* with Jimmy Page, he did Kiss *Alive!* one and *II*, he did Humble Pie, *Performance: Rockin' the Fillmore*, and he produced the third Angel album—and engineered it. And so working with him and doing that was great. We used the Record Plant mobile unit, and

rented a castle up above Sunset Blvd. for about three months and we recorded it up there. And so creatively, the sound, the production values… that was much closer to what I intended Angel to sound like in the beginning."

Continues Frank, painting a brave face on the record's distorted sound (even if Mickie seems to like it), "It was our attempt to try something different and it was good for us to try something different. We learned some stuff working on that album with Eddie Kramer; we learned sounds and what each room had to offer. Some stuff worked and some stuff didn't work that great but it was a good learning adventure for all of us."

Seconds Punky, "That was interesting and a weird story. We were out at the castle that was in *Wizard of Oz*, because Eddie wanted to get that big drum sound, that castle sound with all that ambience and echo, I guess. So we used the mobile unit and we put all the amps in the *Wizard of Oz* castle (laughs). I don't know, kind of an odd experience, really."

"Maybe he brick-walled it; I'm not sure," continues Meadows, referring to a compression process, where the highs and the lows are squashed to the middle to make, in effect, every frequency seem "loud." "A lot of people like that album. I was never that crazy about that album myself, you know? I think we got Eddie because he was on the heels of Kiss, because he did Kiss's live album. But that whole thing was a haze. Because we were getting rid of Mickie at the time too and we were also doing some filming with Casablanca and we were on the road a lot. But I never listen to that album. Of course, I never listen to much Angel anyway, myself, because it's just who I am. Anytime I listened to Angel, I think *White Hot* and *Sinful* more than anything else. But I like 'The Tower' and 'The Fortune,' all those songs, 'Rock & Rollers,' those first ones—I love all that stuff too."

The combative, buzzy sound of the album was at odds with the record's gorgeous cover art. *On Earth as It Is in Heaven* debuted the band's ingenious new logo, which read the same upside-down as it did right-side-up. Additionally, sumptuous blues and greens framed the dramatic mirror-image band shot. The theme was continued on the two panel/two page poster enclosed, which also worked righted or flipped over. Japan did not offer the cover-themed two-panel poster, but rather a larger poster of the band in street clothes posing on some rocks (note that there is a song on the album called "On the Rocks"). No alternate titles or art concepts for the album were considered for the record, according to Frank, "because the whole thing with that was to introduce the upside-down logo. That's why we went with that idea."

Explained Larry Harris from Casablanca, "Well, the story on the logo is that they were playing a gig, and some fan came up to their road manager with this logo, where, if you turned it upside-down it said Angel, and if you turned it up, it said Angel. He just gave it to the band as a gift, and nobody realised how cool it was until somebody actually held it up and looked at it in a mirror, and realised. They found this kid in the audience and they got the rights, paid him, I don't know, $500. Angel paid him or something for the rights to use the logo. It wasn't a brilliant idea from the band or the record label—it was a fan."

"That album cover concept was easy after we got the logo," elaborated Frank, in conversation with John Parks. "What happened was, we were on the road, and our tour manager J.R. Smalling came to us backstage. I don't even remember where the hell we were but a fan sent something back for us to look at. We used to get that kind of stuff happening all the time with J.R.; he'd come back while we were getting ready for the show and putting stuff on backstage and be like, 'Oh, you guys gotta check this out.' So we were like, 'Come on, J.R., we're trying to get ready—get outta here' and all that, and he's like, 'No, guys seriously, you *have* to see this.' So he gets this Angel logo out and we're like, 'Yeah?' And he's going, 'Keep looking, keep looking' and he starts turning it, you know, upside-down. Everyone in the room just stopped. We said, 'Whoa, do that again.' So he does it again and we were just, 'Wow, that is *so cool*. Who

did that?!' So we had this guy, Bob Petrick, come back and
we talked to him, and we paid him to use it and credited him
on the cover which was easy to come up with of course with
the mirror image of us upside-down. We figured if we put
the upside-down image of us on the front, then people would
figure out the logo!"

As for the David Alexander-shot photography of
the guys, "Frankie had gotten into a car accident and hurt
himself pretty bad," relates Punky, "and that's why the
album cover is shot like that. Because he had black and blue
marks and we had to put all this kind of weird makeup on
him and shoot him with that kind of lighting. That's why
that album cover is kind of strange. We're all in really heavy
makeup. He was in an Audi or something, a nice car, with
his girlfriend at the time, and they were out that night and he
came flying around a corner pretty fast and bounced off some
parked cars. She went through the windshield and she got
pretty banged-up and he got banged-up pretty good too and
so his eyes were kind of black. Luckily they weren't terribly
hurt, but enough to where it was a bad deal. And we had to
go in and do a photo shoot because we had done the album.
That's why it looks kind of surreal but cool at the same time.

And then of course they had the upside-down Angel logo. It turned out good. We took a half-empty glass of water and made it half-full."

Once you're finished flipping the cover art upside-down a few times (note that the flipped shot of the guys becomes, necessarily, an incorrect, left/right "reversed" picture), and then done it a few more times with the enclosed poster, the album opens with "Can You Feel It," a nasty rocker which plays up a penchant for odd drum sounds at the hands of the aforementioned Eddie Kramer, he of Zeppelin, Bad Company, Jimi Hendrix and Kiss fame.

Barry is heard unadorned at times and you really get a taste of the tone—it is indeed very Zeppelin-esque but is it good? One could argue both ways, and indeed, add everything else on top and there is a palpable muddiness and lack of treble. Still this one's a killer rock track, even if it's a bit shackled and smothered into a Kiss zone by the thump of the thing. Bits of acoustic guitar and piano are massaged  in for no reason, but all is made well by a screeching twin lead solo and the irreverent heavy drinking lyric. Of note, it's kind of interesting that lyrically "Can You Feel It" works like a direct sequel to "Feelin' Right" from *Helluva Band*, both essentially about drinking alone and a lot. Furthermore, both have "feel" in the title, both are side one/track one, and in both hard-hitting songs, our soused host takes it upon himself to propose a toast!

"'Can You Feel It,' we did the vocals on that in New York," notes Frank. "Actually that was a fun vocal. It was coming from a little different area than what we were doing previously. It was a lot heavier, because of the chord structure and stuff. So the vocal had a chance to sing on those open chords, and it gave me a lot of room to move around. So it's a bit bluesier—a lot of fun doing that one."

"She's a Mover" is extremely poppy, and here the production reveals itself as next to dreadful. I don't know, maybe the idea here is to have something that ploughs through the disadvantageous environment surrounding AM radio technology, but there's a definite displeasure consuming this one at the hi-fi range.

"Big Boy" follows with a funky lope that enters stripper rock terrain, even if the song lightheartedly ends in a double murder crime of passion. "The record company all the time was saying we needed more radio stuff," sighs Frank. "And you kind of want to compromise, but you hate compromising. Yeah, that one was kind of funny, one of those songs where we decided to come from a different area. We put the slide guitar in it and I remember doing that part with the vocal going up."

Essentially "Big Boy" is a Gene Simmons-styled Kiss song, although the amount of funk to it takes it toward Aerosmith in "Last Child" mode. Frank vamps through exhortations of "Big boy, let's do it again," which just asks for a gay controversy, akin to various things Freddie Mercury would sing, or at least *ways* that Freddie would sing, not to mention the simple exercise of calling his band Queen. It's a standard glam ploy, Angel already doing as much with their whites, the same way Sweet had done it with their ridiculous clothes and makeup, on top of Steve Priest's provocative pouting (of course, Angel had their own pouter, one that would soon be celebrated in a Frank Zappa song). Then there's Roxy Music, David Bowie and even, yes, Paul Stanley, somewhat feminine and masculine in manner at the same time, all by design (and when I say all, I mean every example just cited).

And the compromise continued unabated with a glam ballad called "Telephone Exchange." It's nonetheless a catchy tune, with a semi-smart Boston-style break sending it upmarket, this section combining vigorous acoustic guitar strumming plus twin leads, which recur later in the track as well, just before the final wind-up. "Like I say, that one was a lot of fun. We got some unique sounds in different rooms. I did the vocal for that one in this small round room, and we hung a microphone from the top. It was a very high ceiling, and we hung the microphone from above and got this strange kind of whirling effect that we used."

Frank adds the mic placement to get the phasing effect on this one was Eddie's idea, referring to the room as *Rapunzel-like* and cylindrical. Additionally, on the Kiss-like chorus, Frank harmonises with himself.

Side one ends with a frantic high energy funk rocker that would have fit fine, pushing and shoving the songs on Aerosmith's *Draw the Line*. "That was a song we did when we first put the band together," says Frank. "Punky had done that with Bux as well (an earlier version was actually on the aforementioned lone Bux album, *We Come to Play*, issued on Capitol in 1975). He had written that with Ralph Morman, and that was one of the songs we did initially when we were playing clubs."

"White Lightning" was a song that I'd been playing for so many years," affirms Meadows. "I played it in The Cherry People, I recorded it with Bux, as a matter of fact, with Ralph Morman, and I think we needed some more songs for *On Earth*, I don't think we had enough songs yet. So I said, why don't we try work up 'White Lightning?' Because we were on the road all the time, and we would come back, they would give us like a week off to rest up, and we had to write songs for the next album, and pre-production. Then into the studio, finish the album, and then go and

rehearse to go back out, and it was a cycle. It just kept going over and over and over again and it never quit. It got to be pretty rough at different times. But it's funny, when I hear it. I'd kind of gone away from all that stuff and never listened to it, and then I got on Facebook and there was all this research about Angel and this and that. So I started listening to the songs. People would post them and they all came back to me and I started digging them myself. I thought, I could see why people liked that band. It renewed my interest in it and I then became prouder of a lot of the stuff we did, I would say."

Despite there being friction between Eddie Kramer and Mickie, Punky uses "White Lightning" to illustrate that things might have gone differently with Mickie. "I wrote the bass line to 'White Lightning,' but when I played it to him, he picked it up quickly. Because the guitar is going like this (sings it), and I just said, 'Why don't you just cut that in half?' So that's half of what I'm doing. It's still a bass part that's a good

part and he picked it up really quickly. Because I remember when Eddie Kramer started hollering at him in the studio. Mickie would look at me, like, 'Help me. What should I do here?' I said, 'Here, just do this and just do this and we'll be fine.' And so I showed him because he was my buddy. I loved him. I showed him that and he did it and then he got it."

Also, word at the time had the inclusion of "White Lightning" on the album being a bit of a dig at Columbia for issuing the Bux album even though the band was long over. Obviously it was an attempt to feed off the shinier new band's success, but no artist wants to see their old tapes put out when they've long since moved on. What's more, Punky and Mickie weren't even in the picture of the band used for the cover.

Side two of the original vinyl opens with a middle-of-the-road rocker called "On the Rocks," which again edged the band closer to the rudimentary pleasures of heavy Kiss, far, far away from "Pressure Point" and even farther away from "The Tower." Chuckles Frank, "It's a little bit embellished, but 'On the Rocks' is this story where you had this guy we knew who gets caught with his girlfriend in a house, when her parents came home. But it just so happened that her father was a cop, so it was always an interesting funny story." In the lyric, the father is a sheriff and the perp actually ends up on the chain gang, literally "on the rocks."

"I know that I did the vocal to 'You're Not Fooling Me' very, very late at night," says DiMino, moving onto the record's highest quality ballad, one with Queen-like flourishes, especially come Punky's solo. At the lyric end it's essentially a treatise on boredom. "You know, back then, we would stay in the studio until four or five in the morning. And you're going in there late in the afternoon and coming out when it was getting light out and we never saw the dark!"

Which can play on the mind, to be sure, although some creative people flourish at odd hours. "I think it adds a certain kind of… it's easy to get locked up in it. Sometimes the hours go by very slowly, and sometimes they go by very quickly. But when you're doing stuff and staying in the studio that long, a lot of interesting ideas creep up. You don't feel so inhibited for some reason, maybe because no one else is around. But I used to love doing that, just going in the studio and staying there until you get tired and say, 'I'll finish up tomorrow' (laughs)."

Additional odd scheduling confronted Frank when he went back to The Record Plant in New York with Eddie Kramer to mix the album. "It was New Year's (laughs), and I think we got finished at around 10:30, 11 o'clock at night, and it was just me and Eddie Kramer and we met his wife and some people down in the village. But it was funny coming out of there, because it's right near Times Square and people were going crazy."

Frank adds that "You're Not Fooling Me" was rarely attempted live, with "She's a Mover" and "Telephone Exchange" being two of the definite live favourites of the set from this difficult album.

"That Magic Touch" continues in the same vein as the track before it, again Queen-dramatic and predictive of the rise of "pomp rock" a couple of years hence (and note the Mellotron part, which takes us back to Angel's previous era). Again there are guitar licks like Brian May, but the synths and the perky chorus are all Styx. Lyrically, our not very angelic little angel of a narrator is hitting the sauce again, although cloaked in more of a wistful sense of romance than back at "Can You Feel It." This track was launched in April '77 as the album's only single, backed with "Big Boy." Failing to chart in the UK, it did creep to a No.77 placement in the US.

"'Magic Touch' was done very quickly," says Frank. "We were sitting in one of the bigger rooms in the castle, and I think it was Gregg that came up with the front part of that, and then Punky and I worked with him on it. It came out pretty quick. It had a nice pop feel to it and I ended up playing with the vocals, getting that kind of Andrew Sisters triple, three harmony thing, that I wanted to do. And then on the end of it, I actually ended up putting the third on the top, so it kind of opened up at the end of it. The third harmony. You know, I split up between thirds and fifths and stuff, and I ended up putting the third on the top of that one, like I say, at the end."

Additionally, Frank told John Parks that, "Gregg had been messing around on this huge grand piano that was there in the castle and Punky and I heard him screwing around with that galloping piano part and we said, 'Hey, what's that? Let's do something with that" and we took it from there. There were a few other songs that *didn't* end up making it on there but that was one that we ended up finishing."

Following "That Magic Touch" was the album's storming heavy metal fantasy piece, "Cast the First Stone," easily the biggest throwback to the note densities of "Pressure Point." Remarks Frank, "'Cast the First Stone' was, I think, a holdover from the second album. We reworked it a little bit for the third album, and yeah, that was always a good one to play live. That song was actually a typical live song that we really got off playing on. At that time I was reading a lot of science fiction, like the Moorcock stuff, so I wrote a lot coming from that area." Of note, this one's not exactly science fiction, more like a conquering Viking or King Arthur thing, essentially a fine Dio-era Rainbow track. Additionally, it's considerably similar in sword-clashed vibe to "Mirrors" from *Helluva Band*.

I asked Frank who really contributed to the songs the most, in terms of writing the musical tracks.

"All three of us were involved. I can't say that anyone wrote this and someone else did that. It was pretty much always the three of us sitting around after a rehearsal or before a rehearsal and just banging away. Whether it's on piano… I play piano and guitar, so I can fool around with either one. And Gregg had his set-up, and we had a grand piano at the rehearsal place, so it was mostly done at rehearsals. No one else really got involved with lyrics. And Barry and Mickie didn't really write. I don't know why, really, but yeah, we would work out songs in rehearsals, I would get a basic idea, and they'd be like, okay, just take it home and finish up the lyrics for it. If they had ideas lyrically, we could throw that stuff around, but then I would take it home and sculpt it a bit more, try to make it more lyrically suitable."

Evocations of Deep Purple are all over the song, but most definitely they are bold come the first break, where Gregg does his best classical-loving Jon Lord but on synth. He is accompanied by Punky doing the same run. This gives way to a solo section where Punky puts aside any Tony and indeed Ritchie and just does Punky, adding a couple of nice twin lead licks. Then, nice and geometric, it's another blast through the multi-part break and—you guessed it—time for Gregg to solo over that same musical foundation where we just heard Punky. And I suppose it's more suitable that we say Gregg, rather than evoking Rick Wakeman, is doing his best Tony Carey!

"We play 'Cast the First Stone' live now," Punky told me in 2020, "because that's a great song to play. Eddie was looking for that big drum sound but Eddie was also kind of a taskmaster. I felt bad for Mickie because he would say things over the mic, on the headphone about Mickie because we would do so many takes and he could never get the take just right. And as I said, Mickie would look at me for help and I would show him how to play the bass line. But Eddie was kinda tough on everybody. He had Todd Fisher who was Eddie Fisher's son. They had the mobile recording unit up there at the castle and he made Todd Fisher cry and everything else, 'cause he would holler at him. But Eddie liked me and he liked Frank a lot so it was a fun album for us."

"But we had to write on the road and then get quickly into the rehearsal studio with all these songs together, and then get to the studio. We were pretty prolific, I guess you could say, but *On Earth as It Is in Heaven*, like the first two, was also under the gun. We would write and do pre-production, then go into the record studio and record, then come back out and have a couple of weeks off and lay in the sun for a little bit. Then we'd have to go into the rehearsal studio and rehearse to go back on the road. We'd go on the road for six, eight months and then we would come back and the whole thing would start all over again. It was pretty tough, but we were young and full of piss and vinegar and we were up for the task. But yeah, working with Eddie, he was great. I remember when he first came to pre-production, I was playing some Hendrix stuff and he loved that 'cause he loved Hendrix and I loved Hendrix."

For Frank, last track on the record, "Just a Dream" is an album highlight from a lyrical standpoint, DiMino offering three reveries, in the still of night, by a stream and from a hilltop. "I did the lyrics on 'Just a Dream' on the train going home. We took a break, and there were two vocals I had to finish there as well. 'Just a Dream' was one of them. I kept playing with that one, going back and forth with what I was going to do with it, and I ended up writing a whole new batch of lyrics. I went back to Boston to see some relatives and stuff, because we took a five-day break or something. So I went back to Boston, and at that time Amtrak had an express train from New York to Boston. So I took a train and I wrote the lyrics on the train back."

This one's yet another ballad, but a little darker and proggier, melancholy perhaps with spooky synths and a thespian performance from Frank, a nice, wistful way to end an album with many, often frustratingly incompatible directives.

Offering a recap of the album, Frank figures, "*On Earth* reached expectations in many ways and fell short in a lot of different ways too. Because you are always expecting a bit more. Yet when you look back on it, I think we achieved a lot more than we thought we did at the time. It was actually a lot of fun recording it, and then what happens is, once you've recorded and you start mixing it and you start going over stuff sound-wise, you've got so many things going on sonically that it's difficult sometimes to get all that stuff out there in the mix. Now you've got computer mixes and it's a whole different thing."

"An interesting thing happened. As I said, we were mixing it at New Year's. But we had to do a quick mix of four of the songs because the Japanese label wanted to release it earlier because we were going there; we were touring in Japan in early '77. So they released the album, but we were still working on some of the songs, and in order to get things finished, there were like a couple of other songs that needed to be mixed a little bit quicker. So what we did was, we did a quicker mix of two songs—'Can You Feel It' was one of them. I think we knew what we wanted to do with that one, but we had it on the back burner. The things that you know you want are easier to get to. So we mixed 'Can You Feel It' and one other song, and we sent Japan that. So those two songs are a different mix than the rest of the album." Of note, the sequence of the tracks was different on the Japanese issue as well.

Incidentally, Angel never had much in the way of non-album rarities. However, says Frank, "There's one off of *White Hot* that never made it, called 'Better Days,' kind of a ballad. And another one called 'Emerald City' that was recorded for *On Earth*, but never made it."

Neil Bogart and Larry Harris kept getting Angel into the business-to-business industry publications, with Record World writing, "A heavy metal quintet produced by Eddie Kramer. Lead vocalist Frank DiMino is ever at the fore, with guitarist Punky Meadows and keyboardist Gregg Giuffria helping mould the sound into blazing fare. 'Telephone Exchange,' 'She's a Mover,' 'Cast the First Stone' and 'White Lightning' flash through."

After conducting and interview of the band for Circus, Michael Gross was subject to a playback of the new album, noting the record's "strong rhythm section. Mickie, I learned, had the punch he needed for such a loud face. You gotta have something to back it up, my Uncle Meyer used to say, and each member of Angel's got it. Punky's guitar? Sublime. No other words fit. Frank's voice? Turn up the volume too high and it could be Excedrin headache No.57 with an anchor. Mix it right and it's a siren's song. The arrangements? Like vintage Yes filled with surprises enough to make any joker stop and listen. Gregg's synthesizers and keyboards are the key to the mind control. Yes, I thought, Angel will do. In a few more months, following yet another tour that'll put Freddie Mercury and his band of limeys back into diapers, they'll be ready. I'll come see them again. See, 'cause I got a secret. I wanna take all the rock critics who can't see beyond impotent folk singers. I wanna put them in a room and lock the doors. I wanna let Angel play at top volume and teach the professors of pop a thing or two. Teach them that rock ain't dead. Even angels know how to burn."

And then it was time to tour, not that it was in support of promising early album sales, or indeed generous airplay of the album's lone single, "That Magic Touch." Still, Angel were a huge visual draw, both as a back-up band to the era's huge acts and, by this point, as a select headliner. I asked Frank if the band had problems keeping all that white wardrobe clean.

"Oh yeah, absolutely (laughs). We had two sets. One of the guys we had, a holdover from the Tommy Bolin tour, came into our dressing room and it was like… to find a dry cleaner in some of the towns that we were in was really impossible! And none of us were going to wear those things for two nights in a row—they would stand up on their own. So yeah there was some crazy stuff. We would always like to make bets to see if he would come back in time in certain cities we were in. Are we going to have to wear the other clothes? Are we going to have to wear the dirty ones?"

As DiMino alluded to, the guys had to rush-release the album in Japan, because they were on their way over for their first (and as it turns out, only) tour of that Kiss-mad country. From February 7th through the 15th, they played Hiroshima, Osaka, Fukuoka, Osaka and Tokyo.

As Frank told Hit Parader's Timothy Green Beckley at the time, "Our records were receiving an exceptional amount of airplay over there. We even had a half-hour promotional film shipped over and that was played several times on television, and so the Japanese kids knew what to expect. They love rock 'n' roll. Always have. This went over fantastically in Japan. We followed shortly thereafter, receiving an even bigger reception. When we arrived in Tokyo, they were waiting at the airport—huge screaming crowds. And when we finished each of our concerts, the management had to sneak us out a side exit in an unmarked van because the fans would crowd around the limousines we were supposed to be leaving in and were rocking them back and forth."

"The major acts in Japan at the time were Kiss, Queen, Aerosmith, Cheap Trick and us," Punky told Ken Sharp. "It was like Beatlemania when we went to Japan, just total craziness. We'd arrive at the airport and there were thousands and thousands of fans out there, screaming. On the run to our limousine, the kids started pulling my hair out of my head. It was really scary. They wanted a physical piece of me, a souvenir. We had to rent two floors in the hotel, and we couldn't go out anywhere. We had five bodyguards apiece. When we'd look out the windows, we'd see a sea of fans."

Into March, April and May 1977, Angel criss-crossed America, playing with the likes of Manfred Mann's Earth Band, Utopia, The Runaways, Cheech & Chong, Piper, Head East, Sammy Hagar, John Miles, Nils Lofgren, .38

Special, REO Speedwagon, Styx and Atlanta Rhythm Section, with multiple dates logged with Rush and Max Webster.

"We were touring pretty extensively, including a lot of shows with Rush," continues Frank. "They were pretty nice to us. We had fun with them. There were a lot of drinking games we were doing in the hotels after (laughs). You've got to count, and, pass, and if you miss, you gotta down the drink (laughs). I think Rush were the ones who came up with the game, if I'm not mistaken. We did a few gigs with Aerosmith; they were okay. We used to have good banter with Starz. I mean, Richie, still to this day laughs about it. There was some funny stuff going on back and forth. At that time, there were rivalries going on all the time."

"We did like 60 Rush dates," explains Mickie (bear in mind this covers multiple sort of tour "legs"), "and a lot of times, depending who was biggest in which market, Rush would open for us and then we would open for Rush. When we went up to Canada, we opened for Rush, anywhere in Canada, because Rush was still opening for Kiss down here. But when I first saw Rush, they were already headlining 20,000-seaters in Canada. Because their first album went gold and platinum very quickly up in Canada."

"Geddy Lee and I had kind of a distant relationship—we kind of got along," answers Jones, asked about the level of camaraderie with the boys. "They were good guys; I never talked to Alex Lifeson much. And seeing as how we were on the road a lot, I mean, it was a little unusual, but then again, Geddy Lee and Neil Peart… you couldn't slip a piece of paper between them playing live. Standing on the side of the stage and watching those guys play was pretty amazing. I would always want to pick Geddy's brain—I would pick anybody's brain. I would want to get him alone and have dinner with him. Billy Squier (then in Piper) and I would hang out, and he wouldn't want to hang out with other guys in the band. Geddy Lee would hang out, and he wouldn't hang out with anybody else in the band, because basically, when I wanted to talk to somebody, we wouldn't go out and have beers and get high or any of that stuff. We would sit and

I would want to pick their brains and we would want to talk about technical things, you know?"

"One story about Geddy… you know, a lot of people were getting really loose during that period, and I remember Rick Derringer and a couple of his buddies and his bass player Kenny Aaronson, they came into Geddy Lee's room, and they dumped out a bunch of coke on the table. And I remember Geddy looked at it and looked at them and said, 'Get your shit and get the fuck out of my room!' (laughs). They were really straight guys. All of those guys were really straight. They didn't drink, they didn't do drugs… that's just a little story for you."

"Same with Gene Simmons and Paul Stanley," continues Mickie. "I never saw Gene Simmons pick up a drink in my life. And I used to spend a lot of time with Gene. I have a lot of funny Gene Simmons stories, but they're not drug and alcohol stories. I went to have breakfast with him one morning, at the Sunset Marquee. We were all staying in the same hotel and I knocked on his hotel room door (laughs), and it was ajar. So I opened it up—and this was back before they fixed up the Sunset Marquee, and there was a living room and bedroom, because at one time I think it used to be apartments—and he said, 'Oh, Mickie, I'm in the bedroom.' So I went in there and he was butt-naked, you know, with some girl, and he didn't even miss a beat. He goes, 'Oh, I'll be finished in a minute' (laughs)."

But again, Mickie would talk to some of the big bass players at the time about music. With respect to Gene, Mickie says, "Gene was serious about the music from the standpoint… how can I put this? You've got to understand, this is a Mickie Jones editorial, you know what I mean? So who knows. But my take on it was, Gene was a constructor. Gene was an orchestrator of the construction of songs, really, to make that song have a verse, chorus, middle eight, chorus, whatever. And to have really simple hooks, things you could remember. It didn't matter if they were artistic or not. You listen to the early Kiss stuff, you know, 'Meet you in the ladies room.' You listen to that and you think, oh my God. I mean, personally, I wouldn't write that down on a piece of paper. If I did, I would tear it up and throw it away. Those guys would put it on an album, and amongst other songs, that album would become a hit."

Touring by this point had included dates with Rainbow, with Frank pretty sure the band never did any dates with Deep Purple before Tommy Bolin died, mercifully ending what had been an unravelling incarnation from the start—Tommy's last show was December 3rd, 1976 in Miami.

"Yeah, Rainbow with Ronnie James Dio, Jimmy Bain, and Tony Carey," recalls DiMino. "Going back, when Deep Purple were rehearsing next to us, that's when Tommy Bolin was in the band. I was one of the first guys back then to get a digital delay, and the one that I had

was one of the first ones that came out with the variable digital readout. The other ones before that had pre-sets, whereas with the dial I could move it to any millisecond delay that I wanted. So Tommy Bolin asked me if he could rent it from me for the tour. He did a solo tour after he went out with Deep Purple. And actually his tour manager was, at one point, going to be our tour manager, but somehow our tours were going out at the same time, so he ended up going with Deep Purple. But another guy from that crew that took care of most of the dressing rooms and stuff ended up coming out with us. So it was like, back then, everyone knew each other and worked with each other, although (laughs) when bands played with each other it wasn't that friendly. There was actually a lot of animosity going on with some bands back then."

Disco mega-queen Donna Summer (as discussed, also on Casablanca), like Deep Purple, also rehearsed in close quarters with Angel. "I don't really know Donna that well," says Frank, "but we met a few times. Where we rehearsed, in the Gower lot, it was an old lip-syncing place, where they used to do the add-on audio for movies, and I think Casablanca bought that after awhile. We rented it for awhile and then Casablanca bought it at that stage, and I knew that her band used to use it right after us. And then for a while the Village People rehearsed after us. We would be getting done and they would be getting in. Her band… those guys were really nice guys. Like I said, we would be rehearsing in the same place. But I only met her a few times, at functions and stuff like that. She seemed very nice."

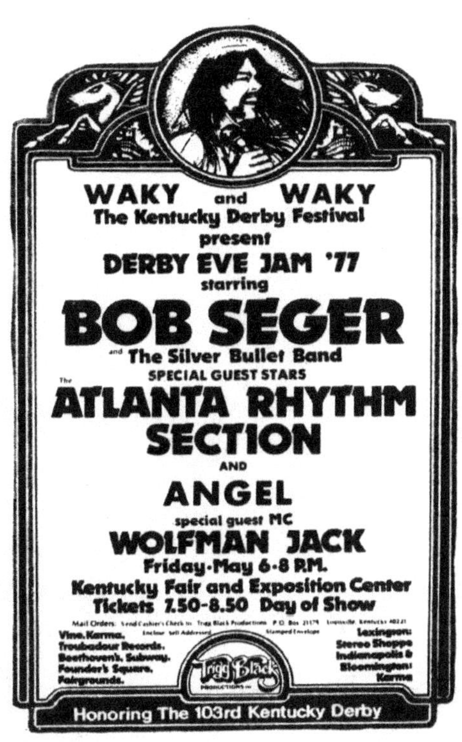

Summer died in 2012, from lung cancer. Although she smoked when she was younger and inhaled tons of second-hand smoke playing clubs, she had been a long-time non-smoker. She was convinced her cancer came from poisonous dust and fumes inhaled after the 9/11 attacks. There was also some genetic history of cancer in her family.

Continues Jones, generally on the subject of Angel's touring history, "Some of the most amazing dates, actually, were having Slade open for us in the United States. They did 'Mama Weer All Crazee Now' and 'Cum on Feel the Noize,' which Quiet Riot later made hits in the States. But they were huge hits in England. I mean, those guys had 14 hits singles in England, and they were already very wealthy because of that, because of their success in England and most of Europe."

Reviewing a show at the Palladium in New York, Billboard's Roman Kozak wrote that, "It was the battle of the power chords April 16. Angel had the best show, Piper played the most pleasing music and Legs Diamond had technical problems."

"A lot of money has been put into Angel to make it an arena attraction. How well it pays off depends on the band's musical development. Visually it is stunning. Church bells, a heavenly choir and a voice from the ages quoting ersatz scriptures preceded the group's arrival onstage. And the entrance itself was accomplished through a neat magical trick that made it appear as if the five individual members of the band materialised inside stacked empty boxes. Angel plays very loud, with the vocalist, guitarist and bass player up front, and the keyboard artist and drummer on a platform behind them. All members of the band, tall, thin, and dressed in white, look very good. Frank DiMino, who provides the band's high vocals, is a professional who knows how to work the Black Sabbath type of audience the band attracts."

"Angel performed 12 tunes in the 75 minutes of its show," continues Kozak, "with the songs 'Magic Touch' and 'Can You Feel It' among the most interesting. Throughout its show, they used a variety of technical gimmicks and stunts. The most spectacular was a moving hologram that made it appear as if the neon-framed angel face suspended above the band actually spoke. It was good fun, and if only the band played slightly better, it would've been a very enjoyable late night—Angel came on stage at the stroke of midnight. But as it was, the band was not that tight, or that good together. Too often Angel just powered its way through passages where a little subtlety and control would've gone a long way."

In the same Hit Parader piece previously cited, Gregg hyped how great the band was live. "It wasn't just Kiss. It was everybody! Nobody wanted us. We got kicked off more tours because they said we were too good. It really blew our minds. This put a big financial burden on us because we realised we had to make it on our own. In other words, headline right away.

Unlike a lot of other bands who tour the country two or three times before they start making money, building up a following a little at a time, we knew we had to do it in one shot or else it would be too late."

"We can be bigger than Kiss," Gregg told Bill Gupton, in '78. "Things are just getting started. The keyboards give us an edge and a musical balance that most hard rock bands just don't have. It has made us much more versatile musically while not taking anything away from the raw energy of our show."

Again, there's that show of self-confidence—and in a couple of directions—from Gregg that might have made fans, critics and other bands a little offended. It's a theme throughout, this idea that Angel were hyped (strike one), and that they felt the hype was deserved (strike two) and that it *was* deserved (strike three, given the influence of a little green monster called jealousy).

More of that self-belief came hard 'n' heavy from Punky, who, also in 1978, speaking with Dennis Hunt, proclaimed, "You've got to have an angle in this business if you want to get ahead or you get lost in the shuffle. On stage we all wear white. We're flashy, very flashy. We use a lot of special effects. We play up the Angel concept, but we're not really angels on stage. We're very aggressive and we play slam-bang rock 'n' roll. I know we're awkward in the studio, but we're working at getting better. That takes time and so far we've been so busy on the road. We haven't had much time to spend in the studio. It's hard for me to spend a lot of time in the studio because I don't like it. I'd rather be on stage."

Explaining that he honed his craft in the clubs, Punky says that, "You have to work to make customers pay attention to you. They come to the bars to get drunk and pick up people. Music is secondary. So you really have to bust your butt to get some attention. That's where I learned all my stage moves and how to manipulate an audience. Also, we want to have a good-looking group. That's part of our appeal. The guys in Angel are chosen for their looks as well as their talent. If they weren't good-looking, they wouldn't fit the band's concept. I came out of the womb this way. I came out with hairspray and makeup on. Man, this is me, the real me."

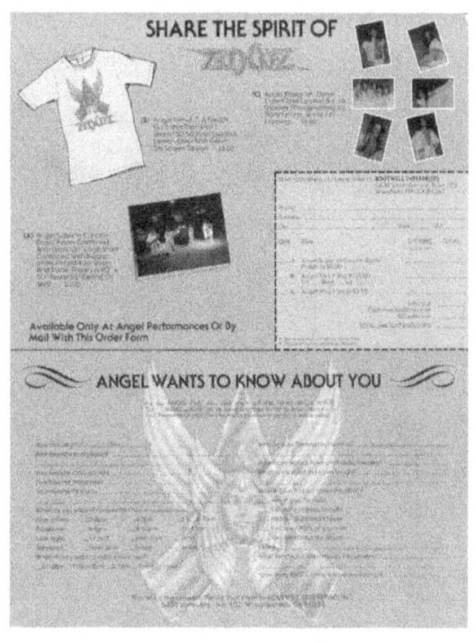

"We don't follow any guru," added Mickie in the Hit Parader piece. "We just want kids to come to see our show and really get lost in the environment we create. We just want people to attend our concerts, and we want to show them a really good time. It's a fantasy—fantasy is what Angel's all about. In Cleveland, where we sold out 11,000 seats, a lot of people in the audience responded by dressing all in white, just like we do on stage. We try to create an exciting atmosphere."

"The clothes and the hair and all of that," stressed Punky, "well, that's us for real. It's not an act! We're sincerely

into the music and what we're trying to put across. It's not just
a money-making venture or something our record company
put us up to. We were always the boys on the block with the
band and not some hula hoops or some silly overnight
sensation. We really believe in what we're doing, and I think
we get that point across to those who come to see us."

It's pretty interesting, really, how much the guys played up to this beyond-pretty boy image. Ben King Jr. of the San Antonio Express interviewed Punky and Mickie as the band were getting dolled-up before their show

in the Municipal Auditorium, writing, "By applying a touch
of lipstick and a daub of rouge, guitarist Punky Meadows is
achieving the 1970s version of the American success story.
Sort of a Horatio Alger with a limp wrist, Meadows is on his
way to becoming a millionaire by capitalizing on a 'beautiful'
image that calls for him to carry a complete makeup kit. Most
rock groups are currently trying to personify the punk image
by looking like they were scraped off the street and handed
electric guitars. But ask Meadows what he thinks of the punk
look, and he will recoil like a five-year-old girl being handed
a slimy bullfrog."

And it seems Punky was buying that assessment,
telling King, "We've always prided ourselves on our beauty.
We're all naturally good-looking guys. The public wants you
to put out. The kids want a show they can really dig. The
theatrics and makeup have always been something I liked
and wanted to do. I'll admit when I put on the makeup, I get
into a sort of bisexual fantasy, but that's as far as it goes. As
for the people who get upset about it, I don't give a (expletive
deleted). We're good enough musicians, but the music
isn't that great that it would be enough if we didn't have
something to go along with it."

Curiously, Mickie reveals that this tendency goes way back. "Until 1975 we were just playing in bars around Washington, DC, getting no place. Back then, Punky and I wore makeup on stage, but we had troubles with the other guys in the bands we played with because they wouldn't." "They were just closed-minded about the whole thing," added Meadows."

Reviewing a show at the Bay Theater in Green Bay, and contrasting the band with opener Piper, staff writer Warren Gerds concentrated not on the band's looks but the obvious money being thrown at them to make them a success. This is indeed the other narrative that we've experienced thus far, from within the band and from those looking on, namely a certain degree of envy and subsequently resentment.

"Angel is different," begins Gerds. "It is visually oriented and its music expands on the recorded product, in this case, *On Earth as It Is in Heaven*. Angel is new and being pushed like crazy. For instance, got a call from Los Angeles Monday afternoon. Did I get Angel's album, pictures and publicity package? No. It came Tuesday afternoon, air express. More: Angel is fresh out of the rock band mill, and yet you could already buy Angel T-shirts ($5) or Angel posters ($2) in the lobby. There is heaps of money in this band from Washington, DC. Just looking at the photos and artwork associated with the group and you get that feeling. Most impressive: the Angel nameplate. Right-side-up or upside-down, it spells Angel. Nifty."

"On stage you see $$$$$ too. From the tips of their manicured hairdos to the toes of their platform shoes, Angel players reek of rock fabrication. Satin-white and sometimes skin-tight outfits give them an other-world look. And: specially made all-white microphones. A synthesizer that looks like it's from 2001. Echo mic gear that highlights singer Frank DiMino's high pitch. Put together, it's really gross. This from the people who brought you Kiss. I really hate to say this because the record company people want copies of this 'review,' but Angel will probably go over. *Big*."

"Tuesday night, this five-man outfit had the place smokin'—sweaty, feverish, hand-clapping, foot-stomping, yelling, whistling, hooting, smokin'. Angel has the look, the feel, the players, the lead singer, the fresh energy, the good ol' $$$$$ to carry it on to bigger halls. Not Bay Theaters. Angel is on a tryout tour, playing small places. Judging from Tuesday's reaction, the Bay would be too small if it comes this way again."

Continues Gerds, in his perceptive piece, "What is striking is Angel carried it off despite blowing virtually all the lights in the place (which is striking in itself—you would think the band would've blown the sound fuses first). The key to Angel is DiMino's voice. It has the rock pyrotechnics—and he has the frenetic party action—to appeal to that element of our society which goes for this modern-day Fantasia. Meanwhile, my wife and child were at a grade school talent show. From the description given, the sensations were four boys—with makeup and lighting effects—doing a take-off on Kiss. Such are their heroes. Such is our society today. Read it and weep, mom and dad."

"I think we started it for the third album and continued it with *White Hot*," Frank explained to me, over to the band's much lauded disappearing trick prop, by the sounds of the above review, not in use in March '77. "We would change the album cover with whatever one it was. So I believe it started with *On Earth*, because we went to Japan and headlined there. How it worked was, there was this kind of stage thing that they would wheel out, and the album cover would come down. It was hanging there but no one could see it until it started to come down. So it would come down and land on this mark on top of this kind of staging. There were steps on each side of it, and after we did the last encore, we would put our instruments down, walk up the steps, each one of us, split up three to two. As we got to the top, each one would go there, wave, go into the album cover, and as soon as the last guy would go into the album cover, the album cover would rise and then explode. Both sides of the album cover would open, and we would be gone (laughs)."

Asked if it ever malfunctioned, DiMino says, "No, actually it didn't. That was one we never really had a problem with. What we were going to do though (laughs), when we recorded the live album at the Santa Monica Civic, what we wanted to do was put five dummies in there, with costumes on, and when the thing exploded and opened, we were going to have the five of them fall (laughs). But no one would let us do that. We thought it was a great idea."

So that's getting Angel off the stage. Getting them on-stage was much more dramatic, or should I say, melodramatic, involving a long and thundering narrative introduction and some magic cubes that the guys "magically" emerged out of.

"The magician, Doug Henning, designed all of our illusions," Punky told Ken Sharp—these were then built by Sid and Marty Krofft, of *H.R. Pufnstuf* fame. "The house lights would be on in the concert hall and the roadies would start rolling out these clear cubes, which would be scattered all over the stage. These cubes were made out of plexiglass and you could see through them. There were no trap doors. The music from *Ben Hur* would be playing while this was happening—that was always our opening music, because it was really angelic and biblical-sounding, with all the angels singing. So the roadies are building columns with the cubes, and the lights start going down.

There was narration by this guy with this really deep voice— his voice was used on a show from the late '60s called The Millionaire. He'd do the narration, like Gabriel, and he'd say, 'Go forth and play your harp, Punky Meadows.' Once he said my name, the lights would illuminate inside the cubes and I'd burst out of one of them, and the kids would go crazy, 'cause they had no idea how that happened. The crowd was always stoned; you would smell all the pot everywhere, so everybody was totally freaked-out."

"The narration would continue, and each individual band member would come out that way. Then Barry would do a drum roll, and then we'd hit the first chord of 'Tower' and all the flash pots would go off. Back then, the only bands doing that kind of a show were us and Kiss. A lot of bands had lasers, but they weren't doing all the elaborate things we were doing. Midway through the set, the giant logo would rise up and speak. From the audience it looked like a hologram."

This was Gabriel, about four feet wide by six feet tall, raised on a 1500 lb. scissor lift, rear-projected to get the facial motion.

"Then, at the end of the show, a giant painting of the cover of whatever album we were promoting at the time would come down. We would all go 'into' the album cover and go up in the air slowly and wave goodbye. Then the whole album cover would blow up and fall apart. We wouldn't be there, of course, and then we'd come running back onstage and the audience would be screaming and going crazy."

"They put five cubes on top of each other," DiMino told American Music Press, as further explanation on the opening sequence. "Chaser lights would go on, then a light would come on inside the cubes and one of us would appear. Then they'd build the next one and another guy would appear. So, you had five chances to figure out how we did it."

Pretty soon it wouldn't be Mickie magically appearing out of the cubes, but Felix Robinson, last seen looking over Eddie Kramer's shoulder as Kramer cursed Mickie out.

Reflects Jones on his ouster from the ranks of Angel, "I mean, historically you look back to what I said about where I formed the band in the beginning. It wasn't just my word saying that. You see, there's one common denominator between all those bands and it's me, and if you're smart, you put me and Punky Meadows together, and then before that, if you include Max, I was in four bands with Barry Brandt. I was in a band called Earth with Barry Brandt. But the band started getting scared—because of Gregg's influence. I mean, you've got to hand it to Gregg in one respect. And I fault myself when I say this—I had control in the beginning. Not that I wanted control over anybody, but I just wanted it to maintain its own natural course musically. And Gregg wasn't really so much of an artist, although I can't put Gregg down musically. But Gregg was more like Gene Simmons. There was a huge hole in Gregg's soul. But he did serve a definite purpose, and Gregg, God, he constructed things in such a way, he pulled us away from Leber Krebs and got us with David Joseph, and then when the first couple of Angel albums didn't have a hit single, it started to worry Gregg."

For his last album with the band, Mickie doesn't really think anything qualified as a hit single, even if the guys were caught red-handed striving for one. "I think 'Telephone Exchange' was the one. I think that was the first thing they released. I don't remember really hearing what I believed was a stone hit single off that album. I don't think Angel wrote great hit singles, I really don't. I think the song

that I wrote, honest to God, having nothing to do with the fact that I wrote it, but 'On & On'… you go back and listen to 'On & On' and hey, I completely nicked that riff from a Queen song, I think from 'Father to Son' on the second Queen album. I didn't nick the melody or anything, but I got the riff… and I mean, everybody does that. But that was the closest thing that I can remember to what I thought turned out sounding like a hit single."

As mentioned by Punky earlier, Angel in fact used to cover "Father to Son," as well as Procol Harum's "Simple Sister," which also employs a descending melody line.

And Mickie, if circumstances were different, would have wanted to be writing more. "Definitely, it became… how can I put this? I told you about how Gregg kinda took the situation over. Because that's what his intention was. Yes, definitely, I was pushed out. I would've liked to have written with Punky Meadows—actually, with Barry Brandt sitting there playing guitar with Punky Meadows. Because Barry Brandt could play guitar, really good guitar. So having him playing guitar, and having Punky Meadows just playing his style of guitar, sitting on chairs. And having Frank, but with Gregg just playing in the background, piano or something, while we were writing. Because if you let Gregg dominate… Gregg's ego was just completely out of control."

"This is the real story," begins Jones, on how the axe fell. "I went to Punky Meadows alone, and I wanted to get rid of Gregg. Really, out of all those guys, Punky was the only one I did hang out with. In fact, that is the *only* guy I hung out with. And I had mentioned it to him, and he thought, you know, I had gone to Punky Meadows and got him to leave Daddy Warbucks to form Angel. And he had just introduced me to Gregg. And Gregg wanted to join Daddy Warbucks. Gregg didn't want to form a new band. So Punky thought I was crazy then, but he still went along with me. But he thought, at this point, that maybe I was going a little bit over the deep end, and that getting rid of Gregg would've been just over the top."

"But I didn't think so," continues Mickie. "I think Gregg was just… without going into too much detail, there were a lot of things going on that weren't cool. And Punky went to Frank DiMino, and Frank DiMino went to Barry Brandt, who went to Gregg. They called a meeting in the office, and Gregg looked at me and said, 'I hear you want to get rid of me.' And I looked at him and said, 'Yeah, that's right.' And David Joseph got up, in his little whiny Australian tone, he had a tirade, and I pretty much left. I split. I definitely was not fired. That was all bullshit."

"Oh yeah, Gregg was like… you might as well have taken a magic marker and drawn a little moustache under his nose (laughs). Oh yeah, Gregg was crazy, man. And that is no bullshit. Hey, I let him get a foothold, and he took off with it, and by the time I trusted him, by the time I knew what was going on, it was too late. So I blame myself! I really do. I don't point the finger at him to say it was his fault. I mean, by the time I realised what was going on it was like hey, there was nothing I could do about it. When you take up so many frequencies on a 24-track board for keyboards, and you bury the crunch of the guitars and the crunch of the drums and the bass guitar, it starts sounding spread-out and kind of muffled."

Asked if Gregg was a good businessman (which he definitely proved to be later, with his gambling technology business), Mickie says, "Oh, without a doubt, without a doubt. Now there you go. Gregg definitely was a suit-and-tie guy. I mean, Gregg could have had short hair and a suit and tie on the whole time. Absolutely for sure. And Gregg and I in the very beginning… that's where Gregg and I came together personally—in the very beginning. We were both on the phone with each other. He wanted to join Daddy Warbucks, but then we decided we were going to join another band, so we were on the phone at least six hours a day. You know what I mean? Masterminded the whole thing."

And what really irks Jones is that he thought, given the right moves, Angel could have turned the corner right about then.

"The thing is, it didn't have anything to do with the music. It didn't have anything to do with the look of the band, certainly, for sure. It had to do with the timing. MTV had not come into existence yet. And there should have been a live album. A live album should have been done when I was still with the band. That *Live Without a Net* should've been done when I was in the band, way back when. The same year, or a little bit before. Like from Japan, Tokyo, we should have done a live album. It would have twisted people's minds here. And in essence, that's what you do. If they don't get it on their own, then you *make* them get it. You don't do it by deception—you do it by showing them really this is what this is so they look at it. That's what Kiss did. That was not false, what they did. What they said was, 'Hey, if you don't get it, look at it! Here's what it is. Hey look, Mickie Jones can sit here and pontificate about all this stuff, right? But the fact of the matter is, history is the way history went. Like I say, MTV had not come about yet, and had it, or had we done that live album, then I would own this block that I'm sitting on. And I would've been on *The Apprentice* instead of Gene last week (laughs)."

To be sure, Kiss issued their live spread after three studio albums, as did Rush, Ted Nugent and Blue Öyster Cult. As well, these live records generated much talk and decent sales in this sort of '75 to '78 pocket, and the bloom was off the double live album somewhat, when you get to 1980, the year *Live Without a Net* was released. In fact Foghat and Blue Öyster Cult (now with a second live album, *Some Enchanted Evening*) notched the best sales of their careers with live albums, both in 1978, and these weren't even doubles.

""It was unfortunate," sighs Punky, still pained 40 years later, about the firing of Mickie. "I hate to say this, but Mickie was a big personality—like Gregg. Mickie could manipulate people too because Mickie was a real promoter. Mickie was the one that helped us almost get a deal with David Krebs and all that kind of stuff. So Mickie had the gift of gab too, maybe even more so than Gregg, and people liked Mickie and Mickie was very personable and could do a lot to really promote things and get his way. That's the thing about Mickie: he was all for the band, all for us, you know what I mean? He would do whatever he had to do to promote us and make us happy and get us a management contract or whatever we had to get—Mickie was good at that. And that's what I liked about Mickie."

"But unfortunately Mickie and Gregg clashed because of that, because they were both very strong personalities. Mickie did all kinds of crap. That's one of the reasons he wound up getting the axe. He did too many crazy things. Mickie and I were best friends growing up and I loved Mickie. We got into a lot trouble together too, but it was always fun. That's what I loved about Mickie. It was never a dull moment. But he was a thief and everything else, you know what I mean? (laughs). We would do some crazy shit together. But that's when we were kids full of piss and vinegar. We were just wild and having a blast."

"When we got together as a band in DC, we were a gang and we stuck together," continues Meadows. "We thought we ruled the world, that we ran the street. Like Danny

(Farrow, current Angel co-guitarist) always say, 'We run the streets.' Well, we ran the streets then, when we were Angel. We were a gang. But when we went out to LA and we got in the big time, then you started having all these people pissing in your ear and shit and saying, 'You know, you don't need this guy. You're the star.' And then it's, 'Gregg, you're the star—you don't need this guy.' So people start believing that shit. And that's what happened. And you wind up breaking up. Mickie was as good a bass player as Gene Simmons is. Gene Simmons is not a great bass player. This is the truth I'm telling you. Mickie might not have been the best bass player anywhere, but he could hold his own and was good for what Angel was doing. We weren't playing really complicated. I mean, we could; some of the stuff was complicated as far as writing, but as long as you could hold the bass down, you were doing okay. And Mickie could and all that. I always felt bad about what happened to Mickie. And before he passed away, we talked a lot and I told him I was really sorry about all that, because Mickie was my friend."

White Hot

"Those guys were looking at Angel and saying, 'Hmm, I can take a scalp here.'"

"It's kind of a long story with Mickie," continues Punky, on the changing of the guard. To be sure, *On Earth as It Is in Heaven* is a fairly neat and tidy—but in and of itself messy, even sloppy!—transitional album, between an era marked by a pair, and another era marked by a pair, both featuring new bassist Felix Robinson.

"And I don't really want to… because Mickie and I were brothers; we grew up together. And I love Mickie so much. Like I said, he was my brother, but Mickie rubbed people the wrong way a lot of times. Mickie was a real hustler, kind of a go-getter. I don't want to badmouth Mickie because I love the guy, but anyway, it just didn't work out with Mickie. We were in the studio with Eddie Kramer, and Eddie didn't like Mickie, for whatever reasons. He didn't think Mickie could cut it on the bass. So he kind of pissed in everybody's ears and stuff, and the consensus was that we had to get rid of Mickie and get somebody else."

"Our manager, David Joseph, knew Felix from this other band I think he was auditioning for, and he went down to see Felix play, and he saw him and of course he was great. We loved Felix and he fit right in, so we hired him right away—we didn't look anywhere else. Because the thing about Felix, a lot of bass players in rock and metal are just thumpers, you know what I mean? They just bang the low note. Where Felix actually plays bass. I mean, he can play melodies on the bass, and he complements the songs. And there's nothing greater than a great bass player. Watching Motown players… those are real bass players. Not just thumping on one string all through the song, like a lot of bass players in metal do. So Felix was just a great decision."

Punky confirms that it was indeed Mickie playing all of the last album though. "Yes, yeah, he did, but it was really difficult, because Mickie couldn't cut the bass parts a lot of times. It was kind of sad. We would do a song, and we'd have to go over one song 15 times, and Eddie Kramer would say through the loud speaker at the studio,

'We have an endless solo out there.' That kind of thing. And he was directing it to Mickie and it was a rotten thing to do. Mickie was never a great bass player—he was a star. He had a lot of charisma, and he was definitely a star, without a doubt."

"He was an okay bass player, but he used to watch me play in The Cherry People, and my bass player was an English cat. He was an amazing bass player that nobody could even touch, one of the greatest bass players that everyone looked up to. So Mickie used to watch Jan (Zukowski) play all the time, and Mickie and I became friends and we always wanted to start a band together. Mickie would sit in every now and again and we would play some Jeff Beck songs or whatever, Yardbirds songs. Mickie and I got along so well, we saw eye-to-eye with a lot of things and we liked the same kind of music. But Mickie just was never… he never really sunk his teeth into practising and playing bass that much. But there were a lot of bass players in those days that weren't all that great either and they got away with it, you know? Because bass was not an instrument that was really explored, unless you were Geddy Lee (laughs). As I said, even Gene Simmons in Kiss wasn't a great bass player. He held the bottom down and stuff but he wasn't Bootsy Collins."

"But back to Felix—Felix is a very talented musician," continues Meadows. "Not only is he a great bass player, but he's a really good singer, he's a great keyboard player and he can play guitar well too. So he's an all-around talented musician, a pure talent. He's underrated. Nobody knows what a great musician Felix really is. He used to intimidate Gregg. Felix and I would show up to rehearsals early, and he would sit down at the piano and he would play like Ray Charles songs, 'Georgia,' and he would sing them too—he can sing all that stuff. Felix comes from the same school I come from, where he plays all different types of music—soul, country, blues, I mean anything. He didn't play just heavy metal where a lot of the heavy metal bass players just thump along on one string, boom, boom, boom. They're not really playing melodic stuff. And so we related really well with him. He can play blues and he can play rock and he can play Motown and country and everything. And he appreciates all that stuff too. So we bonded."

The new guy picks up the story of his somewhat gradual easing into the ranks of Angel. "One of their roadies, the keyboard roadie, Lon LeMaster, he and I shared a house in Venice Beach, along with another guy who was the drummer of the band, The Word, who are all from back in the St. Louis area. And so Lonnie, keyboard roadie for Angel, is coming back home in the evenings/afternoons. The band had just returned from Japan. So they got the Japanese tour in. And I think that Japanese tour was fomenting a great deal of resentment towards Mickie, within the band and within the organization. Apparently he had been behaving in certain ways that had caused difficulties, you know, among a lot of people. Consensus is that he was more preoccupied with being a rock star than he was being a member of a band. He was complaining about other people getting attention and trying to, I guess, direct everyone away from whatever they were doing and let himself take responsibility for a lot of these things. And frankly, they were all tired of his behaviour."

"I had met and gotten to know, a little bit, Frankie and Punky and Gregg. I didn't know Barry that well. I'm not sure who it was that contacted me, but they said, 'Felix, would you like to come and work with us to put together songs for a new album?' Which turned out to be *White Hot*. And I said yeah, of course. And we started woodshedding at Gregg Giuffria's house. He had a piano and a keyboard set up and I brought my bass and little amplifiers. We sat around, mostly in the living room, banging out tunes. Somebody had a hook, somebody had a verse, somebody had a chorus. I'll have to tell you that I had a lot to do with the formative versions of those songs. That happens when several people are together and songs are being worked on. You don't just sit there with your mouth shut and not contribute something. So I did, but I was not a member of the band. I was just a co-contributor to the development of those songs. So that was developing."

"So I'm still playing in that band, The Word, and getting together with the guys to work on these songs, during which it's becoming increasingly obvious to me that I'm there because the other bass player in the band—*the* bass player in the band—is not there. And I wasn't going to say, 'Well, why isn't he here?' I didn't need to say it but it was quite obvious it was because they didn't want him to be there. They needed a competent bass player to be part of the assembly and construction of the songs. And that was an example of what Mickie was both unwilling—and I'll add, unable—to do."

"There may have been disparaging remarks made during those periods of time; I don't recall them. I do remember having the thought in my mind, here I am, we're getting to know each other, getting friendly, sharing the experience of writing the tunes—I should probably make the most of this moment. And I did say at one point, 'Guys, you know, I'm going to write my own sort of bass parts here. I can't play this as if I'm trying to prepare for Mickie to come in and replace these bass parts. Because what I'm playing, I don't know that he can do, that he can replicate them.' And I seem to remember the guys saying, 'Well, yeah, of course, please play what you need to play. You're doing great.' And then a subsequent comment on my part was, 'Well, if you need me to come in and record the tracks when you do the album, that would be fine with me. Although you may want to consider replacing your bass player.'"

"So we finished working on the songs," continues Felix. "I don't know that we did all the songs from the album but a good portion of them. Time was moving along. They were still working on writing the songs for the album and I was still playing with The Word. We had gigs and that band sounded great. I mean, The Word was terrific. We had original music and we could do covers that were, you know, better than or equal to the originals."

"We were playing at a really great club up in Santa Barbara, about 75 miles north of Los Angeles. I think we were there for three nights. And in walk Punky, Gregg and Frank, my songwriting buds. They come in and sit at a table not too far from the stage. And of course to me, that was just… I felt great: they came to see the band. We had spoken about the band. They knew that the manager of the band was their road manager, the tour manager, Bill, so the guys know each other. So we, The Word, went ahead and played, did our couple sets. I would go back on the break and sit with those guys, see how everything's going, make small talk. I think they left before I saw them again. Maybe a week or two or even three weeks went by, not a whole lot of time. And, I think we might've gotten together once more to write tunes. And here's where it gets a little sketchy for me. I believe we got together at the soundstage at Columbia, a lot where they had a big rehearsal studio. And I think I came down and played live with them in the rehearsal room. I'm almost certain I did that once before they asked me to join the band. In other words, we had worked together. I brought songs. They had come to see me perform live. I think I got together and played with them. I could be wrong; maybe that came afterwards. But nonetheless the familiarity there, it was good, it was high."

"I got a phone call; I was at work," continues Robinson. "I had a day job, very brief. I'd only been there a couple of weeks working in a speaker cabinet factory in the valley building speaker cabinets, wearing a lumberjack shirt and a pair of dusty jeans, covered in sawdust. I got a phone call, 'Felix, it's David Joseph calling for you.' That was announced over the loudspeaker system in the factory.

It wasn't a big factory. And, so wow, David Joseph. And I looked across at my buddy, who was the drummer in The Word and had gotten me the job in the speaker cabinet factory. One of the partners in the speaker cabinet factory was Lon LeMaster, the keyboard roadie for Angel. 'Felix, it's David Joseph on the phone.' And I look over and I see my drummer looking at me. He goes, 'You son of a bitch.' He was just, you know, giving me daggers but in a friendly, loving way."

"And I went in and picked up the phone and it's, 'Hi Felix, this is David Joseph; I'm the manager for Angel.' And I said, 'Oh, hi, David, how are you doing?' 'Well, I have an important question for you.' I didn't realise it, but all the guys in the band Angel were sitting in the room with David at that very point in his office at the ICM building, and I'm on speakerphone. And he says, 'Well, I have a question. How would you like to be the next bassist for Angel?' And I said, 'Well, let me think about that for a minute—okay.' Or something similarly stupid. And yes, that'd be great. He said, 'Well, the boys are in the office here.' They were at the ICM building, top floor. 'And we'd like you to come over right now.' And I remember looking at my clothing thinking, oh my God, this is just embarrassing as hell. I said, 'Right now?' He says, 'Yes, come on over.'"

"And I said okay. And I kind of brushed the sawdust off of my shirt and my pants best I could as I'm walking to my car, which was a '65 Mustang. I get in the car, I drive down to Hollywood, Beverly Hills, wherever it was, or is. I think that building's still there and my daughter lives in West Hollywood, so we're there frequently. I went up the elevator and walked into the office—took me a half-hour, 45 minutes to get there. They probably took a look at me and went, 'Oh, there's no photographs today.' But it was great and we talked about how great of a fit this was going to be and how comfortable it felt and all that stuff. As for what happened to Mickie, my recollection of what I was told was that they had met with Mickie previously—might've been that day, might've been a very short time before on the previous day—but they said, 'Mickie, it's over,' and he had gotten very upset."

Meanwhile, there was always something cooking in the Angel camp, and at this juncture there was a movie that got shelved, to be called *Angel at Midnight*.

As Punky explained to Ken Sharp, "Casablanca had us do a movie with Candy Silvers, who was the daughter of the comedian Phil Silvers, but the film never got released. There was a lot of footage of us playing live. Candy Silvers loved Angel, and they shot these dream sequences where she would be backstage touching our costumes and having these fantasies about us. Then we would show up and put our arms around her and she would be thrilled. So the film comprised all these different dream sequences, along with us playing live. It was shot in a bunch of different cities including Cleveland. The local radio station put out word that if you came to the Angel concert dressed in white you'd get in for a dollar, so the place was full with all of these people dressed in white. There were also all these white balloons that said Angel."

"The film was being done right around the time that Mickie Jones was getting ousted from the band, unfortunately. They wouldn't shoot any footage of Mickie and it got to be really awkward. I think the plan was for the film to be shown in theatres. Casablanca did a lot of filming and spent a lot of money doing it. Then it just came to an abrupt halt and never went any further and it was never finished. It never got released, and the footage got put into storage somewhere. I would love to see it."

Adds Felix, "I don't recall much about *Angel at Midnight*, but I was talking to our tour manager Bill Schereck a few months ago and he swears he remembers how they were rushing to shoot me separately for this famous movie that was never released, this music video of Angel that they had to reshoot because I had just joined the band."

As for Frank's recollection, "I remember they were trying to shoot around Mickie, which was kind of uncomfortable because we were talking about maybe having to replace him, so there was a lot of shooting around him. But the bigger problem was, after we shot it, it was never finished. I don't know why it was never finished. We never found any of the film for it and I still don't know where the film is. There was a lot of live footage that was shot in Cleveland, where we had everyone out in the audience come down dressed in white, which was great. And then we shot close-ups when we got back after that tour, on a couple of the sound stages at the Gower lot where we rehearsed, you know, in costume and everything. But I don't know what ever happened to that film—it was never finished and it's never been found. And I never quite saw the script of it. I know they shot some scenes with Candy, the daughter of Phil Silvers who was Sgt. Bilko, and there was some dialogue and stuff. It's one of those strange things that's almost floating somewhere out there. Either that or it's disintegrated by now."

Back to the next Angel record, I asked Punky back in 2016 why it came to pass that *White Hot* would mark such a more directly commercial, poppy, accessible style for the band.

"Well, I mean, I played in club bands my whole life," explained Meadows. "I was like the hardest working musician. I had a group in the Washington, DC area and around there and I would be in the house band. We would play in one club for three years straight. And in those days, there weren't DJs, and the only time the band would have a break, they would have like a little jukebox in between the time. You could play five or six sets a night and you could learn your craft well. We had to play everything from the Beatles to Zeppelin to the Stones, even some country songs and a lot of Motown. So I learned to play everything, and I learned to love and appreciate that stuff too. I love nothing more than a cool Motown song with great background vocals. So I kind of like to put all that in there. *White Hot* was the beginning of being a little more commercial but more guitar-driven too. Well, not completely. Because there are a lot of keyboards on all of those songs but, yes, a little more guitars to it. *White Hot* was still fairly heavy. But sure, it was getting commercial with the Rascals song, 'Ain't Gonna Eat Out My Heart Anymore' and 'Don't Leave Me Lonely' on that record. We started writing songs more in that vein then, which was a lot of fun."

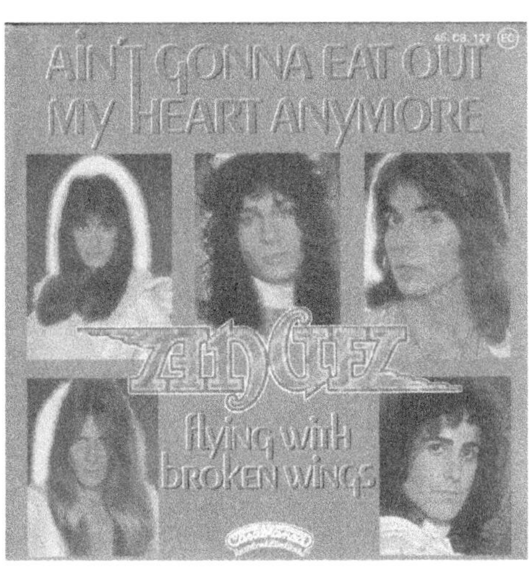

"*White Hot* is one of my favourite Angel albums," avows Meadows. "Power pop is what I call it. I kind of figure Cheap Trick were a power pop band and I loved Cheap Trick. I love that shit like crazy. Whenever 'Surrender' is on, I crank the radio to sing right along with it like everybody else (laughs). I mean, you can't resist it. To me, that's what music is all about. It inspires you, it makes you want to sing along and that kind of thing. You want to play it over and over again."

Indeed all the guys in Angel were admirers of what Cheap Trick had accomplished, as well as their sound, which rubbed off on Angel for the present record and even more so for *Sinful*. But when Angel were cooking up *White Hot*, the beloved band from Rockford hadn't broken yet. Cheap Trick's second record, *In Color*, from September '77, wouldn't go gold until August 1979 (and then eventually platinum), and the debut, from February '77, would in fact never certify. To be sure, however, as Angel began to fizzle in 1980, Cheap Trick had to their name *Heaven Tonight*, *Dream Police* and the smash *At Budokan* live album, and Angel could only look on glumly at what could have been, and more bummed about it when they thought about their own successful visit to Japan.

"By the time you got to the fourth album," says Frank, "we were pretty much comfortable with being in the studio. We had two guys that were really listening to what we were like: Eddie Leonetti and Lee DeCarlo. Lee was the engineer, and Eddie had done a lot of stuff with Jack Douglas. But we got along really well and we were comfortable enough, like I said, in the studio. These guys would listen to us and we would listen to them. It was a really good working relationship. We tried all kinds of things. Whatever we wanted that made sense, they went along with and tried to make it better and made it easy for us. We had a good feeling going into the studio for that. That album was the best, as far as working conditions and working together and getting things done goes. That album might be my favourite of all of them. It's a toss-up between that one and the first one. Because there is so much stuff on the first one that I think was a pretty good strong statement of what we were about when we first started."

"It had to be," answers Felix emphatically, asked if he felt *White Hot* and *Sinful* represented a new era for the band stylistically. "It just had to be, because the dynamic that developed with my coming into the band made it different. There was a lot more energy. When I first heard them, I remember thinking that everything is plodding along. This bass player is just keeping time and not very well at that. When I came in and got to hear Barry play… I'm not sure how much you think about bass players, but I'm a very aggressive musician. I'm a guitar player. I'm a keyboard player. I had a long history as a musician before I joined Angel playing multiple instruments. My old band with Phil Driscoll, I was both guitarist, second guitars, bass guitars, I played piano on a lot of songs and I played second trumpet, all instruments that I had have had training in. I was reasonably competent with a trumpet, but not so much as the other instruments. So when I came into Angel, I really had my thoughts pretty clear on how I was going to mix into this. And realizing how Barry played drums was an important key element to how I was approaching my parts, and it was not to do what Mickie had been doing."

Felix is making total sense here. Despite the songs being squarely less heavy metal across the two albums, there's a new bite to the rhythm section, making for a unique chemistry and style, an aggressive pop, sort of like Cheap Trick in the meaning of those two words "aggressive pop" put together, but not sounding anything like Cheap Trick at the same time. In other words, the rhythm sections of both Angel and Cheap Trick evoked the articulation of The Who's, if not the chaos, or at least not nearly as much of it.

"With Mickie, Barry was sort of uncontrollable," continues Felix. "There was nothing to keep him centered, with timing, and he just was nuts. He played more with the guitar and somewhat with the keyboards because Barry and Gregg used to get together before rehearsal and play like Emerson, Lake & Palmer style, loud keyboard parts with the bass part that was there, but not integral to whatever music they were playing, but more like keynotes (sings long, low straight notes). So Barry was playing like that in warm-ups or working through song ideas—Barry would just play like a maniac."

"Barry's style of playing, I would liken more to Keith Moon, or for somebody who's just on the edge of fusion—a lot of everything which I loved. Barry has such tremendous talent and independence, as drummers describe independence, like four-limb independence. And you know, his speed, his ability to go into some type of a drum fill that you don't know how it could possibly be resolved or how he can come out of it but he does, *and* playing with power. There are great drummers that can do that, like Billy Cobham and Lenny White. Both these guys I've heard live and both of them I've seen play drum fills that I would say are some of the best that you can imagine."

"Of course there are other great drummers that do amazing things, but Barry was close to that league in terms of being able to pull off tremendous drumming ideas that are not just complicated rhythmic patterns. Barry can hit the kit and make things happen. Now, keep in mind, he'd been playing with a bass player who just played pedal tones, quarter notes, no bass fills, really. If Barry was going to play a lick on the drums, Mickie was not going to follow that; he was just going to get along. But you want more colour than that as a musician, and we did that. He wasn't able to shake me."

As for the impression of his new band mate Mr. Giuffria, Felix opines that, "Gregg has a good background in music, somewhat educational, definitely had played in bands that had made use of his skills as a more classically-oriented keyboard player, but he also has a feel for rock 'n' roll. Like the B3 sound that he got was the right sound, with a bite to it. So the texture of the keyboards, with him in rehearsal and recording, was always fitting in with the sound of the band. Keep in mind that with any rock band there's a sonic landscape; there's the guitar, where are the drums? Where's the bass, where are the vocals and where are the keys?"

"And Angel was never a band that had a battle going on. There was a battle between guitars and keys, but we were all part of that sonic landscape. For example, my bass is always up in the mix with a bite to it, because that's the way I play. I don't play with a tubby bottom end, so that it's all low end. And then, you know, high end with cymbal crashes and keyboards way up there. Unfortunately some of the songs could have been better and our basic tracks usually sounded better than the final product."

"That put aside, talking about Gregg's keys, Gregg spent a lot of time working with programmers to get the synthesizer sounds that were current, meaning using synthesizer sounds for the time that were at the front edge of technology. Remember, synthesizers had not been around that long. But Gregg always had a good blend between somewhat traditional sounds, and then utilizing assistance and expertise in programming. And I'm glad that he did that because Gregg's a keyboard player and of course he became a great programmer because that's what his business has been since then. At that point, we were going into the studio and spending hundreds of thousands of dollars on recording time and people with very good engineering skills. We had Lee DeCarlo and we were using the best studios. And Gregg understood the requirement for bringing in the right expertise to program the complicated synthesizer that he was using. We were using very good quality equipment, and Gregg made sure that everything sounded cool instead of having to be made sound to sound good afterwards."

What Felix refers to is the proverbial "We'll fix it in the mix" work ethic, or lack of work ethic as it were. Instead the band were going to play it right and record it right from the start, to the point where on the basic tracks, Punky would even play his rhythm track, launching into a solo and go right back to playing rhythm, as if this were a live situation.

On the subject of writing credits for the record, asked specifically about Punky and Gregg, the two main music guys, Felix says there was conflict "only in a healthy way. And it came from the dynamic that happened when Mickie was there. Mickie having been in the band up to that point caused Gregg and Punky to become a little more isolated among themselves, along with Barry, so that their teamwork approach to doing what they were doing had to become more solidified. So only in a healthy way. When we would talk about sounds or parts, they would have very brief arguments, 'I'm going to do this' versus 'Well, I think I should do that; you take that part' and 'It needs more of this or that.' But you know what? They worked through that quickly and decisively and it didn't turn into lingering resentment."

Capturing all this was Eddie Leonetti who would work with a bunch of bands roughly of this ilk, including Rex, Moxy and Legs Diamond but also Artful Dodger and Skyhooks. But doing the heavy lifting would be Lee DeCarlo. "There's a guy that is a natural producer engineer," remarks Robinson, "understands the music in a very technical way, perfectly suited at that time to be the guy. He just had a way of managing the responsibilities of engineering that went far beyond just tweaking knobs. He understood how we played and he found it a very amusing atmosphere that we created with him. He was part of that. Lee was more one of the guys. We spent a lot of time laughing and having a good time together apart from being in the studio. I just have great memories of working with him, and he went on to a lot of very good successful work, with the likes of Jack Douglas."

Noted Gregg in Hit Parader at the time, asked about Leonetti and the importance of a good producer, "He's the overseer of vibes. It doesn't matter how positive everyone's attitudes are when they come in, the producer creates the atmosphere and a bad producer can ruin everything. That's why we have a lunatic for a producer (laughs). But we achieve a 'live' sound because of the way we record. We don't pad everything and play like we're isolated. We play like we're live."

As for the writing of the record, Giuffria said that "certain tunes were written individually and others are composite efforts. There are a lot of different colours on this album because we've all had a lot of different inspirations. The music has come at different times; we haven't tried to force it."

Onto the release of the album, rock journalists of the day who might have gotten a free copy of *White Hot* for review would have also received the Casablanca Records press materials for the album, which amusingly paint the band as the guys with the best hair in the business. Sure, wait five years and we'd have actual hair metal, but Dokken and Ratt had nothing on Angel.

"*White Hot*, that's the password today into the spectacular world of wonder and imagination from those modern rock Gabriels known as Angel," trumpets the bio, slicker than usual, but that's Casablanca for you. "Yes, Angel, the group spawned in 1975 somewhere over Washington, DC, is a band grounded in the inspired belief that rock music is a communication, a special sound enhanced by super visuals and a mind-tingling experience that is simply out of this world. Angel has toured for three straight years (after one-and-a-half years of rehearsal preparation prior to their maiden voyage of '75), honing their skills, confronting the challenges, testing their wings, often spending their hard-earned proceeds from one night's performance totally on better illusions and special effects for the very next audience. They have always felt that it is better to give than to receive, and their generosity has resulted in a groundswell reception from fans around the world (they are one of Japan's supergroups, for example!). The result has been constant growth, development and creative transfusion among the five members who religiously believe in friendship and teamwork first in the torrid rock nether regions."

"Now, with four fine albums under their collective belts on Casablanca (*Angel, Helluva Band, On Earth as It Is in Heaven* and *White Hot*, plus a live album on the way), Angel has embarked on perhaps the most ambitious stage show in the young history of rock, with priceless settings and illusions like none seen on earth before."

"And now a word from our own 'Earth Angels,'" continues the bio, although the guys are barely allowed to speak. "Punky Meadows: in the beginning, God created the heavens and earth—and Punky Meadows! Punky created Angel with a little help from his friends (see below). Edwin Lionel Meadows, known to all you insiders as Punky, swings the big guitar ax for the group. He was born on February 6th 1952 in Washington, DC with a full mane of brown hair, which he's had ever since. His eye colour matches that of his hair. This Angel is an Aquarius whose favourite pastime offstage is Farrah Fawcett-Majors, the only person in the country with hair to rival his!"

This is of course a reference to the greatest pinup star of the late '70s, rivalled only by crooning folkie Linda Ronstadt, or maybe Farrah's co-star in Charlie's Angels, Jaclyn Smith, or even Kate Jackson, for those who tend to prefer Mary Ann over Ginger, or Betty over Veronica. There's also famed Wonder Woman of the day, Lynda Carter and, back to rock, Ann and Nancy Wilson. Indeed the vamping and puckering pictures of Punky at the time really did have you wondering if this particular Angel member was crossing into a transvestite zone, trying to look like a woman.

Continuing, "The two-tone tresses belong to Gregg Giuffria, who has 88 or more tones to display out of his keyboard. Gregg hails from Gulfport, Mississippi. 'If ya blink twice ya miss it.' He claims he has two blue, slightly glazed eyes, and likes football and dames in his off hours. 'Which don't come very often,' Gregg informs us, since the group must arrive at 8AM in the morning to rehearse the spectacular special effects for each new concert date. 'It's got the script and stopwatch timing of a Broadway musical,' says this Leo, who was born July 28th 1953, springing from the forehand of a Steinway piano."

"Then there is Frank DiMino, an angel with a bit of the devil in his eye, the lead vocalist with the dark hair and brown eyes and an ivory microphone stand to match his outfit. Frank dropped in from Boston, Massachusetts, on October 15, 1951, and says he is an 'unlisted Libra' and that his favourite occupational side of his angelic mission is watching reruns of The Gong Show. Frank believes every concert is a separate artistic event and should be a total escapist magic carpet ride for all who attend."

"Barry Brandt is the shy, retiring Angel until you put this black-haired, blue-eyed Scorpio behind his drums, where he proceeds to beat all Heaven out of them. Born in Washington, DC on November 14, 1952, Barry said he discovered Frank singing out of a tiny Fender amp in a junior high gym in Boston, making all the teeny girls scream. Barry's favourite hobby is being mistaken for Frank, and his best friend outside the band is his Corvette."

"Felix Robinson is the newest member of the group. Felix was a young Virgo cat reared in St. Louis from unknown sources on September 14, 1952. Felix especially favours the lighting used in the group's stage show, which resembles a ballet 'played like an additional instrument by the stage designer.' Felix's brown hair holds its own with any found in this band, and with his green eyes, he likes to watch Daffy Duck cartoons and young girls, in that order, puh-leeze. Well, that's the latest chapter on Angel, but the story has hardly begun. They wish you a fond 'Halo' 'til next time."

Punky Meadows makes no apologies for a write-up— or send-up or wind-up?—like that.

"Yeah, I love it and still do," begins an adamant Punky, who really spells out the crux and credo of what Angel were about, once and for all. "I mean, we started that shit. Because before that, bands were like Lynyrd Skynyrd, wearing T-shirts and with holes in their jeans and stuff. But Bowie was the first one, along with Jagger, when he started wearing makeup and eyeliner and stuff. But Bowie and Mick Ronson, I fell in love with that. I remember the first time, dude (laughs)—I might have been 22—and I decided I was gonna put eyeliner on. I put it on and I looked at and I said, 'That is so fucking wrong, it's so fucking cool' (laughs)."

"Because all of a sudden I became androgynous me; I became a character almost. Which is really cool. And then of course, the New York Dolls came out and everything went from black and white to colour again. I jumped on that stuff right away and then made it bigger with the hair and stuff, which… I really got my thing from Keith Richards and Ronnie Wood. I remember reading an article about how Ronnie Wood got his hair to stick up—those guys looked like crows, with their hair straight in the air like that (laughs). I remember first seeing him with Jeff Beck and Rod Stewart when they first came out. I thought that guy looks cool like that, man, and I read this thing where Ronnie said he would put Coca Cola in his hair and pull his hair and it would get so stiff from all the sugar (laughs)."

"So yeah, I dug it, I was into it," continues Punky, underscoring the preoccupation, specifically, with the band's hair, as stated in the label materials and subsequently in the press. "When Elvis Presley first came out, he had his hair all greased-up into a pompadour and ducktails in the back. If you see pictures of Elvis Presley sitting next to anybody else, it looks like he came from Mars. So fucking beautiful. Everybody else looked like hillbillies. He was so beautiful with all of that jet-black hair hanging down all greasy and shit. And then when the Beatles came out, hair got cool. Then Brian Jones and the Stones came out with the bangs and stuff right across. I always thought Brian was the coolest one of the Stones. That's what rock 'n' roll was—it was bigger than life. You were *supposed* to be a star. And so I lived it. There were guys when I played in bands that would wear their suits at work in the daytime and would put the rock clothes on at night. Me, I wore mine in the day, because I remember, Keith Richards once said, 'A real rock star lives it. He's a rock star in the day and he's a rock star at night.' And I lived by those rules."

And important to the Angel saga, Punky's deep appreciation for star quality visuals necessarily had to extend to who he would choose to hang with. "Yes. Mickie was my biggest fan too. I told you that Mickie used to come down and watch me play in The Cherry People all the time and became my biggest fan. He loved me and I loved Mickie too, you know? And then when we played together in Bux, he would always try to look like me on stage and I was honoured by that. It's a funny thing. I don't know why that happened but it did. And to this day I notice that a lot of people tend to be drawn to me for whatever reason. I'm just doing what I do. Like I said, I never looked to try to be the most popular guy in Angel. I just did my thing and it just happened that way."

"But when I started the band, everybody had to be cool-looking. Like, I never got a really fat guy in the band. The Cherry People were the same way. Everybody was pretty nice looking. In fact, they tried to sell us as The Monkees at one point. Because when I first saw the Beatles, everybody was cool-looking; the Rolling Stones, everybody was cool looking, even Herman's Hermits. I love The Dave Clark Five. They were fucking heavy. They were the best of those British rock bands at the beginning—they qualify with the best, man. And they were heavy as shit, big drum rolls, fucking bad-ass, man. But they all were cool-looking too. So when I started my band, everybody had to look cool. That's why when I went down and saw Barry, Barry looked cool, and Frank looked great and Gregg looked fucking cool and Mickie looked cool. That's how we wanted it—we did that ourselves. We wanted to be like the Beatles or like the Stones. We wanted everybody to look cool at the same time. That's what rock 'n' roll's about. Listen, it's an image business, dude. Everybody knows that it's an image business. That's why Lady Gaga is so fucking big. That's why Taylor Swift is so big. It's an image business, and if you don't know that you're a shmuck. But the thing is, that's what we all love anyway."

"I'm the first one to say Elvis is beautiful," chuckles Punky. "I fucking love to look at him. He's great. Jagger's beautiful. He's great. I love looking at Bowie, or Freddie Mercury. I have no problems about saying it because I'm secure in my manhood. They're beautiful and I love those fucking guys for that because they perpetuate that thing and keep it alive. That's what it's all about. You know, when these guys get all grungy and shit, the girls don't go to the concerts. It's just all guys and the girls are the ones that buy the records and that's what happened. That's why the girl thing got so big with Lady Gaga, Taylor Swift and Ariana Grande because they're pretty to look at. The music's good too; Lady Gaga is actually a good singer. But the thing is, if they're nice to look at, all the girls want to look at them now. But in the '70s and '80s, the girls wanted to look at the guys in the bands because they were good-looking. Yet they were androgynous. If you look at a Bon Jovi video, all the girls in the front are pulling up their blouses and shit, and they're all hot. But if you look at a Nirvana video, it's just a bunch of guys moshing in the pit banging their heads. No one gives a shit about it."

Back to the record at hand, past the gushing label materials we are confronted with the *White Hot* album cover, which displays the band illustrated very much like the Bon Jovi band Punky just described. But this is still the '70s, Angel is on Casablanca, and so *White Hot* also looks a lot like *Destroyer* and *Love Gun*. As Frank told John Parks, "We had gotten tired of the whole 'put a photo of the band' thing for the front covers so we thought we'd like to do something a little more cartoon-ish and more artistic rather than just a photograph of us on the front. We had this idea to find someone who could paint something that was in our heads, which was this city burning and all these people watching us getting burned at the stake, all dressed in white. You know, to be as sacrilegious as possible (laughs)."

"That's by David McMaken," explains Felix—of note, the Kiss ones just cited were by Ken Kelley, also known for his Rainbow and Manowar covers. "Now David, he had been in California for some period of time and the other guys all had a chance to sit and have the artist see them and do a rendering to be included in the final painted version. But I was not available at that point. I might've been back home in St. Louis visiting family. Either way, I had to fly to the Berkshires where David McMaken lived. It was a very arduous journey. I had to fly to Boston and then take a train or a limo to his house—I think it was a limo. It was like a cabin out in the woods, in the beautiful wilderness of Massachusetts during the winter time, as I recall. So it was very beautiful and he had this beautiful calm studio. And when I came into his studio, there was a portrait already sitting on the easel and it was Arlo Guthrie, which would be much more appropriate to that kind of thing. So he took Arlo's portrait down and put up a fresh piece of canvas and I sat in a chair and he painted me. Or actually it was a rendering, a sketch, at that point. And if you look at the cover, we're all kind of caricatures. Are they true to life? No, they are embellished, you know, sort of like artist interpretations and we all look terrific and in fighting form (laughs)."

"That's Notre-Dame de Paris, Notre-Dame cathedral, which is about ready to be lit on fire, which is so ironic because it was just on fire a year ago. The hordes of people around us are all complaining that we are being burned at the stake, which is a reference to the French revolution." The back cover of the album featured a darker and more violent image, a close-up of the rioting horde with the city on fire behind them. Inside there was a gloss colour inner sleeve with the guys all in their tidy whites, credits and group shot on one side (Gregg front and centre), individual head and shoulders on the other side along with the band's logo rendered in fresh red, yellow and green. Also included was a merchandising notice imploring kids to join the Angel Earth Force, this band's version of the Kiss Army.

Into the music and the listener is confronted by a very different Angel than the band who penned, from upon high, "The Fortune." As discussed, the label was gunning for the band to break, to achieve some approximation of what Kiss had done and indeed to get a taste of what newer bands like Boston and Foreigner were achieving. Even Styx, REO Speedwagon and Kansas were finding some success finally in this new "corporate rock" era.

First track on the album, "Don't Leave Me Lonely" reflected the poppiest parts of the previous record, but with a new directness and clarity of sound that seemed, on paper at least, to be the ticket. One definitely hears the sharp edge from the rhythm section Felix describes, but melody dominates, especially come the chorus, which above anything else on the album, leaves an indelible stamp.

"When Barry wrote 'Don't Leave Me Lonely,' he did that on a Silvertone guitar at the house where he lived," explains Felix, "and I was with him when he was first starting to play that song. We sat on the couch together and all he had was, you know (sings some chords) and he would play that over and over and over again. So we went into the rehearsals and Barry said, 'I've got this tune' and he sat down and he picked up maybe his guitar or Punky's guitar, and he played 'dada dada,' like that and it got restructured. Songs that start with other elements were always getting restructured, rearranged. Sometimes it would be me; sometimes it would be somebody else. 'Let's make that be the chorus.' 'Let's try to put a solo in right here.' 'Let's try to expand on that solo or come out of the solo into a quiet part that builds into a chorus.' My recollection is that happened quite frequently. I was a catalyst for some of those things, but we all did that together."

Remarked Barry in Hit Parader, "Writing my first song was difficult, and it took a long time. But I'm really happy with the way it came out and I want to write more in the future."

Adding some specifics in his chat with John Parks, Felix said, "I just thought that the chorus wasn't working out right. So we kept working with the verses and decided to have that sort of 'break' part kick in the chorus. As soon as we had figured out how to go from the verses portion to the chorus, as soon as we figured out the snap/break-in part to the chorus, I thought, 'Man, this is really gonna be a great song.' That should have been the first single but they wanted us to cram in 'The Winter Song' thing for that, which wasn't even supposed to *be* on the album."

At the lyric end, the song is apparently about what happened when Frank DiMino got locked in the bathroom with Goldie Hawn at Jack Nicholson's house on Arnold Schwarzenegger's birthday! "Don't Leave Me Lonely" was issued as a single, non-picture sleeve in the US, featuring "Stick Like Glue" on the B-side. The same two tracks were used for a Japanese single, which was issued in a picture sleeve featuring on the cover the same group shot from the inner sleeve of the LP. The track was not floated as a single in any other territories.

Next was "Ain't Gonna Eat Out My Heart Anymore," a cover of a Rascals tune (penned by Lori Burton and Pam Sawyer), and quite a mouthful of a title that is hard to remember by correct name. Nonetheless, the song was issued as the album's first single, backed with "Flying with Broken Wings (Without You)." The song got to a No.44 placement on the Billboard Hot 100, spending eight weeks on the charts.

"Angel didn't play covers live," Frank told me, "but that old club band vibe would find its way to the surface during rehearsals. We did 'All the Young Dudes.' I mean, we used to do a lot in rehearsal, fooling around. 'Ain't Gonna Eat Out My Heart Anymore'… that's how that ended up on the  album. Because we used to play around with that song, as well as 'Got to Get You into My Life' and 'You Better Run'—it was a toss-up between 'Ain't Gonna Eat Out My Heart Anymore,' 'Got to Get You into My Life' and 'You Better Run.'"

Also considered was "You Really Got Me." Frank had told me once that he remembers talking with Eddie Van Halen about covers once and bringing that up as a possibly Angel pick and then, lo and behold, the Kinks classic shows up on Van Halen's debut out just a month after the release of *White Hot*.

"Ed Leonetti, I believe, had brought up the idea of doing a cover song," notes Felix. "We were listening to 'You Really Got Me,' which became a hit for Van Halen, right? We were around them; they were around us. So Ed came in like, 'You know, why not do a cover song now?' I'm not sure who it was that said that Rascals song would be a good one. I think we all voted this way or that way on a couple of different ideas. I know that the guitar part of that song that Punky came up with pretty much sealed the deal. When he did (sings a riff)—that's classic Angel. And that was an easy song to do for us; it had the energy level that we needed. We wanted to carry that through—one of the filters that Angel specifically had was that the energy level had to be there. We couldn't do a song that turned into a poppy kind of come-down or bring-down or slow-down. 'Broken Wings' was probably the only ballad thing like that that we did up until later songs on *Sinful*."

Next is "Hold Me, Squeeze Me," which again courts this strange hybrid of poppy melody and thundering drums and busy bass. There are background vocals, some synth licks but little in the way of audible guitaring, save for Punky's solo, which is manic and almost panicked, like C.C. Deville on a Poison joint that doesn't need the noise. After Punky comes a similarly energy-infused solo from Gregg, but alas, one wonders if this overt display of Rick Wakeman-isms isn't becoming an anachronism by 1978, or whether it belongs on an up-tempo pop song. And it's frustrating to the fan of the old stuff, because the first 30 seconds point to a sure-fire rocker arriving, but then the song collapses into a sort of two-chord R&B verse and it's all over.

Figures Punky, "'Hold Me, Squeeze Me,' you know, that's a great fucking song. Angel was a very special band, and I have to say, Gregg was a big part of that too. There was a lot of cool stuff coming out of everybody that was really good and it's hard to find things like that. Gregg was a good musician, but he was a good songwriter too. He had a lot of cool ideas, and a lot of those songs, like that one, Gregg and I would put our heads together."

"'Hold Me, Squeeze Me' was derivative of a groove that Barry and I created," explains Felix, "and you'll notice that the bass part on that song and the very fast drum part, it's really quick, it's hard. But it's hard to listen to now. I'm sure digitally it sounds a little better on a good sound system, but if you can hear the bass drum and the bass guitar parts, I mean that is fast work and gets back into the topic

of what Barry and I were really good at, which was playing really tough, fast, hard rock rhythmic parts with a great deal of precision. You know, we were not deviating. We were not sloppy when Barry and I locked in; it was making use of his tremendous speed and energy. Remember I said before about how out-of-control he was; well, I was the guy that came in and made it controllable. I forced it into grooves and we would just go over and over and over those parts in rehearsal until they became rock-solid. There was no deviation from beginning to end. We could play that part for 20 minutes."

As for the amount of melody… I mean, this is a chorus so directly teenybopper, Kiss didn't even go there.

"We knew the album needed to be a breakaway," defends Felix. "We had meetings with Neil Bogart. We had meetings with other people in Casablanca, and David Joseph, of course. 'What are we going to do on this record?' I mean, there were production meetings with Eddie Leonetti as well, Eddie and David and the band. We had to go into that record with a concept, a purpose behind what the album needed to be, and then what was Casablanca going to do with it? Some of the elements from that album and in those songs were the result of that leaning towards commercialism."

"Now here's where my opinion has to be stated," continues Robinson. "I don't think that should have happened in some cases. I think some of those songs should have been left with the driving hard rock element left untouched. 'Hold Me, Squeeze Me' might even be an example of that. If you read the lyrics, if you listen to the vocals, it's a pop song. 'Hold me, squeeze me?!' Change the title. 'Kill Me, Kill You.' Put something demonic in there. I mean, now you've got a very heavy rock tune that is not cute at all. You put 'Hold Me, Squeeze Me' in there and it's a cute pop song. But it's too heavy to be a pop song. That's not Top 40 radio. And that happened on several songs on that record. It became, I think, a confused direction within the record itself. When you put that in the hands of an A&R person, who's got sell it to a radio station, you know, what are they going to pick out? They're going to pick out 'Ain't Gonna Eat Out My Heart Anymore' because it's a re-do of what had already been a Top 40 hit. And that's fine. But you know, it's not a follow-up song. Maybe it's a lead-in, right? Where's the hit song? Where is hit radio going at that point?"

Felix makes a good point here. This is a song arranged and played like a hard rock band with chops, fusion chops even, as we've heard, with a Tony Iommi-like guitarist and a synth wizard surrounded live by a near comical amount of keyboards, not to mentioned dressed in white with long blond hair down to his ass. He's off base with respect to how heavy the underlying musical track is, however—no amount of ritualistic murder in the lyrics could make this song "demonic." But Robinson's assessment of "confused direction" across the record is represented in microcosm right here. If Frank had any complaints, he figured Eddie went a little overdub-crazy in Studio C after the fact. But then again, to reiterate, no amount of molten Punky guitar or other changes in arranging could make these songs sound heavy rock—if the Ritchie Blackmore riffs ain't there, they ain't there.

"I don't think there should have been any singles," continues Felix. "That should have been an album of much more progressive hard-edged rock 'n' roll, taking the musicianship of the band and pushing it off into the areas that it could have gone, which would have probably given us much more credibility

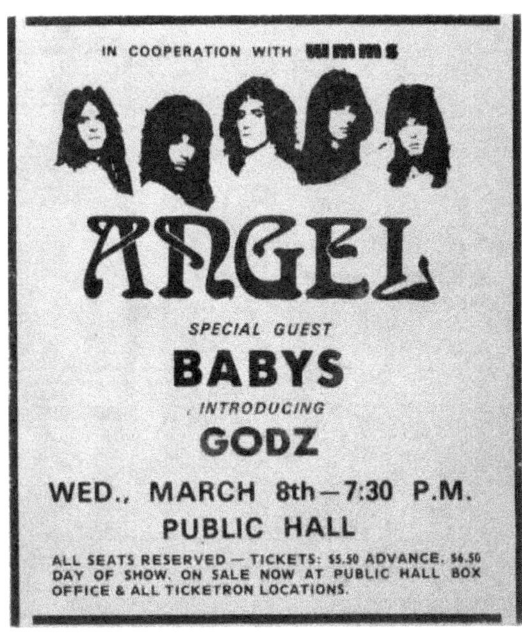

and recognisability, maybe like Rush. Hard rock at that point was turning into pre-metal, driving rock 'n' roll. Punky could play guitar great. Gregg is that good of a keyboard player. I'm sure the rhythm section was… you know, Barry and I, I don't remember seeing very many other bands that could match Barry and I as far as bass and drums. I know there's some bold statements there, but I heard a lot of bands. I had seen a lot of bands and we had that edge, I think, over a lot of people who may have been considered as the top musicians in a lot of those bands that went on to heavy, heavy rock reputations instead of pop music. I believe Angel could have eventually gone in that direction. But we had to get airplay, airplay, airplay. That was the mantra. That's what Eddie Leonetti was hired to do—make a record that gets airplay. But you look at AC/DC—they had hit records, but they had hit records because they were so damn good. They were a hit record machine, but they were true to the form and didn't make pop songs."

Felix's two examples there, Rush and AC/DC, are of course radically different from each other, but it's funny, Angel might have excelled as a band twice as proggy as they were on the self titled debut, and they also might have succeeded with the more straight-forward and Kiss-like hard rock sound of say the heaviest songs from *Helluva Band* and *On Earth as It Is in Heaven*. Then again, with

the rise of Cheap Trick and pomp rock, bleeding into the new wave-lite of The Cars and The Knack, this current direction might have worked as well, except, one feels that the costumes would have to go. Then again, back to *all five guys in the band*—none of them were suited, deep down in their musical bone structure, to that kind of music!

However, having said all that, "Over and Over" brings Angel back to mid-intensity Kiss, the type of song Gene Simmons would write and sing. Perhaps dating it is the cowbell as well as the synth tones, although there are flashes of the kind of keyboard shading here that would make Styx and Journey household names. All told, this is a no-nonsense guitar rocker for the stage, right down to the crowd participation segment and the handclaps.

"You're going to laugh, but I like to listen to 'Under Suspicion,'" says Punky, asked to name his favourite song from the album. This one indeed comes next, and comparisons with Kiss carry over, this one sounding like one that Peter Criss might sing, or, sure, once more Gene. The groove is slow, and the riff has a bit of southern rock to it.

"I came in with a riff," recalls Punky, "and we all sat down. Generally, Gregg and Frank and I did all the songwriting. I would come up with the riff, to plant a seed, and then Gregg would come up with a bridge or something. And vice versa—Gregg would come up with some kind of a song and then I would help him, and then Frank would sit down and write the lyrics and the melody."

Recalls Frank, "For 'Under Suspicion,' that was the time that we put the drums in… it was like a vocal booth but a little bit bigger, and it was all mirrors in it. *White Hot* was a good experimental album for us. After doing the third album in the castle, we were always up for finding different sounds using different rooms. So we tried to see what it would sound like recording the drums in there, although I don't think it worked for that song. So what we did was we set up Barry on the stage in Studio C and recorded… we had a big PA system brought in so that we could get the biggest sound we could. And we tried to hang up mics here and there kind of like 'When the Levee Breaks,' and that's how we got that drum sound on 'Under Suspicion.'"

Felix gets a credit on the track as well. "Do you hear the drum part at the beginning of the song?" begins Robinson. "That's the way the tune started, with Barry and I doing a lick that we probably came up with as part of a jam session in rehearsal. And it was like speed it up, slow it down, figure out what works best. Punky's coming in with a guitar part that is reminiscent of a Stones tune, I suppose, like a Keith Richards-style thing (note: "Can't You Hear Me Knocking" comes to mind). And I'm finding a way to pull that together into a three-piece groove as it is, and then carrying on towards more chords, more transitions, where's the vocal gonna come from now? Frank would be listening. I remember so many times Frank sitting there with a pad of paper and a pen and he would start writing down lyrics. And sometimes he would just come to the mic and start singing."

"By the way, I don't know if I explained this to you, but we would rehearse at full volume," continues Felix. "We tried to turn it down, but it would rarely stay there because we had a large PA system facing right at us, what for most bands would be considered a concert-level PA. And Punky had all of his SVTs, I was using a good combination rig that I had custom-built. You remember that I was working in a speaker factory. Well, the guy that owned that factory was a design engineer

from JBL and he was a brilliant design engineer for speaker cabinets. And so one of the first things I had happening when I joined the band—I mean, literally the first thing, because I inherited Mickie's old amplifier—I didn't have anything big enough to rehearse with, and Mickie's amp was sitting right there. And it was horrible; it was just a horrible amplifier, but I had to use it. So the first thing I did was call up Richard Guy, the guy who was working there. I said, 'Richard, build me an amplifier.' And he loved that. I was his employee. I think I was making $8 an hour there and I'm giving him $8,000 to build me an amp (laughs)."

"So, you know, nonetheless, we rehearsed at full volume and so now we're banging out these rhythms on that particular song and Frankie would sometimes come to the microphone and start singing rhythmically, with scat singing, not real lyrics. But everybody does that, I'm sure. I mean, the Beatles, Paul McCartney, sang 'Scrambled eggs' before he sang 'Yesterday.' Whenever Frank was singing,

I couldn't understand it anyway because we were just incredibly loud. But that's the way it came together. That's the way it sounded right to us. You couldn't turn that down and sit in the living room and do that song. So when earlier we were writing songs together, before I joined the band and we were sitting around with acoustic guitars and a bass and a small amplifier and no drums at all, now we've got those songs being portrayed with big amplifiers and loud drums. I mean, Barry even had a drum monitor system, a big one, in rehearsal, with big speaker boxes. So some songs came together like that, like 'Got Love if You Want It' and 'Under Suspicion,' whereas some songs started out with a more acoustic feel to them."

Speaking of fusion chops, that's exactly how "Got Love if You Want It" starts, completely non-fusion title notwithstanding—there's that weirdness with Angel song titling again. After a full minute of this we're into a sort of "secret agent man" riff for the verse (carried mainly by Felix's biting bass), helping make this track probably the heaviest song on the album. The chorus takes us back to a sort of spirited, showy pop, and it's not a great fit to the dark verse. Throughout, once again, Barry is driving the thing like his life depended on it.

Again, intimates, Felix, this sort of thing could start from Brandt and himself crafting a geometric rhythm. "Barry started seeing what I was doing, listening to what I was doing, and sometimes the rest of the band would have to stop playing because Barry and I would just take off. We would keep staying with the basic rhythm of where the song had been and we would take off into these fusion rock jams. It got to be almost like nobody could follow. We would do that for a couple minutes and then Barry and I would start laughing hysterically. The guys would stand around watching us and go, 'Come on, knock it off.' We were in a fantasyland of rhythm with bass and drums, but the songs had to come together in a way that utilised some of that energy. So when you asked me the question, what sort of changed in the way the band was playing? I think you can hear that in some of the arrangements on that album, and definitely 'Got Love if You Want It,' where the band starts out with more of a musical introduction that turns into a song. That was a jam session that Barry and I had created that had been then pulled into the song; we were taking from one part and putting it in with another part. Bands had been doing this for ages. Of course engineers and producers are the ones that usually can make that happen as George Martin did so many times with the Beatles."

Second track on side two of the original vinyl is "Stick Like Glue." This one sounds like happy party-rocking Lynyrd Skynyrd, with its R&B/boogie rock chord structure, its horns and its barrelhouse piano, a southern rock trope.

"There's a song that didn't end up as it started," notes Felix. "It began with a basic bar band rock 'n' roll feel, and I heard a horn section, a horn arrangement, all through the development stages on that song, maybe tied to my bass part (sings the riff). That sounds like a

saxophone part to me. Well, we don't have a horn part and we don't have a horn player in the band. So when we got to the studio and were doing basic tracks, I remember Bill Schereck, our tour manager, saying, 'Well, I play sax.' And I said, 'Really? Do you play baritone sax?' 'Yeah.' And he said, 'Well, I can play any sax.' I said, 'How good are you at it?' He said, 'I'm not very good.' I said, 'Could you do half notes?' He said, 'I probably can.' And I said to the engineer, 'Call up SIR; see if we can get a bari-sax over here.' Which was really easy to do back in those days; you could get anything from tympani to you name it."

"So we had a bari-sax show up within about an hour. I took Bill into a smaller studio at the Record Plant that was not in use at the time, along with a… I guess it was a two-track, a dupe of the band playing the rhythm parts, and an assistant engineer. And we sat down in that little room and Bill had to get acclimated to using the sax. It was hard for him because it takes a lot of breath to push air through a sax. I don't know if we had a tenor and a bari or a tenor or a bari. So anyway, I took Bill into this small studio and had him record the sax part—I got a horn part and that's Bill playing the sax."

"Edgar Winter was going to play on 'Stick Like Glue,'" recalls Frank. "He was in Studio B next door to us. We wanted to put a sax on the there and someone said, 'Well, how about Edgar?' So we went in there and he said, 'So, let me hear the song.' So we brought him into Studio C and he listened to the song and he said, 'Yeah, I got it; I can do that.' And we said, 'Oh okay, great. We just gotta do a few things, tidy up some other tracks, and then we'll call you in about an hour—we'll be ready to throw it on.' He said, 'I'll be in the studio.' He went into Studio B and we never saw him again. We couldn't find him (laughs). We found him the next morning sleeping under the console in Studio B. So as Felix says, we got Bill Schereck—who knew that he played sax?"

Adds Punky, "'Stick Like Glue' is a funny song. I was trying to write like a Motown song but it didn't really come off the way it should have. You have to be a

certain kind of band to pull off a song like that but it didn't come out right. It doesn't matter."

"Flying with Broken Wings (Without You)" is Angel in full-on Beatles mode, which prompted the missive on the inner sleeve that reads: "'Broken Wings' inspired by J.P.G&R. yeah yeah yeah," questionable punctuation notwithstanding. The Beatle most part and parcel of this one is George Harrison, but the almost proto-power ballad full-band crescendo bit is, as Felix frames it, a tribute to "Hey Jude."

Explains Robinson, "I had a lot to do with that song, especially in the recording of it, because one of the songwriters that I've always been partial to and at that point had been listening to, was Jeff Lynne. At that point, ELO was really just breaking. I was a fan of the band and The Move, which he had come from. And so we got into this song, 'Broken Wings,' and to me that was a tribute to the Beatles all the way, other than in certain parts, which for me was also indicative and somewhat reminiscent of some of the ELO stuff. I was doing the background vocals on many of those songs, and you'll hear me in this one. Frank would double many of my parts, and Barry of course sang as well. He has this very high, reedy falsetto, which blended well with Frank and I. So a lot of the background vocals were Frank, Barry and I. Sometimes the background vocals would be Frank singing them and me singing with Frank. I mean, Lee DeCarlo was able to use all these different versions and blend things together to come up with an assembly of background vocals that worked well for the band and for the mix in 'Broken Wings,' which was always about acoustic guitar."

Further on what Eddie Leonetti was bringing to the table, Felix explains that, "Lee and Eddie both came to rehearsals, but Eddie came to a lot of more rehearsals when we were in the process of building these tunes; he would be there at formative steps and make recommendations. He would say, 'You know, this song needs more of a chorus. This song needs an ending. That is more powerful. This song needs an introduction that has, you know, something that builds from other parts of the song. And then it comes back to remind you of what the introduction was.' And if you listen to *White Hot* from beginning to end, you'll hear those thematic adjustments that became part of what Eddie contributed, which was intelligent, thoughtful, organizational arranging."

"Eddie was good at that," continues Robinson. "That was one of his best contributions as well as keeping what I'll call an atmosphere conducive to productivity. Now what does a producer do? In film, the director is keeping the team working; he's keeping an eye on where the final product needs to be and he's fulfilling the goal of the screenplay. They come in with a vision, they know their beginning and end and where the

adjustments have to happen. But somebody has to ride herd on this whole process. Eddie was doing that and most good producers of albums would do that. Arranger, part-time director… they're making it work with the small details and the big picture too."

"When you get into the recording studio, where's the producer? He's sitting in a chair in the control room, and Eddie was always in that chair. He always had the New York Times crossword puzzle, right? Either in his lap or at the table next to him. He might've had coffee and he had a comfort zone. While we're a bunch of crazy rock 'n' roll guys, climbing all over this place, laying on the couch, some of us with hangovers, some of us in weird moods, some of us laughing… but Eddie was always there. And he knew when to say, 'Let's get to work' and he knew when to make it jovial; he knew when to make it funny—he has a good sense of humour."

"You Could Lose Me" is along the lines of "Over and Over" and "Under Suspicion," in other words, fairly heavy but sluggish and steeped in an early part of the 1970s, similar also to "Big Boy" from the last record and "Chicken Soup" from the one before it. But it's got some heft, due to the powerful production from Eddie and Lee, along with the muscular rhythm bed provided by Felix and Barry. Amusingly it starts with video game sounds from Gregg (or is that "Polymoog courtesy of Buck Minger, Norlin Music?"), and very quickly Barry's absolutely cracking snare whacks. There's an acoustic break which again evokes images of resplendent and progressive Styx passages, before the band goes into a solo guitar section and then another round of the chorus with Barry hitting everything in sight, followed by a final prog rock flourish.

"For 'You Could Lose Me,' we did do an alternate of that breakdown," recalls DiMino. "When I did the vocal, I had like five different endings to each one, and each one was more profane than the last, for the guys. Each one of them, I'd go, 'No, no, no, no, the next one.' And then the next one was worse than the last one. But that middle part was recorded off the telephone. I was on the telephone for the recording; I put the mic on the phone in the control room and recorded that little part off of there."

More than anything, *White Hot* is known for its closing number, "The Winter Song." "The original idea was a Christmas song," begins Frank, "which you can hear on *The Anthology.*" What DiMino is referring to there is a version called "The Christmas Song" which is pretty close to "The Winter Song," but for a few words changed.

As he explains, "That was written and finished before the rest of the album was done. And the intention was to put it out to the radio stations as a Christmas thing for the fans, and also to bring in the fact that the *White Hot* album was coming out in January. But I got talked into… you know, the record company, 'It's a great song, it's a great song, but we want to make it better.' How do you tell me it's a great song in one sentence, and then in the next sentence, you want me to make it better? What does that mean? 'Well, we want to put this on the album. We think it will help sell the album, and we want to release it as a single, but we want you to change it so it's less seasonal and more like a winter kind of thing rather than Christmas, where it can only be played at Christmas time.' And I said, 'That's the whole idea. That's what it is. Why change it?' So you go back and forth with them, and then you say, I can't... I've got to give them some ammunition, if that's what they want. And then what happened was, they didn't do anything with it! So I mean, it kills me when stuff like that happens."

Adds Felix, the idea was, "'Why don't we do a Christmas song?' Neil Bogart loved that idea. We recorded it as 'The Christmas Song' and it was decided that it was a little too specific. Make it a little more generic; call it 'The Winter Song,' re-record the vocals—we did that. We had the California Boys Choir. There's a photo of us, and among the young boys, stage right, is Lenny Kravitz. He was in the California Boys Choir. That was maybe his first, you know, recording as a singer. He still remembers that. And then we did *American Bandstand* with it."

As Felix elaborated in conversation with John Parks, "I really thought it was a terrific idea to put out 'The Christmas Song' because at that time, nobody was doing that type of thing. Back in the day it was a cool thing to do every year with the Phil Spector groups, the Beatles and all these bands doing those kind of 'message to the fans' type things. I thought it had been a while so let's try it again in 1978; my feeling was that it was perfect timing. So it was only recorded to be issued to radio stations. The DJs were supposed to play it as a thank you to the fans and alert them that, as Christmas was on its way, a new Angel album was on its way because it was almost finished. We took another song *off* the album called 'Better Days' to put that on (laughs). It was one of my biggest disagreements with Casablanca. I didn't want to take that song off the album and I really didn't want to change the words."

"The Winter Song" was issued as a single in a myriad of territories, backed, variously, with "The Christmas Song" and "Can You Feel It." Canada, in fact, got the non-LP track

"Better Days," which is a sort of pomp-rocking piano ballad, actually, structured very much like a Guns N' Roses joint, when Axl is included to tinkle the ivories.

As Felix mentioned, the band "did" *American Bandstand*, which meant sitting on stools and lip-syncing to the studio version of the song, to a man, looking uncomfortable. Once this exercise is dispensed with, Dick Clark bounds over and talks to the guys. Frank introduces what Dick calls "this handsome young man next to me" as Punky "Get Down" Meadows. Gregg next informs Dick that the California Boys Choir had "36 little guys (that) sang along with us," adding that the band came up with the idea for the song in the studio and knocked it out in a couple of hours. Dick then asks them about being compared to Kiss and then how they do the disappearing act at the end of the show, to which Frank replies, "It's magic."

"Dick Clark was great; he was cool," recalls Punky, with respect to the band's brush with TV stardom. "That was a funny experience. At that time Dick Clark was doing *American Bandstand* on the West coast, but he was also doing *$20,000 Pyramid*, that game show, on the East coast. So he would take the red-eye all week long from the East coast back to California. So he would do like four or five *American Bandstand*s in one day. I remember we were sitting in the dressing room back there, getting makeup on, and he was telling the makeup girl, 'Can you please get rid of these bags under my eyes?' And I said to him, 'You look great.' Then he goes, 'Listen, Punky, I'm flying back and forth and I never get any sleep. I'm on the red-eye. I'm in New York one day and then in LA the next day.' He was really cool, man. But for some reason they had an applause track on *American Bandstand* and somebody had left those speakers on in the makeup room there. And Dick goes, 'Somebody turn that God-damn applause track off!' and somebody runs in there and turns it off."

During the band's brief interview segment, Punky has to think on his feet and reel of a bit of "Rudolf the Red Nosed Reindeer." "Yes, how that happened, years earlier, I was in the studio and actually showing Jim Sullivan how I would finger-pick stuff with my steel finger picks. And he finger-picked too. So I watched him play 'Rudolph the Red Nosed Reindeer' a few times and then I went home and I figured it out myself. And it came along just in time because when Dick Clark asked me about, you know, the No.1-selling song—'Blue Christmas' or whatever it was—I froze, and said, 'But I can play this' and I started playing 'Rudolph the Red Nosed Reindeer.' So luckily that worked out good. Being on TV, you're already nervous anyway; you're lip-synching and you're not playing. So you're trying to make that look real and it never does. The people in the audiences are clapping, they're singing, and then he comes up and he introduces each one of us and you don't know what he's going to say. Luckily I pulled that off and it worked out fine."

"ZZZZ. Hey, who woke me up?" wrote Record Mirror's Robin Smith, reviewing *White Hot* over in the UK. "God, is this album still playing? Must have dropped off after the first track on side two. Angel are a sort of poor man's Rush only prettier. Stateside heavy metal fodder for headbangers of the first order There's not really a lot more you can say about Angel except they're a group of gents with immaculately coiffured long hair who pose around a bit in white suits. If you've heard Aerosmith, Kiss or Rush, then this album is an amalgamation of all three. Take any track and you will see it's a simple re-hash of what's gone before. Sweet dreams."

Billboard, unsurprisingly, gave a thumbs-up to the band's more accessible sounds this time out, proclaiming that, "This five-man, flash heavy metal group comes up with some tasty surprises here. Most of the tunes are class rockers as the playing is more cohesive, especially the guitar riffs of Punky Meadows, and an ever-present synthesizer. Lead vocalist Frank DiMino is the gut and drive of the band with his dynamic vocal renditions. Apparently, the band's music can now complement its stage performances." Billboard then goes on to recommend "Winter Song," "Don't Leave Me Lonely," "Ain't Gonna Eat Out My Heart Anymore" and "Stick Like Glue" as the best songs on the album, adding a message to the industry that "Angel is a label priority."

There was a positive notice in Circus from Max Thaler, who said that "Angel are here to stay. Their newest album for Casablanca, *White Hot*, is the fastest-breaking LP for the group. Augmented by the California Boys Choir, a better production and an important personnel change, Angel sound and feel like a real rock band, not just a bunch of namby-pamby white-suited make-believers, a not infrequent charge before. On this album, they more than prove themselves. Entertaining, aggressive and talented, this quintet will be around for a long time to come."

However it was also Circus who gave a thumbs-down, and this in the official review of the album, penned by John Swenson, who lamented that, "*White Hot* finds Angel perfecting a production strategy and running out of ideas. The band has always been, if not good, at least competent in the mindless sort of way perfected by its stablemate, Kiss. Plenty of unmitigated garbage passes for commercial hard rock in the late '70s on the strength of its meticulous presentation and shrewdly manipulated production values, and this is the commodity void Angel helps fill. The band's attempts at coining a musical identity on its first three albums were dutifully recorded by producers Derek Lawrence and Eddie Kramer. But on *White Hot*, Angel has given up its search for a style and instead mines rock history for some proven formulae to hook songs around."

"The list of steals is as obvious as it is shameless," continues Swenson. "To wit: 1. 'Don't Leave Me Lonely' moves from the characteristic Yes vocal cop to Queen-like sonic ambience and lyrics. 2.'Over and Over' steals the cowbell-over-drums intro from Mountain's 'Mississippi Queen.' 3.'Under Suspicion' matches the chord structure and intro to the Rolling Stones' 'Sway' to Robert Plant vocal imitation from Led Zeppelin *II* ('You Could Lose Me' is also based on a standard Zeppelin chord pattern). 4. 'Flying with Broken Wings (Without You)' is built around a virtual duplication of George Harrison's transition theme at the end of *Abbey Road*'s 'You Never Give Me Your Money.' Don't get me wrong. There's nothing wrong with being influenced, or even outright stealing, if you do something interesting with it. But in this case, Angel is using proven formulae in lieu of coming up with its own style. Angel was voted best new band of the year by Circus readers on the strength of an extraordinary live presentation. But you have to *listen* to records, and that's just where these guys run into trouble."

A review like this in Circus did not portend of continued career ascension for Angel. Rolling Stone had ignored the band, Hit Parader cared somewhat, and Creem mostly poked good-natured fun. Circus on the other hand, was the most influential voice for the band in America, and had been quite supportive with column inches, as they say, thus far.

Negativity from the press toward Angel at this point might have been seen as logical—or destined—for a few reasons. First, Angel had been around for a while now and their transition toward radio rock might have been seen as desperate and opportunistic. Second, new wave was the trendy, exciting thing, something seen

as more artistically valid. The dire state of Manhattan at the time was a story in and of itself, and the city had a vibrant music scene, built of this music and its more belligerent strain, punk. It was also still very much a media centre of its day and alas, the package and concept of something like Angel seemed a spoiled world away. Third, coupled with this rise of the spiky-haired, the press was aligned against "corporate rock" bands like Boston, Foreigner and Styx suddenly doing very well indeed, and Angel was hitched to that critically toxic bunch of well-dressed bands, even if they enjoyed but a tiny fraction of their record sales.

Still, it was Creem's coverage of Angel that turned out to have really creative ramifications. Their "running gag" with respect to making fun of Punky Meadows and how he was often seen in pictures with his full-puckered pout (this would become a hair metal trope a rock 'n' roll generation later), resulted in Frank Zappa writing a song called "Punky's Whips."

As Meadows explained to Ken Sharp, "We had just come out to California and were rehearsing on the ABC Studios lot. Casablanca had a rehearsal space there. Dale Bozzio (later of Missing Persons) came down and said her boyfriend Terry, who played drums in Frank Zappa's band, saw that famous picture of me with my pouting lips and he loved my whole look (laughs). Dale said Frank wanted to write a song about me. Later, Frank sent us a tape of this new song, and I thought it was really cool and also very surreal. The other guys were kind of envious, because it was about me. It was originally called 'Punky's Lips,' because of that photo, and Frank changed it to 'Punky's Whips.' I can't remember why. Zappa was gonna play 'Punky's Whips' as the last song of the night at a show at UCLA, and he wanted me to come onstage in full costume and play. But the rest of the band didn't want me to do it. I think they might have been a little jealous, because I used to get a lot of attention anyway."

Asked by Sharp if he was at all offended by the "tribute," Punky says, "I understood Frank Zappa and was into him when I was a kid. I used to sit on the floor with a friend and smoke joints listening to Zappa and go, 'My God, this guy's a genius!' So I'm at the UCLA show, and they had this huge scrim behind them that was covered by a curtain. At the end of 'Punky's Whips,' flash pots went off, the curtain dropped and there was that gigantic picture of me with those pouting lips (laughs). It was really cool. I went backstage after the show and met Frank and Terry. Frank said, 'You're a really good sport. Come up to my house sometime; we'll drink some beer and make some music.' I was honoured by the song because with Frank being a satirical writer, you needed to take it with a grain of salt. He does parody and that's what he's always done. A lot of people hear it and they don't get it and they think that it's a put-down, but I knew better."

"Punky's Whips," all 11 minutes of it, was set to go on Frank's *Zappa in New York* album, but got yanked by Warner Bros. at the last minute, much to Zappa's consternation. The label, it seemed, was worried about getting sued by the Angel camp, and of course was already used to dealing with Frank on a legal basis. Frank not only vehemently disliked being censored, but he was doubly ticked-off that the song wasn't replaced by anything, making the album 11 minutes shorter, which caused complaints in the press and with fans who didn't know the whole story. A few copies had leaked out initially in early 1977 in the UK with the song on it, but remaining copies were quickly withdrawn. The track was gone when the double record came out in the US, March 3rd 1978. However subsequent CD reissues of the album have the track restored and in place, beginning 13 years later, in 1991.

Back to Angel, it was time to hit the tour trail, which seemed to help, because *White Hot* turned out to be the band's best-selling album to date, even though it fell just short of RIAA gold certification.

In a feature for Circus in June '78, Punky stressed to the writer Daisann McLane how important the live show is to the band's success. "It's true we're better live than on record," admits Meadows. "Our performances are what made us New Group of the Year. We all live for those moments on stage. Recording is like work to us. So we figure we've got to get out there and play in order to break. And we're not afraid to tour; we're not afraid to sweat. There's no way you can stop Angel when we get on stage. When I feel that guitar shaking on my body, well, it's like I'm preaching a religion. I feel tremendous. Like the king of the hill. I'm living my dream right now. Seeing Elvis changed my life. I stood in front of a mirror for weeks after that, holding a tennis racket as if it was a guitar, trying to copy his moves. I decided right then and there that I wanted to make it in rock 'n' roll no matter what it took. I knew I was destined for this, and I'm prepared to work my butt off to get all that's coming to me. I'm not afraid of anything. Except flying—I just close my eyes and grit my teeth."

When not gutting it out through turbulence to get through a tour, Punky says, "I'm no different when I take off that costume. If I go out to the supermarket, I don't comb my hair back. I live what I am. I stay away from bars and the party scene. I guess I spent too much time in bar bands to enjoy hanging out anymore. I come home to relax, watch TV, play with my cats, ride my bike around the beach, just normal stuff."

Manager David Joseph is quoted in the same piece as well, amusingly telling the story of making Punky leave his guitar at home when he's called in for business meetings, as the constant strumming drove him to distraction. "What I saw in them was their incredible energy level," noted Joseph. "I had been managing groups like The New Seekers, but Angel just bowled me over. Secondly was Punky's musicianship. Punky's the first to go run out and buy a new album; he's always interested in what other groups are doing."

Added tour co-ordinator Tracy Gold, "I've never seen a bunch of guys so committed, so dedicated to rock 'n' roll. In Lexington, Kentucky, for instance, their gig was cancelled suddenly. Then 20 minutes before show time, we got word that the performance was on again. In 20 minutes, everybody was in costume and makeup and ready to go."

"A critic once said that if our props got much better, we could stay at home and send our show on the road," laughed Gregg, speaking with Deane Zimmerman. "But I take that as a compliment. If people come to see the effects, then they're going to get the music too. At the beginning, everything we did was scaled down. We were in a tiny club in Washington, DC called Bogies and we spent all the money we made each week to get lighting and a giant sound system. We had people make clothes, we used smoke bombs, anything we could do. So in a way, it was similar to what we do now, but on a smaller scale. Our attitude was that we weren't going to settle for anything but the best because we'd been on the road with other groups, playing in bars, doing just about everything for almost ten years. So when we got together, we just said, 'This is it—let's do it right.'"

"Even though we set our goal so high, it didn't seem unrealistic to us at all," continued Gregg. "We were like a football team going out on the field. We were going to do it and we never thought about the negative side. We were so sure of ourselves then that sometimes we were *too* cocky. Now that we are successful, our goals are still high. We're still looking forward. The people at Casablanca had the foresight to see what we could do. Most companies would've said, 'Okay, do an album, we'll put it out and then you can go out on the road.' But Casablanca realised that we could create an entire illusion, a whole new dimension of live entertainment."

Columbus, Ohio bad boys The Godz also entered Angel's orbit on this record's tour cycle. If Angel were Casablanca's heavenly answer to Kiss, The Godz were the label's dirtbags on bikes.

"Yeah, yeah, yeah, that was a funny tour," recalls Frank. "We were in Alabama or something. And Eric Moore had made a comment to the audience. He lit up a joint, and said, 'If y'all got one, light 'em up because there's more of us than there are of them.' And something happened with the cops, and the cops wanted to get us, and so they had called us, called our tour manager before we got to the next city: 'You better tell that guy and rein him in or whatever, because there's going to be cops there.' So we just mentioned it to them and they got all freaked-out. It was just one of those times where we looked at each other and said, man, I hope there's no trouble. But there was no trouble."

There in fact was an incident, however, that is part of both Angel and Godz lore.

"Yes, what happened with me there on that tour, in San Diego, there were all these kids, and there's one point in the show where I ask everyone to stand up. And I told security what was going on. I explained everything. I used to do that before the show so they know what's going on. I told everyone to stand up, and everybody started coming closer to the stage. And all of a sudden this one security guard decided that he was going to stop everybody from doing it. He was grabbing kids and throwing them. And he picked up this one girl and threw her. I pointed him out and started yelling at him. So he came towards me. He was down on the floor and I was on the stage. He came towards me, he gave me the finger, and then sort of reached up towards me, and I hit him with the mic stand in the chest."

"And after I did that, he started to kind of lunge forward, and two of our big roadies just flew off the stage and a whole kind of mess ensued; I mean, it was a mess. And I'm hanging off the side of the stage and I'm kicking this one guy off one of our guys. The band threw their instruments down. Barry was the only one who kept playing (laughs). So finally we get back on stage, and I started talking to the audience and I said, 'We're going to play as long as we can. I know they're going to want to pull the power, but we're going to play as long as we can—get really kind of crazy.' And it got kind of crazy. They wanted a piece of me after that. So what happened, The Godz and their crew and our crew made this line so no one could get past them backstage. So when we were finished, they scooted me off in-between this lineup and right to the back room so no one could get to me. Those guys definitely wanted a piece of me…"

Recalls Moore, bassist and vocalist for the Godz (deceased May 17th, 2019), "We did a tour that was Judas Priest, The Godz in the middle, and Angel. And they called it, you know, the Heavenly Tour or something like that, because it all had some kind of relationship to Christianity or something. Angel, to me, was just a caricature of a '70s rock band. I was never crazy about the material or anything, but when you are on the same record label and you've got the same agency… we toured for a time with Angel. As I said, one time we were with Judas Priest, Godz, and Angel, this heavenly heaven and hell thing, a bunch of dates doing that, and that was Judas Priest's first time here in the States and they were happy to do it. We had fun. But Angel, they were a little 'fem,' the way they came off, and we were just opposite, which is one of the reasons they paired us together."

"And yeah, we had to get them off stage and we had to get them out of bar fights. They didn't know when to shut up (laughs). When you're around a bunch of bikers in some place like El Paso or Laredo, you know, those guys were looking at Angel and saying, 'Hmm, I can take a scalp here.' So yes, we got them out of trouble a few times."

"Well, it was kinda like *Spinal Tap*," adds Bob Hill, Godz guitarist. "Angel all looked perfect in the morning, hair sprayed and makeup on, while we looked… well, 'experienced.' I will tell you that I am not that sociable and especially on tour I thought that I was a star and that I would not lower myself to be a 'fan' of any other group. So, I minimised my contact with both the audience and the headline groups. But we were in the same boat with the label. Casablanca would hire people to do stuff in your name, and you pay for it, and you had no input whatsoever. With Parliament and Kiss it worked, but with us and Angel and Donna Summer, we never saw the stuff that came out of Casablanca; so it was constantly fighting with them."

Felix recalls this story as well, explaining that, "We were headlining at that point. So a lot of bands opened for us, most often Judas Priest. They were a very small outfit. They were opening, plus The Godz. They were trying to break that band, and they were a lot of fun. They were definitely a heavy metal forerunner, with their biker background. They stood up for us in San Diego. Frankie got pissed-off at one of the bouncers, because the bouncers in that arena had been very brutal to the little girls up front; these bouncers were all Cal State football players. They were just monsters. And they were just grabbing these girls and throwing them two and three rows back. And Frankie went up and punched one of them in the head with a mic stand. And this bouncer reached up and grabbed the mic stand and started dragging Frankie off the stage, at which point, my bass roadie, Steve

Brooks, who was about six-four and about 250, 280, he goes
flying past me off the stage into these guys. The next thing
you know, it's just a major brawl going on right in front of the
band. We're still playing. It was a great scene."

Filling in a few details in their interview with
American Music Press, Felix said that, "By the time we
got back up on stage—nobody was hurt very badly, just
ripped-up a little bit—the house lights were up, and the
Fire Marshall was standing next to my amp, giving me the
cross-the-throat thing, 'Cut it!' We played one more song.
The audience was screaming! In approval! There were still
fights going on in front of the stage. The house lights were
still up. There were security people all over the place and
the fun wasn't over yet. We had to get back to our dressing
room—about a 40- to 50-foot walk. The original guy who had
provoked us had gotten five or six of his friends together to
jump us between the stage and the dressing room. The Godz,
a very disgusting bunch of bikers from Ohio who carried
loaded weapons with them everywhere they went, had been
backstage cheering us on. And, I might add, they were really
impressed! They had decided they were going to protect us."

"The Godz and our road crew made a chain," adds
DiMino, "and we went right in between them to the dressing
room. The Chief of Police came back and wanted to arrest me
for inciting a riot."

"I stood up and said, 'Yes! Let's go to jail! This is great
press!'" says Felix. "Our manager said, 'We can't go to jail. Frank
will have to make an apology. Frank has to go out front and
try to get calm restored.' Frank went back on stage and said,
'You gotta cool it, the show's over, we gotta leave, we love you
all, thanks for coming, be careful and stop fighting! One of the
funny anecdotes of this was, my mother—who had never seen
the band before—was living in San Diego and had come to
the show with my aunt. They were both in their 70s. After this
whole thing had died down, I went outside and found them.
My mom says, 'Is it like this every time you play?'"

Chuckles Punky, "The Godz had guns out and stuff
and they ushered Frank out; Frank had to go to jail overnight

because of that; of course we got him out. But The Godz were great—'Put a shell in the chamber!'"

As for the rest of the tour, Felix explained to me that, "I think we did a couple of co-headlining shows with Styx and I believe Ted Nugent and Blue Öyster Cult. This was a transitional point for Angel because, you know, we had the magic show, we did a big production. We appeared on stage. We disappeared at the end of the night. It was a major part of what Angel was at that point. So taking Angel, the rock band, the good band, the 'whatever you think of us' band, the records, if you don't put the special effects into our live show and put that down on that stage at that point, then you're missing a big part. You're missing almost half. The reason for the impact the band had at the time was because we had incredible sound, lights and magical effects and nobody else was going there. You know who we should have played with? We had the same photographer, Barry Levine, who did us and Queen and Kiss. If not Kiss, why wasn't there a package between Angel and Queen?"

"I know the answers when it comes to Kiss," continues Felix, familiar with the frustrating history with Gene, Paul, Ace and Peter before he had ever joined Angel. "It's not like it has never been discussed. Neil Bogart didn't want to mix us up with Kiss. They were two separate marketing schemes, two separate identities. Kiss did not want to appear with us. We might have said we didn't want to appear with them. I think that would have been a big mistake. And I think it was on our part plus a big failure on the part of Casablanca. I think that Neil could have said, 'No, those two bands have to appear together.' Even if it was just a festival event. It would have been a great time."

Other than this miscalculation, it couldn't be said that Neil wasn't fully behind Angel and gunning for their success. "Yes, when he sold Casablanca to Polygram, we owed almost a million dollars. That's how much money was spent to break this band. The band made money selling records and the money all went back into promoting the band. And I could give you all kinds of conspiracy theories and tell you stuff that I've heard. But the reason we're talking nonetheless, it's because the record company people spent a lot of time and a lot of effort—certainly a ton of money—to break Angel. There was no effort to bury them. And I know they believe they did everything they could."

Maybe some portion of Casablanca's woes can be chalked up to shifting musical sands. Asked about the new wave, Frank recalls, "I know that we did some shows where The Jam opened up for us a few times. That was more the beginning stages. The audience was still figuring that whole thing out, whether they liked it or not. It wasn't really full-on at that time."

Indeed punk rock in '78, now a couple years on, was persisting but also evolving, at the same time making what Angel was doing look perhaps a little old. That's fine, new musical things happen, but just don't call Angel uncool, says—or at least implies—Meadows.

"Right, well here's the thing," explains Punky, persistently positive. "Punk rock was the funniest thing. I remember, when we first came out with Angel in '75, it was before punk. Or you could say that punk was just kind of starting up. But before that it was Queen, Aerosmith, Angel and Kiss. When I wasn't playing on stage, I always wore a black motorcycle jacket with scarves and shit like that. Always. I wore that back in 1973, '74. That was my shtick when I wasn't playing. And then I went and got one in the surplus store, and it smelled like the surplus store (laughs). Those places always had like a warehouse smell to them. And I tore the lining out and took it to a tailor and had him make it really tight on me. I wore that thing all through Angel and everything else. So we're on the tour bus and we're coming into New York City and Frank wakes me and you know, the Ramones had come out, and they're all wearing motorcycle jackets. I didn't really pay much attention to it, but Frank wakes me and he's looking out the window and he goes, 'Punky, look, all the people in the streets are wearing your jacket.' I just started laughing. And of course, my name was Punky. Which I'd had since I was a baby. I was Punky at one and Punky at two; I've had that since I was a child."

"And as I mentioned, David Krebs wanted me to join the New York Dolls. And I remember Steve Conte, who went and played in the New York Dolls later on when they got back together, he was a friend of mine and he said to me, 'I always thought you would have been a great fit for the New York Dolls. I always wished you would have had taken that position because it was a great fit.' But I don't know if it would have been or not, really. I was a little more progressive in my play than Johnny Thunders."

"What I didn't like about the punk thing was that it was very trendy," continues Meadows. "That's one thing I don't like about the music businesses. Like when Elvis was big, I loved Elvis. And then out came the Beatles and did I think Elvis was not cool with me? Well, no, you're wrong. Once you're cool, you're fucking always cool. So what else may come along? It may be cool too. I don't like when all these fucking elitists come out and they want to say, "Yes or Genesis—they're no longer cool. This is cooler.' No it's not. When punk came out it was all about how loud you could play and maybe make some political statements about doing whatever you want to do and spitting on people. Is that something that's going to make you really cool? That wasn't cool to me. And then they had to put down Pink Floyd and all these bands that were actually fucking great bands."

"So I didn't like that. When I like something from the past, I still appreciate it. Like when I first learned to play the blues, people said, well, you've got to listen not to Eric Clapton, but you have to listen to B.B. King and those people. So I went back and listened to that stuff, the roots, and then I would hear people playing later on just copying Eddie Van Halen and I would think to myself, dude, go back a little farther and listen to what's going on there. Listen to that. Eddie didn't start that stuff. Neither did I. Go back a little further. All that stuff was cool and is still cool. That's what I always thought about blues players. With country musicians it's the same way—they appreciate and admire where their stuff comes from."

"Whereas rock 'n' roll is very trendy and faddish: this is not cool now. We'll stick safety pins in our T-shirts and our cheeks. Those other guys aren't cool anymore. These guys are cool now—it's not true. Elvis was cool then, Elvis is cool now, Elvis will always be cool. Cher was cool then, Cher is cool now. You know what I mean? If you're cool, you're always going to be cool. Your coolness doesn't go away because some critic says you're not cool anymore. Fuck that. It's not the way it goes. Otherwise you're just never going to never be able to appreciate anything. All you do is you stick yourself in an envelope and you seal it off."

Sinful

"It's harder to write a three-minute pop song than to write a heavy riff."

"So, you know, here we're done with *White Hot*, the album's getting airplay and we're riding a wave," begins Felix, setting the stage for what would be the last Angel studio album of the classic era. "'Ain't Gonna Eat Out My Heart Anymore' had done pretty well but not fantastic. We have this album, *White Hot*, and it's all over the map—and I'm going to say now, not in the best way, but not in a bad way."

"But I like commercial rock," continues Robinson, not entirely in revolt against the version of the band in which he found himself. "I definitely enjoyed doing it and I definitely played those things and I thought that it made the band sound better. Whatever I was doing was leading the rhythm section towards making those songs much more legitimate, but less hard rock, 'cause they were not hard rock songs. I'm talking now about the songs on *Sinful* that were much more ballad pop songs. And you know which ones they were. We were having a good time making better songs and we weren't so much trying to make live concert songs. We were making a studio record, and we were doing it because we were in the studio over and over again, and in different studios. So we were working on songs that became better songs, and that's why with the *Sinful* album, you can listen to that from beginning to end and it sounds like an album. It's very, very playable, with the way songs lead from one to another. But it's AOR made for airplay, it's pop music, it's not heavy rock."

Over at head office as well, at Casablanca, cracks were beginning to show. As part of what was slated to be a notoriously bad year in the record industry and the economy in general, it was looking like the party was over.

"We never made a profit," Larry Harris told me, "even with the disco boom, and you know, we had all the big disco acts. We were doing 30, 40 million dollars a year but we kept putting it back into the business. We were also pretty well-known for the fact that everybody that worked for us flew first  class, used limos, a lot of drugs. We were definitely heavy-duty into the drug culture. Even when we sold half the company to Polygram in 1978, and we used their money to even grow the company bigger. I mean the Village People and Donna Summer and Parliament were huge. We had three movies out. One was an academy award winner, *Midnight Express*, and our first movie was *The Deep*. We just spent tons of money because when Polygram bought us, the deal was, they bought half the company and in five years they'd pay us ten times the profits after five years, to buy the rest of the company. So Neil being the big gambler decided that he was going to roll the dice, and spend their money to see how much money we could make. As it so happens, Kiss started to slow down in sales and disco started to slow down in sales, all at roughly the same time. So things weren't so good."

And notoriously in 1979, Kiss tried their hand at disco as well, with "I Was Made for Loving You," from *Dynasty*, issued five months after Angel put out *Sinful*. "Yeah, a lot of hard rock people started to do disco songs because disco was so popular. And sure, Kiss did one, which pissed off their audience. Cher went from being a rock 'n' roller to having a disco hit, and there were numerous other bands who decided to do a little disco thing here and there. It took away some attention and resources from the hard rock. There was even a station in Chicago that switched to a disco format, and New York as well, which led to the famous disco album burnings. Because that disc jockey who was fired from the rock station because it went disco was pissed-off and he got a job at another station, and he did this whole thing against disco. But we also had people burning Kiss albums because they thought they were the devil and Satan, down in the south. That was fine with us because they had to buy the albums to burn them. So burn them all you want—go enjoy yourself."

"But the economy went into recession," continues Harris. "A lot of people didn't have money to go see the shows. That generation was also growing up and having kids and getting jobs and having more responsibilities than they initially had. That changed everything over a little too."

In parallel you had the rise of The Knack and The Cars and Cheap Trick, with a whole different sound *and* look than the long-haired rockers of the mid-'70s—and God forbid if you were dressed in self-important semi-matching white "costumes." The era of the Irish-style "showband" was over, if it ever existed in America in the first place.

"Yes, you had that new music coming in that wasn't heavy metal," agrees Harris. "It wasn't straight rock 'n' roll—

it was a mix. The Police were coming in and there were a bunch of bands like that. But you also had people like Springsteen who were doing fine. The Stones were still touring and doing fine." Larry is right, but you could name bands all day, including old bands and new bands, but the common denominator is that there's not much in the way of hard rock or heavy metal that's doing well in 1979, outside of Van Halen. If Angel were going to succeed, it seemed like the sensible thing to do would be to double down on the pop, move even further from *Helluva Band* in a direction that at least appeared plausible, and that would be toward Cheap Trick, or, in fact, that of another new band with Kiss ties playing their hand in '79, namely New England, who would nonetheless make modest inroads with a very Angel-like song called "Don't Ever Wanna Lose Ya."

"We were still selling two or three million albums with Kiss," continues Harris on the state of Casablanca circa '79. "But the Kiss solo albums had come out and none of them sold well, but that had nothing to do with heavy metal music. I mean they were four albums that sucked. So they were four terrible albums that even their fans didn't want to come close to. The best-selling of the four was

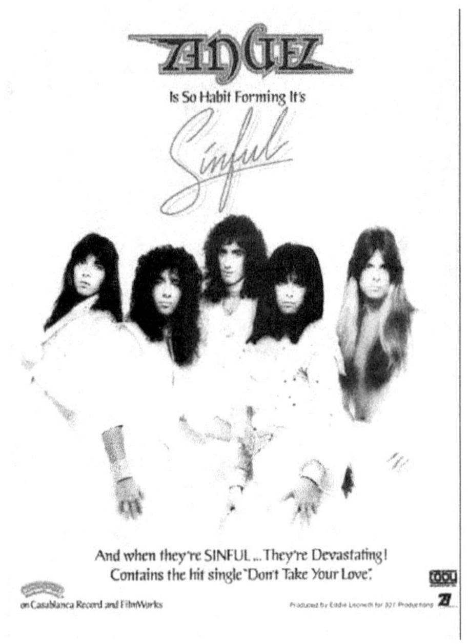

Ace's because it had a song called 'New York Groove' on it, and that didn't sell that well. So we shipped over a million albums on each album and we got back almost all of them on all the albums. Even though we… what sold was the Kiss picture discs. We said they were limited edition, which was bullshit. We wound up selling like a quarter of a million on each picture disc, which was amazing. Initially we were going to sell like 5000, but they kept selling and selling. The kids wanted the picture discs, not the music. And at that point that really hurt Kiss a lot. I think kids were starting to get a little tired, but they were still selling a lot of albums in '78 and '79, and they were still selling out gigs wherever they went in '78 and '79."

It's interesting, because although Larry is talking about Kiss, most definitely my memory of the situation is that Angel was going the same route, exacerbated, to be sure, by the music getting poppier, but also because of the association with a Kiss that was running out of steam, with both being associated with a label that was losing its lustre with hard rock fans, due to its growing association with disco.

"Now 1980 is when Kiss started getting into trouble," continues Harris (but again he could be talking about Angel). "In '78 they had done that *Phantom of the Opera*-like movie for TV (*Kiss Meets the Phantom of the Park*). It was terrible. It was not a good idea. Somebody talked them into the fact, 'Oh you're big enough, you should have your own TV movie.' Fine, it didn't work. But the amazing thing about Kiss, when everybody counted them out and said they were going downhill, a few years later they came back and they were the biggest grossing band in the world on the road and they had another hit, and they're still doing it. I mean it's 35, 40 years later. It's amazing to me. I never would have thought that they would still be selling out shows all over the world."

Angel at Midnight, *Kiss Meets the Phantom of the Park*, *Foxes*, *Sinful*, *Unmasked*… Angel was on the same road to ruin except without the early success. Plus there would never be the redemption Harris just outlined. Aerosmith periodically didn't even exist in 1979 and 1980. Angel doppelgangers Starz were already gone—their *White Hot* and *Sinful* period was represented by the shocking pop turn that was *Attention Shoppers!*, from which they never recovered, despite returning with one last heavy album called *Coliseum Rock*.

"It's kind of human nature that after you see something, even if it's shocking at first, after a while you get used to it," muses Larry. "And with all the magazine stuff going on and TV appearances and constantly being in the news and gigs, eventually Kiss just became, really, a caricature of themselves, and people got really used to it and they weren't shocking any more. They had to go. Somebody had to take that next step to be more shocking. And how far can you go? Maybe cut your own hand off or something, I don't know."

Which is a different story, or many stories, about a bunch of other bands in the '80s and beyond. What Angel was attempting to do with *Sinful* would be what Kiss would attempt to do with *Dynasty* and *Unmasked*, and that's move on, get contemporary, grow up.

As Frank told me, "That was like a transition period, and very weird, because when the transition to the '80s began with our fifth album, the *Sinful* album, all we kept hearing from the label was, 'Oh, let's try for a bit more radio access. Let's get a little bit more radio-friendly.' But at that time the radio stations were changing as well. That's what I think happened. When we did those first two albums, the radio stations were playing 'Long Time,' and that's like seven minutes long. You don't hear those kinds of songs anymore—and it was a deep cut. But there was still an FM-oriented audience. By the time '79 came, it was getting to be more of an AM feel out there versus FM. And it progressively got worse, up to this point now where there is no such thing as FM kind of oriented stations. Even Sirius, to some point, they seem to play different songs, maybe a few deeper cuts, but they seem to play the same ones all the time now and I don't know why. They shouldn't have to."

"I don't know why the record companies put themselves behind the eight ball with that stuff. Instead of being out on the forefront and making things happen, they seemed to go along with it. Guys like Neil Bogart were not so much around anymore. Neil was the guy who went out and made things happen. He wasn't someone who wanted things to happen and then take credit for it. Which, I think a lot of the record companies were starting to go that way. And it seems like a lot of lawyers took over the record companies, because of the money situation, where the record company wasn't making enough money. But what is success? As long as you're making money, you are successful at it. But that's what I remember happening, is a lot of lawyers all of a sudden were the heads of record companies."

"We started trying to get more commercial," agrees Punky. "Because everybody wants hit singles and that sort of thing. And back then, for us, there wasn't any MTV. If we would've had MTV, it would've been a whole different story for Angel. We would've broke wide-open, because we were such a visual band and we could have been seen. Back in those days you had to just tour, to every little city, every little town, and you spent your life on the road, eight months out of the

year, just touring. And then coming back to record another album and write songs and then you go back out on the road again. But we were trying to get some hit songs, because in those days, they weren't playing anything like us. They were playing things like Fleetwood Mac and Peter Frampton. They weren't really playing anything loud. Even Kiss couldn't get any airplay except for 'Beth.'"

"But once MTV came out, those bands like Def Leppard and Quiet Riot, they all broke overnight—because you could see them playing 24 hours a day. It was just rammed down your throat. Whereas when we were out, you had to tour every little city on the scene and be heard. I remember, if there was ever a band on TV, you couldn't wait to see it, because you never got to see bands on TV."

"So then we started writing the poppier songs like you hear on *Sinful*," continues Meadows. "And I love the *Sinful* album. That's one of my favourite albums, because to me, it's harder to write a three-minute pop song than to write a heavy riff. It's just a hard thing to do. I can sit up all day and come up with all these heavier riffs. And put some vocals to it and keyboards. But to write a song that has a really good singable verse, good lyrics, good hooks and good bridge, you know, and lyrics that are memorable and singable too, that's a lot more difficult to me. And I've always loved how the Beatles could construct these beautiful songs, these great songs. And to this day, I still love all that."

Punky appreciated Eddie Leonetti's work on the album as well. "Yes, well, Eddie knew where we were coming from, because he was in that band, Soul Survivors, who had that hit, 'Expressway to Your Heart' (sings it). Anyway, he was a little more in tune with what we were doing on *Sinful*. I would write a song and he would hear something a little different in the chorus, and maybe change the chorus—him and I saw eye-to-eye on that kind of thing. He was good at bringing out more of a commercial side to us. And I'm proud of the fact that everybody in that band could actually come up with good commercial hooks. That's a lot harder to do than write a heavy metal riff."

"But we had to hurry to get that album out because we'd been on the road. We'd just finished filming the movie *Foxes* with Jodie Foster and Sally Kellerman and we did that at the Shrine Auditorium, and so we decided to do the basic tracks live. So you listen to *Sinful*, one side is all live basic tracks and the other side is basic tracks in the studio, with overdubs done in the studio on both sides. So, sonically, it's different on side two than it is on side one. People don't really know that. And a lot of those songs, like 'Wild and

Hot,' were played faster than they really should have been because we were playing it live."

"But we were writing more commercial songs, definitely," continues Meadows. "And having fun doing that. Because I always loved Mott the Hoople and David Bowie and Sweet and all those English bands. I loved The Raspberries, man. One of my all-time favourite songs is 'Go All the Way.' Every time I hear that song, the hair on my arm stands up and I want to sing along with it. I just love melody. That's why I'm really proud of this album. There's a lot of melody on this album, a lot of good hooks and choruses. But there's also slamming guitars all over the place too. I mean, it's a power pop thing as well. It's really heavy with the guitars. When you hear the guitars and solos and stuff, it's heavy, but yet the songs are good songs and some of the choruses you can sing along to. The problem with metal nowadays, is that it's all guys. I don't want to go to a concert, man, where... I want to go where there are chicks too! Where there's chicks there's going to be guys, you know what I mean? And the girls are really the ones who buy records, let's face it. That's why we all started playing guitar. First of all, for the love of the music, but also, we wanted chicks. Everybody will tell you that. And so *Sinful* is geared to that. Girls can sing along with the record as well. That's really what we were striving for."

"*Sinful* was kind of an unsettled album," is how Frank frames the experience. "Neil wanted us to do it half live and half studio. And then what? Are you going to do new songs live that people have never heard of? It was just very unsettling. We were trying to figure out how to do it. What we ended up doing is, we did the last show of the tour. I think it was *Angel at Midnight* at Santa Monica. So what we ended up doing is we brought the trucks in, the mobile truck from the Record Plant, and instead of doing the songs live to the audience, we recorded them at Santa Monica Civic (laughs). They might've been a couple of the songs off the second side, maybe 'Waited a Long Time.' But it just never felt like we settled into that album although the direction was fine. By that time we were all comfortable with our writing and that record was a case of us just writing and getting it down on tape. Some of the stuff was at the Record Plant. Studio C had burned down, so we did some stuff in a smaller studio. But yeah, it's kind of a disjointed effort and I don't know why."

And then it was time for the public to voice their opinion—but not until Casablanca put the spin on *Sinful* for the press and radio programmers. Following is the bio for the record, a spiffy spot of writing that offers insight as to how the frantic front office hoped Angel would fit and then sit in the marketplace of ideas circa January of 1979.

"White satin costumes, cherubic faces, and Angel *still* manages to look… wicked. The type of guys a self-respecting father wouldn't let near his daughter, because his instincts tell him that somehow, in spite

of their looks, they're dangerous. They're playing that loud rock 'n' roll and who knows what they do with their spare time? Angel knows… and it's right up front on *Sinful*, their latest Casablanca LP. *Sinful* follows an established tradition of progressive heavy metal that's won Angel a devoted following throughout the United States and even in far-flung places like Japan. In contrast to the angelic visages displayed on the album's jacket, *Sinful* is actually a tongue-in-cheek title. The content reflects a loosening of the group's attitudes and the return of boyish high spirits and enthusiasm. In short, they've let their hair down."

"'We're having *fun* now,' says lead guitarist Punky Meadows, in a mock Steve Martin voice. 'We've matured and our music's matured. This album is more fun because it's more *spontaneous*.' A big part of that feeling can be traced to producer Eddie Leonetti. *Sinful* is the second album he's produced for Angel (the first was last year's *White Hot*) and producer and group are pleased with the rapport that's developed. Angel drummer Barry Brandt commented, 'He really gets the best performance from all of us. We are very happy with the results, and I think it shows in the sounds and the album's general feel. It practically *bleeds* energy.' The superb translation of that energy onto vinyl is an Angel trademark. Here it's even more unique—many of *Sinful*'s instrumental tracks were recorded during an actual live concert for a harder sound. That approach—of using concert tracks as a basis for the studio album—is enough to make anyone's album something special, but on *Sinful*, it's yet another example of Angel's eagerness to explore a variety of musical techniques."

"Another favoured approach is their attention to arrangement and melody (a direction that really took flight on *White Hot*) and extensive collaboration. Angel's belief in group composition creates a very open climate for ideas, and on *Sinful*, it makes for some great songs. Their sense of musical unity has served them extremely well, not only on their albums, but also on the forthcoming Casablanca picture film, *The Foxes*, where they contributed the title theme to Giorgio Moroder's soundtrack. Angel's cohesiveness and entertainment sense has combined to develop a stage show whose visual effects are perfectly synced with the spirit of the music. When Angel performs, they create a total environment—of sound, light and magical illusions like no other in contemporary music. It's a feast for the eyes as well as the ears… and it's so habit-forming, it's *Sinful*."

If one was to read between the lines, downplayed this time are the band's pretty-boy looks and, really, anything that could align them with Kiss. Instead there's a sort of sober view that the band was maturing and that meant less heavy metal, which aligns perfectly with Punky's aims and subsequent views of the record, instantly at the time and, commendably, steadfast now 40 years later.

As for the purely angelic cover art, well, this nearly swung quite wildly a different way. In fact, take a look at *Bad Publicity* from obscure UK-based garage glam band Pet Hate (also produced by Eddie Leonetti), and you will see the cover art—and title—*Sinful* almost wound up with. "Yeah, that was going to be our cover," affirms Frank. "I hear it's almost an exact replica. That's the one we wanted to use, but Neil didn't want to use it. We had it all planned and Neil pulled out at the last minute. I think they had already pressed like 200,000 of them, something crazy, 100,000 of them, with the *Bad Publicity* cover. Some of the records themselves have a label that says *Bad Publicity*, and they put *Sinful* over it."

Asked if any were sold with that cover, Frank answers, "No, they only got made. I had a box of only the cover. I've seen them at record fairs. The whole idea was to show that we didn't take ourselves that seriously. And what we had was, you know the picture by now, and on the back was all bad reviews; we had all our bad reviews pasted on the back."

Elaborating in conversation with John Parks, Frank explained that, "Neil Bogart did not want us to release the cover of us in street clothes. There was a big argument over the costumes. We felt like the costumes were just a part of the stage show and that we weren't tied to the costumes the same way that Kiss was tied to the characters and the costumes. It just wasn't the same thing. We weren't trying, like Kiss, to avoid being seen out of the makeup or the stage costumes; we were just a rock 'n' roll band. We said, 'We're not like Kiss, that's not what Angel is defined by, that's just a small part of the show, we are not tied to it as individual comic book-type characters, they're just stage clothes.'"

"Our concept was just that: we were wearing street clothes at the Hyatt House and we were gambling, and there was a midget pouring champagne in a top hat (laughs) and we had all these women laying all over and the cops were busting into the room. That was it. Then surrounding the photo and all over the back cover was a collection of all the horrible reviews we had gotten that past year, hence the title *Bad Publicity*. We loved the idea—Casablanca hated it. The cover art of the re-titled *Sinful*, I have no feeling toward whatsoever. It was just damage control with them at that point. Just pick a photo from Barry Levine's bank and get on with it, slap a few songs on it and put it out. Fine, whatever. We would have been much happier as a band had they let us continue with our vision for the album rather than make all this fuss about the cover, so the end result was that we were less invested as a band."

Punky recalls Neil saying, "I didn't sign a punk band—I signed Angel," but as Felix figures, that was sort of the point, to look a bit more like the first name of the band's guitarist.

"We were going to break away from the angelic image and become bad boys," explains Robinson, "along with what we felt was the changing music business at that time. We felt that we had been pushing that spandex white patent image as far as it could be pushed, and at that point we wanted to find something that was different. Everyone agreed with us. But after we had shot the album cover with us being, you know, interrupted in a hotel room party, then the story goes—and I wasn't in touch with Neil at that point; Frank seems to remember this better than me—Neil looked at that went, 'No, I can't do that. I know what works and that's not it.' And for one reason or another we decided—or *it* was decided—that we stay with the white image. So we went back to a photography studio and Barry Levine shot another series of photographs. The inner sleeve, however, included a shot of us standing against the background of a lineup in a police station in street clothes."

Indeed it did, with the guys apparently averaging six-foot-six in height. Flipped over, there was a full set of lyrics, again, suggesting that we take the band seriously as grown men saying something. The back cover of the album itself however was so sinful—excuse me, simple—that it looked like a record club design, or worse, one of those drug deal record company back covers from the mid-'70s (look these up—pretty interesting).

Into the record proper, *Sinful* opens with "Don't Take Your Love," credited to Frank and Gregg, which makes sense, given how prominent the keys are, despite the pushing and shoving that takes place from the rhythm end of things, with a sharp bass sound from Felix and punchy drums from Barry. I hear a ton on New England in this one, although that band's self-titled debut was yet to come out, also in 1979, but not until May. There's also a bit of The Cars here, and indeed that band's self-titled debut was already out, having hit the streets burning rubber back in June 1978.

"That was kind of like a Beach Boys fan thing that we tried to do," recalls Frank, "with a lot of the vocals and stuff, although we kept it heavier, not heavy, a little bit different than that, but you have to keep it within the realm of Angel. Although with Angel we never kept ourselves in one pocket. We would always try to move musically and not keep ourselves in one particular thing, which might've had a lot to do with us being in the situation we were as well. As a fan you weren't likely to put the album on and know exactly what to expect. Our stuff was always music-oriented in whatever direction we went in. When we were writing, we just kept building. We didn't say, 'Oh, we gotta keep it more Angel.' We never approached the song like that. It was always, let's make the song be the identifying factor of it."

"Don't Take Your Love" was issued as a single, backed with "Bad Time," non-picture sleeve in the US but over in Germany, with a sleeve that reproduces the album cover.

Next is "L.A. Lady," a heavy enough boogie-woogie barroom rocker with barrelhouse piano—if you want to know where "7 o'clock," smash hit for the London Quireboys circa 1990, came from, look no further than right here, although really, the precedent before Angel is Lynyrd Skynyrd, not to mention The Faces and Humble Pie… even Kiss.

Notes Punky, "That was a song we wrote pretty much together. We just weren't the kind of band where someone came in and said, 'Here's a song'—never happened. 'Here's a song from beginning to end, learn your part, we're gonna record this song.' We never did that. Frank would come up with lyrics generally to a song that maybe Felix or myself had an idea about. And then the song would come together in a rehearsal or at a songwriting session generally at or after or around rehearsal time. Barry would come in with song ideas and everybody would help. Gregg would have parts of tunes that needed to be completed. That's the way we did it."

"Just Can't Take It" opens deftly, amusingly, with Punky doing his best Pete Townshend (say, "Squeezebox"), playing licks that sound close enough to be a variation on the "L.A. Lady" theme, even though we quickly find out that they are the basis of the next track. Once into the plush recline of "Just Can't Take It," we hear what Punky's on about, namely the fact that the band was maturing as songwriters. Fact is, this is a gorgeous, catchy pop song with artful transitions and hooks for miles.

But then again, the band undermine their shot at success with songs like this through the faceless titling of the damn thing. Frank chuckles at hearing a list of the song titles on *White Hot* and *Sinful,* most with many short words in them, most going in one ear and out the other without much chance of sticking to the memory banks.

"You know, if anyone knew what the formula was to writing a hit song, we'd be writing them all day," he laughs. "You try and do the best you can with it and hopefully it gets airplay. If it gets airplay and people start to kick in and they're wanting to hear it again, then you've got a chance for it to be a hit. But mostly it gets down to radio stations playing it. It's up to the programmers accepting a record, and the company pushing that particular song for a particular reason. I mean, there's so many horrible songs that were huge, huge hits. And then you sit and you listen to some songs and you go, 'How is that not a hit?!' So I don't buy into any kind of formula. There's a formula for writing a pop song. There's a formula for writing a metal song. Sure. But I don't think there's any kind of set formula for writing a hit."

In effect, as Frank alludes to, being part of the Casablanca stable might have been a hindrance at this point. "Yes, I think some of the problem was Casablanca. I don't think that programmers really felt that Casablanca at that time was a company that was going to have any kind of rock band that had any validity because they were a big disco label and they had Kiss. And Kiss was like a novelty act at that time, with a big live show which was not translatable to radio. If you think about Kiss, they never really got a lot of airplay back then. Sure, they were such a big band live and there were so many people who grew up listening to Kiss, that everyone knows their songs. But those songs weren't really played on the radio that much is what I mean. So there's two ways of looking at things. Anybody who knows Angel certainly doesn't know them from any regular play. Because we didn't get a whole lot of that. They know us from coming to see us and buying our records."

Moving on, "You Can't Buy Love" is yet another delectable slice of Cheap Trick power pop featuring big block chords with strong and simple and yet countering vocal melodies over top. Then we're into "Bad Time" and more of the same, namely swaggering chord sequences, biting rhythms and Gregg piling on the syrupy synths, topped finally by Frank's fine voice. Again, I picture a manager growling at the guys saying, "Don't call it 'Bad Time;' call it 'Good Time!'" But even that's a half measure. To beat it into the ground, Angel's titles have too many words, too many small and forgettable words, and too many words arranged to sound negative or self-defeating.

And here comes another one illustrating all three of those characteristics: "Waited a Long Time," which fits the narrative of this record's well-recorded and hard-hitting pomp rock along the lines of Starz-lite, Piper and New England. This one's got prog elements as well although not much in the way of keyboards. And as usual, Barry comes on strong, almost at odds with the song construction.

Next is "I'll Bring the Whole World to Your Door," credited to Punky, Frank and producer Eddie Leonetti. Still, says Felix, "I pretty much wrote the solo section and the B-section, the bridge, and the arrangement was mine pretty much, but I'm not going to say that I wrote the arrangement and handed it to the guys. We arranged it together in rehearsal. I know a lot of the arrangements were me saying, 'We shouldn't do this now. No, don't go there. Let's go there. Let's do this.' That was my contribution. Did I get songwriting credit? No."

"Eddie got me," reflects Punky, intimating how the two of them bonded over pop. "Like I say, he was in that band that did 'Expressway to Your Heart,' Soul Survivors, and that was a pop song. 'I'll Bring the Whole World to Your Door' is an uplifting song about loving somebody and giving them everything they want for their love. Eddie got that kind of thing and he was a cool dude. Lee DeCarlo actually wasn't a big fan of the pop song as much. He was more into like the John Lennon, political kind of stuff. But he was a great engineer. It's funny, because you get a lot of criticism. When people talk about the Angel albums, some people see *Sinful* as their favourite when other people say, 'No, they sold out on *Sinful*' and they'll say the first two are my favourites. I was getting a kick out of it, because nobody saw that we just became better songwriters and we just wanted to go in a different direction."

"And so each album is different. To me, I would say you don't have to look at *Sinful* as a sell-out. Look at it as a different album, 'cause the songs are great. You can enjoy it all. That's why I say you shouldn't pigeonhole yourself with these situations because you're not going to be able to enjoy any shit. For

example, I love country music. When I was a kid growing up, I'd say, 'Oh that wang-dang shit.' I still make fun of it too: 'She broke my heart so I broke her jaw.' But I grew up in Maryland and Virginia, so I heard a lot of country music growing up as a kid and didn't realise how much it influenced me later on. One of the first songs that made a big impression on me was 'Big Bad John' by Jimmy Dean, about a coal mine. And that whole story in there made me think. I also liked the song 'Rumble' from Link Wray. He grew up in my area—he's often called the guy with the first heavy metal song, right? He was from Washington, DC and I used to see him play because he'd play all the nightclubs. And I always said that I wanted to do a song like 'Rumble' and I actually wrote a song like that called 'You're So Cold' and Eddie kind of got it and he recorded it, as a demo. Anyway, he always got me and knew what I wanted to do when I wrote those pop songs."

"But yeah, when power pop kind of became a thing, I was all in," continues Meadows. "That's why I wrote 'Wild and Hot' and all the *Sinful* stuff. I loved Cheap Trick and The Cars, The Knack, all that stuff. That just spoke to me. I would rather hear that than hear Black Sabbath."

Punky also credits Lee DeCarlo for encouraging him, even if, as Punky says, he wasn't one for the pop stuff. "Oh yes, Lee was a great engineer. I used to come in early and I would play some songs and he'd go 'What's that?!' and I'd play it, he goes, 'We need to record that next time. That's awesome.' I'd say, 'It's not finished yet; it's just an idea.' And he would always come out and tap his foot and really listen and go, 'What is that?!' And I'd say, 'That's just something I've been messing around with.' Because whenever I go in the studio playing my guitar parts, I'm just warming up a little bit. I'm messing around and I still do that."

In any event, "I'll Bring the Whole World to Your Door" is mostly standard *Sinful* pop, but the verse is somewhat Zeppelin-esque, both of riff and with respect to Gregg's part, which is very John Paul Jones. The bridge, of which Felix speaks, evokes images of Queen. But again, the sum total is a sort of drum-dominated pop with a passionate vocal.

"I'll Never Fall in Love Again"—there's yet another title that is a mouthful—is closer to what would later be called a power ballad. Again, one thinks of Piper and New England, especially the latter. Barry is prominent as usual, firing off big snare drum fills during the powerful and memorable chorus. This one also has one of those solo sections Punky talks about where the underlying musical structure is a new one, this time, again, sort of pop version of late-period Led Zeppelin. And if that wasn't enough with respect to Zep, Barry closes the song with a gong bash.

Next we arrive at the most famed song across the expanse of *Sinful* and another curious foible of the band's song titling. "Wild and Hot" sounds like a misstatement of "White Hot," which would have made it the title track of the band's previous album. This prompts one to notice that across five records, Angel indeed never had a single title track, which means they passed on another ploy that might have brought them a hit. A title track suggest the song is good enough to name the whole album after this marquee song, plus through the doubling, that title is driven harder into the memory banks. Instead we get the slightly awkward, English-as-second-language "Wild and Hot." To make matters worse, the chorus refrain is the mouthful, 'Cause we're wild and we're hot." Now, the lyric is admirable because it's not referring to the predicable, namely girls in short skirts. But it's also confusing, at least when it comes to the titling.

"'Wild and Hot' was a song that I wrote about my son," explains Punky, "because he was just a kid and he loved Kiss. He loved Angel too, but that's really a teenage kind of song about kids loving the rock bands and that sort of thing. So yeah, I wrote that song for my son, just as a fun song. And I just like the way it goes and how it ends up. It's an adolescent, teenage song, about playing guitars and stuff. I like the simplicity of it and it's fun to sing along with."

So yes, it's a poignant lyric, about all of us who were insane young fans of these bands in the '70s, and written out of love. Plus the music is engaging, sort of hard rock-meets-girl group, like poppy New York Dolls or similarly camp Kiss, along the lines of "Tomorrow and Tonight" and "Then She Kissed Me," which, granted, is a cover.

Notes Felix, "'Wild and Hot' was definitely a derivative from Cheap Trick's first big hit record, 'Surrender.' Listen to Robin Zander. I think we listened to that song and something there was a bolt of inspiration. They appeared to be a pop band to us but a really great pop band and terrific live. Gregg had become friends with Rick Nielsen around that point, or subsequent to that. But I remember listening to that song and talking about it. Punky came in with 'Wild and Hot' and I remember the first time I heard it thinking, well, this is very similar song to a Cheap Trick tune and being told, 'Nah, that's my song.' And I went okay and we learned it. I'm not saying that it was a rip-off, but look, you learn something from everywhere. If you hear a song on the radio that you like and you hear it often enough and if you think about it long enough and you sit down with your guitar, you know, are you going to write a song that might be similar to it? Yeah. But I don't want to make too big a deal out of it."

The similarity is both small and fleeting. First, the two songs are not particularly aligned musically, at the verse nor the chorus. It's really only that Punky's overall idea aligns with the memorable lines, "Mom and dad are rolling on the couch, rolling numbers, rock and rolling, got my Kiss records out." In fact, "Surrender" is a pretty sophisticated lyric all about mom and dad. This line merely mentions that the son (presumably) happens to have Kiss records, ergo the link with Punky writing about his son being a Kiss fan. However—here we go again—Punky doesn't cite Kiss or any other band by name, hence his lyric is not as memorable as Rick Nielsen's.

Continues Felix, "I don't want to step on too many toes here, but I know that when we were in the studio, I was doubling Frank's vocal of the song—Frankie and I were singing it together. I know how I pronounce words and I know how Frank pronounces words—he's from Boston; I'm from St. Louis. I know what it sounds like when I sing. So that's Frank but it's also me; it's Lee DeCarlo doing the right thing, blending two vocals together to make one, versus it just being Frank alone. So that is an engineered vocal."

Indeed Frank went so far as to single Felix out in interviews as a great addition—in fact "a whole new dimension"—to the live show given that they could now explore doing harmonies on stage that had previously been limited to the studio albums.

There's a nice little bonus story about "Wild and Hot," notes Frank. "Yeah, Kiss used 'Wild and Hot' in the *Detroit*

Rock City movie. Got a little royalty check for that. But if you go to see the movie, you'll have a hard time seeing the song."

Sinful closes with "Lovers Live On," another up-tempo pop rocker with a '60s girl group vibe. Once more, Barry is driving the song like his life depended on it and once again we have an Angel title that is forgettable and just a little weird—you're just a tiny bit annoyed and you don't know why, basically, through cognitive dissonance. This one is credited to Meadows and Robinson, and it's Felix's only credit on the album—one gets the feeling the band were a little tight with assigning credit where it was due.

"Frank, Punky and I wrote that on the bus," says Felix, notably bringing Frank into it! "We were sitting in the bunks writing tunes, and we came with that sort of 50-50. You know, I contributed to all those songs. I certainly could have shared writing credits, but the songwriting team of Frank and Punky and Gregg dominated much of that. And so songs were maybe started on one hand and then finished in the studio. As things were progressing pretty haphazardly at that point, I did not assert myself at times when I could have. I know I should have done a better job of that myself. I don't blame somebody else for stealing. I only say I should have taken more credit. I should have demanded more credit and I didn't and that's not their fault."

For what it's worth, Gregg gets credited four times on the record, and Barry twice. The *Sinful* experience… in hindsight, as we've seen, Punky is adamant that writing songs like that was a great idea, but Frank not so much. The record stalled at a lowly No.159 on the Billboard charts, while, conversely, *Dynasty* from Kiss vaulted to No.9, and mostly from the inclusion of a novelty disco song.

"We had a hard time getting airplay," sighs Punky, "like I said, I've always loved melody. Power pop music has always been one of my favourite things. So again, *Sinful* was that kind of an album where I was actually becoming a better songwriter. As I said, when I ask you to write a song with melody that has a verse/verse/chorus, then a bridge, and it's a three- or four-minute song, that's a lot harder to do than writing some complicated riffs. All I'm telling you is if it was easy, everybody would be doing it. So I love *Sinful*. It's one of my favourite albums actually of all of them. Every song on there could have been a hit record, I feel, back in the day, if Casablanca had done their job. When I listen to *Sinful*, I really am happy—the songs make me feel good. They're really commercial-oriented, they're singable and they're good performances, but they're played well too, you know? And so I love *Sinful*. I really do."

"But I also love *White Hot*. I mean every album for Angel has its own personality and is different. There are certain things I like about every album. You can't beat 'The Tower' of course. And we play so many of these songs live. Things like 'Can You Feel It' are great songs to play; they just kick ass and the audience loves it. So every album has its own personality and that's what was kind of cool about Angel. We kept changing. People say, 'Well, they didn't know who they were.' That's not the truth. That's not the way it was. We just kept evolving and changing. And I'm like that now. I don't make any bones about it, man. When we made *Risen*, I said that it has to be diversified."

As for Felix's assessment of *Sinful*… "Here's my definitive answer on that: it was coming from everywhere instead of coming from a direction that it should have been. It's easy now to say where it should have been—hindsight is 20/20. We should have been allowed to write our songs in seclusion instead of in-between tours with very little time. We should have been allowed to rehearse and build these songs. We should have had extra help in songwriting from people who were more crafted, had more ability to craft hit records, which we struggled with. Certainly Kiss did that. In fact, I was in a band with one of the guys who helped Kiss write some of their hit songs—he was a ghostwriter for Kiss. They brought in other people to write songs so that they could have good records, and we could have done the same. You know, where are we going? We're going in every direction all at once. And we were touring too much. Plus the image was confusing to some people. And then when things got tough for us, the money was starting to get lean."

"We recorded *Sinful* at probably four different recording studios. There was Cherokee, there was The Record Plant, different rooms, Record Plant New York, Record Plant Los Angeles, live recording at the Santa Monica Civic Center. We rented the Santa Monica Civic Center. We set up the whole act, the whole band, whole PA, everything. Lee DeCarlo wanted a live sound. They weren't sure whether they were going to use it for a live album or not. They ended up using some of it as backing tracks for some of the songs on the live album, so some of the live album is not entirely live. It's actually recorded in the Santa Monica Civic Center without an audience. But that's not unique; other bands have done that. Other bands have made live albums that were almost entirely done in some sort of studio environment and then added audience sounds."

One song recorded during the Sinful sessions but not included on the album was the band's cover of The Left Banke's 1967 hit "Walk Away Renee."

"I don't know how we came up with that song," muses Frank. "With the Rascals song, we used to screw around with a lot of different stuff in rehearsal because we rehearsed every single day. We used to go through a lot of the Beatles catalogue at rehearsal, and 'Ain't Gonna Eat Out My Heart Anymore' was one of the songs that we used to screw around with. But I don't remember 'Walk Away Renee' as being anything that we did in rehearsal. It must have come up as an idea, 'Well, maybe we can do something with it.' And I don't know if we really were going to put it on the album. I believe it was more like, let's record it and see how we feel about it after we do it. So we worked it up at rehearsal and then went into the studio with it."

"Back then a lot of bands were doing cover tunes," adds Punky. "Cheap Trick was doing cover tunes left and right. Everybody was doing a cover and trying to get a hit, like of course Van Halen with 'You Really Got Me.' So 'Walk Away Renee' of course was a song that everybody loved. As Frank says, we also did 'Ain't Gonna Eat Out My Heart Anymore' because I loved The Rascals. See, my thing was, I always loved the East coast bands more than the West coast bands. I'm not talking about the '70s and '80s but like in the '60s I was never a big fan of Grateful Dead and Jefferson Starship. I liked the East coast bands and the English bands. 'Walk Away Renee,' great song, The Left Banke, and talk about a beautiful melody. That song… you can't stop singing it."

Angel's version of "Walk Away Renee" can be heard on *An Anthology*, issued by Casablanca in 1992, along with two other rarities, "20th Century Foxes" and "The Christmas Song."

Hitting the tour trail, Angel played a mix of support slots (most notably with Ted Nugent) and small headline shows (TKO, Sad Café, Trillion). One of those warm-up jobs found the band ill-paired with Eddie Money, hot at the time with a gold debut (now double platinum) and a second record, *Life for the Taking*, that had just shipped gold (en route to platinum).

"It is rare that a rock concert boils down to something like a contest between cotton candy and prime rib," opined John Cullinane from the St. Louis Post-Dispatch, reviewing a show in July '79. "That was the degree of contrast in a show Thursday night that featured Eddie Money and Angel. You can guess who turned in the cotton candy set."

"It was the musicians in Angel who came out with every wild hair stuck neatly in place. They had the costumes, the bombs bursting overhead and a display of showmanship that could only be the product of divine inspiration. The opening of the group's show was worth standing on one's chair to see—and nearly all the 6500 persons at Kiel Auditorium did so. But that didn't make for great music. It made cotton candy, and we all know what a cheap thrill that is. Angel's Frank DiMino, a talented singer, had trouble piercing the smokescreen of volume laid down by the instrumentalists. He and the boys mostly tried to overwhelm the audience, but to some in the audience, the show was a little too similar to previous Angel shows. They do have a new album, *Sinful*, and a new single, 'Don't Take Your Love,' to offer. To state the obvious, it was Eddie Money and the Eddie Money Band that were the prime rib for the evening."

Then again, if it's Angel supporting Styx, all of a sudden the heroes of our story emerge triumphant. "The opening act, Angel, drew more response," argued Chuck Graham, addressing a Tucson gig in February '79. "This extremely long-haired, somewhat theatrical quintet played like it had just found out the devil was going to inherit Heaven. The electronic dervish of sound assaulted the senses with glee, pushing the enthusiastic audience into hyperspace. Angel's music was shrill, agitated, scraping, devoid of reticence. It was loud and harried, but the emotional effect wasn't obtained just by turning amplifier volume knobs up to danger levels. This dose of melted heavy metal carried the spirit to heights as far beyond pure noise as a rocket ship's performance goes far beyond pure speed."

Speaking with Gregg after Angel's set, Chuck gets told this whopper: "Back East, we headline all the time in 18,000-seat halls and have a theatrical show, so big it wouldn't fit on the stage here. We use a lot of lights, holograms and lasers. There is an eight-minute theatrical production that precedes the band's introduction on stage. Earth, Wind and Fire saw us preparing our show, stole all our ideas and changed them just enough so that we couldn't do anything about it. We were going to sue anyway, but since they appeal to a different market, we didn't."

Graham, incredulous, adds, "Such bravado would seem wholly absurd if Angel had not played so well. Styx just couldn't compete."

"We were starting to do co-headlining and we were starting to open for other acts," explains Felix—don't forget also, these were recessionary times, with a gas shortage to boot, which dampened enthusiasm for kids to drive long distances to see concerts, hence even greater recessionary times for the music business. "So we played with REO Speedwagon, Blue Öyster Cult, Styx and things were starting to get very lean for us. We did a lot of shows and we travelled a lot—that was a good bus and truck tour. We had a large crew and we played some good shows. We opened up but we did headline a lot of the smaller venues, in cities like Chicago, Seattle and Portland and throughout the Midwest and Texas."

"I remember we had long talks about this. Should we go out on tour and open for other bands? And the fact is that we should have never done that for financial reasons. Our management got paid 15% or more of everything we earned, no matter where it came from. And if we opened for Blue Öyster Cult or we opened for Styx, if we opened for Ted Nugent, as we started to do that, he got 15% of every dollar we made and we got a guarantee, plus we got part of the gate at some shows. So he was pulling in the money every time we played."

'But you know what it was doing? It was destroying our image. We were not an opening band. We were a headlining act and that's what we should have stayed. That's all we should have ever become. At that point. We should never have left that. But it was time and money. And of course the excuse was, you've got to keep your name out there. You gotta be in front of people. You gotta go out there and play. You've got a great record coming up, *Sinful*. It's going to be a great record—go out there and perform. I remember that very clearly and I don't think anybody else in the band would disagree with me."

"It was simply one of the biggest mistakes we made," continues Robinson, "agreeing to open for other bands. Because when we did, we didn't have the full effects part of our show, right? We didn't use the whole power of our presentation. We didn't get to a long enough period of time to use different songs and do arrangements of songs and actually express our musicianship for periods of time that allowed us to really put it out there. We had to keep our show at 45 minutes or under. Plus we didn't get the use of the whole PA system. Some of these bands that we performed with, as we did with bands that opened for us, we didn't get the full PA system. We were turned down and we didn't have the impact. Again, it's the biggest mistake we ever made, and as it turns out, we never made another record."

January 20, 1979, Tulsa, OK. Angel were the support act with Ted Nugent headlining. © Richard Galbraith.

The original cover design on the left; the final product on the right.

Hello and goodbye: the front and back cover of *Live Without a Net*, the last album from Angel's classic era.

Publicity still for the *Foxes* movie.

T-shirt image for the ill-fated tour featuring Angel, Humble Pie, Frank Marino & Mahogany Rush and Mother's Finest.

Gregg and Punky on the gruelling Rock & Roll Marathon tour, May 2, 1980, Norman, OK. © Richard Galbraith.

Rock & Roll Marathon tour, May 2, 1980, Norman, OK. © Richard Galbraith.

Frank Dimino, from a solo gig on July 6, 2018 at The Token Lounge in Westland, MI (west Detroit) promoting *Old Habits Die Hard.* © Bill Baran.

Felix Robinson, reflecting on what might have been. Collection of Felix Robinson.

Promo shot of Punky's solo band. Note Angel alumnus Felix Robinson behind Punky to his left.

Angel back in action and promoting their *Risen* album, March 1, 2020 on the Rock Legends Cruise. © Bill Baran.

Live Without a Net
"Disenchanted and drained by the whole thing"

Angel appeared magically at the nexus of the decades with fresh possibilities. Despite the depressed year across the music business in 1979 as well as in the wider economy—Jimmy Carter out, soon to be replaced by Ronald Reagan—the boys found themselves hopeful about their involvement in movies. *Angel at Midnight* died like so many film projects, but a coming-of-age feature film called *Foxes* was nearing completion.

Starring Jodie Foster, Scott Baio, Sally Kellerman and Randy Quaid, the movie was in fact a Casablanca project, winding its way through a birthing process just as the company was imploding. As it happened, Angel's contribution would be greatly diminished, living on through time as two tracks stuck on the soundtrack album.

Explains Felix, "We got into the movie, *Foxes*, as a cameo, but we were supposed to be far more involved. There were scenes shot backstage and other camera work that never made it into the final film—we were edited out. I guess they felt they had enough. They didn't wan to move it in that direction too far. The storyline of course was what it was, but the screenplay started out one way and ended up their own way. Still, I'm glad we did it."

The double LP soundtrack album consisted mostly of Giorgio Moroder and other disco things. Angel contributed

"Virginia" and a full-on disco song of their own called "20th Century Foxes."

"We did the movie," explains Frank, "and they asked us to write a song, the title track, for the movie. We wrote one and then I think Giorgio wrote one. And then Neil said, 'Let's go with the one that Angel did.' So we tried to work it out so that it was a compromise between an  Angel song and Giorgio's way of producing disco. That's what he wanted to do so we struck a compromise."

Adds Punky, "This all happened because Neil Bogart and Casablanca Records went into film works too. They did *Thank God It's Friday* with Donna Summer (issued May 19, 1978). They did *Foxes*, you know, with Jodie Foster and Sally Kellerman, and so they were into films and of course disco was big. Neil Bogart was pretty much the person who spearheaded disco. He'd started out with Donna Summer and the Village People of course. Neil started Casablanca off with a credit card. And his first album was Johnny Carson, I think, a comedy album. And he wasn't making it; he was going down, but then he got Donna Summer and then of course Kiss *Alive!* finally broke."

"And then he became the golden boy of Hollywood," continues Meadows. "Then of course he could do no wrong, right? Even the Stones and Rod Stewart did disco songs. So we were kind of forced into doing one because he wanted that for the soundtrack. And of course he was going to put us in the movie. We did it with Giorgio Moroder who was of course the big disco king producer at the time. We were on the road playing and then we went to a studio in New York and put that song together really quickly."

Adding a bit of detail, in conversation with Ken Sharp, Punky explained that, "We did the basic tracks in one day, and then the next day Frank came back in to do the vocals. I don't remember having much conversation with Giorgio. Then we went right back out on tour. It wasn't the direction we wanted to go in, but Casablanca wanted us to do it and we were told the song was gonna be in the movie. We thought it would further our career. Kiss also recorded a disco song, 'I Was Made for Lovin' You,' and had a big hit with it. I don't really hate disco because I love the Bee Gees. But I think at the time if you were in a rock band, you had to say that you hated disco."

"We were filming at the Shrine auditorium," continues Punky. "Filming is really boring. You get there really early in the morning and sit around all day long waiting to do a ten-minute scene. Jodie was really enamoured by us. The actress Sally Kellerman was there

too, and she used to come to all of our shows. We went in and did our songs and the audience screamed and they'd yell 'Cut!' and we'd do it all over again. It was exciting to be in a film, but it wasn't the same as playing onstage live and doing your thing."

Indeed, initially, *Foxes* was supposed to be *about* Angel, fully as a ploy by Neil to promote the band. But as it turned out, Angel were relegated to a passing source of entertainment as the girls in the film went about their drama-filled lives. Felix remembers how it took forever to get the drums down, due to the difficulty of getting Barry to lock into a disco beat. Ultimately, the movie bombed and at the same time, Neil was diagnosed with cancer, eventually succumbing in 1982.

Both "20th Century Foxes" and "Virginia" have been made available on compilations as well as bonus tracks on later CD issues of *Sinful*. As mentioned, the former is a full-on disco vamp, while "Virginia" is a typical Angel power pop song of the day but strapped to a halting disco beat.

More of an Angel joint, of course, was the band's double live album, *Live Without a Net*, issued concurrently with *Foxes*. The album included "20th Century Foxes" recorded live at The Shrine, but the rest was from two dates, as Frank explains.

"Yes, the best stuff that we had was Long Beach, so that's most of it. We also had Santa Monica, which was just in case some of the other places we recorded in didn't turn out right. We recorded at the Santa Monica Civic, which was the last date of that tour. We had the mobile truck down there, one whole day, and had a whole day to play around before the show. So we had small amplifiers in the back, and we had all these options to go through. It wasn't as spontaneous as the Long Beach show was, so we ended up using a lot more of the Long Beach stuff. But in the end, what was cool, we had a big pie fight with the crew."

"And that was the show… we used to do this thing at the end of the show where we would get into the album cover and the album cover would rise and explode, and there would be no one there. As I mentioned earlier, what we were going to do was put five dummies at the top, and when the album cover exploded, we were going to let the five dummies fall (laughs). But someone thought that would not go over well. You might really scare the shit out of somebody."

"Long Beach Arena, three sold-out nights, that was all recorded," recalls Felix. "We did the Santa Monica Civic Center recordings. Lee DeCarlo, Eddie Leonetti and us periodically went back in the studio and mixed the live album. I came in and out of those sessions. We sweetened up some of those tracks with better solos, in some cases with improved vocal parts, and some cases it's a combination of all that stuff. Some of the live tracks are genuine and inspiring and sound great. We chose the songs that had become part of the live show; we had to do 'The Tower' and had to do 'Rock & Rollers,' several songs that were not songs that I had originally recorded."

"But if you listen to the original recordings and you listen to the live album, you're going to hear bass parts that were enhanced considerably over what Mickie had done. Plus I pushed the bass definitely up in the mix in terms of working with the guitar parts instead of just enhancing the bottom end sonically. I always loved to play those songs. The bass part on 'Telephone Exchange' on the live album is *very* different than on the original record. I was having a lot of fun with that one. I've had people tell me how much they love the bass solo. I didn't think it was good at all. I thought I could have done a much better job with that bass solo if I had been given the time to develop something that was more making use of my skills as a soloist. You know, I'm bored by bass solos like everyone else! And it was kind of like 'Do it, get it over with' as far as I was concerned at the time. Now I regret that. I did not say, 'Stop, that's not good enough.' I definitely should have said stop. But there it is."

It was hoped, obviously, that *Live Without a Net* would do for Angel what *Alive!* and *Alive II* did for Kiss. Toward that end the graphics had that Kiss feel, plastered with live shots front, back and inside the gatefold.

Noted Larry Harris from Casablanca, "If you have a really great live album and you can capture the excitement, it's a lot more interesting to listen to than a studio album, which is so dry and carefully constructed. But if you have a live album that can really capture the excitement of being there, that adds tremendously to it. And in those days we also did tons of videos. I mean, we've got 75, 80 to 100 videos of all the bands that we had. We believed in the visual medium and we used it for television—we used it to send to news shows. Maybe they'd plug it into a news story or something. We were way ahead of the curve on using visual media and videos. In those days it wasn't even called videos, it was film."

Can't say the photograph on the front cover is much of a winner though. The shot is blurry, everybody's heads are turned away except for the drummer's, and Frank's leg is hiked at a disconcerting angle.

"The shot that is on the cover was the one that I had chosen," admits Frank. "But the inside was supposed to be a collage. And you don't know how many days I was at Casablanca choosing and picking all the pictures, and then going back to the guys in the band and going, 'Is this one okay? Do you like this one?' I'd never done that before, taken that much time. But I wanted to make sure that the pictures I used were okay with everyone, and I didn't want the record company to pick the pictures. So I thought okay, I'll take the time to do this. So I was there every day picking pictures and saying, 'Okay, this is okay, that one's not, this one is okay.' And they ended up not using any of them (laughs). Inside there, I don't know where they got any of those photos!"

As for the title, that was pretty good, catchy even, pardon the joke. Six years later Van Halen would call one of their concert videos *Live Without a Net*. Ten years later, Grateful Dead would issue a live album called *Without a Net*.

Everything other than "20th Century Foxes" was captured before *Sinful* was recorded so there are no selections from that record, save for an early version of "Wild and Hot." Otherwise it's a pretty even split between the first four albums, with one wrinkle being a massive ear-splitting keyboard solo from Gregg. Another wrinkle is a live version of "All the Young Dudes," confirmed by Felix to be from the Santa Monica Civic.

"Of course that's just a great song," muses Punky, asked why it's here. "I remember when I first saw Aerosmith. They opened up in Boston and were just a regional band. I was with Daddy Warbucks in Boston, and Mickie and I went to see Mott the Hoople and Aerosmith opened up. It was just a small venue, maybe a 3000-seater. And I remember thinking how cool Tyler and Joe Perry were. And then Ian Hunter and Mott the Hoople came out and they played 'All the Young Dudes' and I thought, what a fucking great song that is. That's another song with melody, in those verses and in that chorus; the melody is just incredible and beautiful in that song. So we did that song too. We picked the songs that we all liked him and thought would work."

    As Frank told John Parks, "That was after Felix had already been playing bass with us for a while, so we were pretty tight as a band and the performances that we had to work with were solid to begin with. I don't mind the album that much. I think it's a decent representation of the live show at that point, with the counter-play between Punky and Gregg and the set list being developed. My stuff with the audience was there and Barry's drumming was great. The set list really tended to change, and still, to this day, what we did back in the '70s is what we still do now: for every new addition, we take out a song that we might be getting burned-out on, aside from those few staples like 'The Tower.' But we change up the set a lot, which is great for us."

    After being somewhat less impressed with the first part of *Live Without a Net*, the eminent Malcolm Dome, working for Record Mirror, wrote that, "Side two is when the band prove they can rock 'n' roll all night with 'Over & Over' and 'Anyway You Want It,' sounding like the consequence of Journey's Steve Perry fronting Kiss. Then it's solo time as keyboard player Gregg Giuffria dips into Keith

Emerson, Larry Fast and Vangelis for a quick instrumental appetiser, which opens out into the hard-driven 'On the Rocks.' Only 'Wild and Hot' lets the side down because the band don't deliver the sort of earthy aggression a song with such a title demands. However, the band save the best for last, closing the album with four real beauties. 'Hold Me, Squeeze Me' and 'Got Love if You Want It' are average heavy metal thrashers raised to anthemic heights through some magnificent overboard playing."

After neither the new live album nor the movie managed to make Angel stars, middle of 1980, the band found themselves on a tour package put together by management guru David Krebs. The Rock & Roll Marathon featured a revolving lineup of four mid-level acts (with regional variations), namely Humble Pie, Frank Marino & Mahogany Rush, Mother's Finest and Angel, who were arguably the biggest of the four at the time, but not by much.

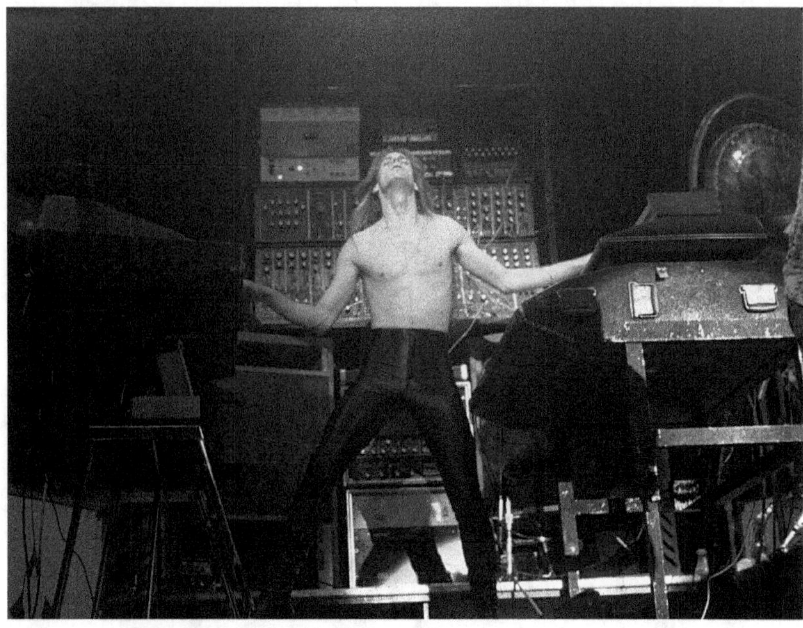

"I knew Angel well," begins Krebs. "I had a concept that ended up costing us a lot of money called the Rock & Roll Marathon, which were four acts, none of which were… it was like taking four acts and hoping that the sum was greater than the parts. So we put together for arenas a 30- or 40-city tour of Frank Marino, Angel, Humble Pie with Steve Marriott and Mother's Finest, four acts that I personally liked, all of which I thought had a shot. Nobody broke off of this tour; it didn't work. But what's interesting is that these guys had all promised—before I did this tour—that they would share expenses so that maybe two bands would be in each of these sleeper buses. Every band then ended up demanding a sleeper bus, so I thought this is fucked."

Asked why he thought Angel didn't break, Krebs figures, "I thought Angel was great, I thought Punky Meadows was great, I thought Frank DiMino was missing something, although I can't tell you what. And their manager, David Joseph, from Australia, was a guy who had managed other kinds of music, if I'm not mistaken. I thought Punky Meadows was a great guitar player and star. I thought Frank DiMino had a voice that was a little too high. But it was good. It was not bad. I don't know, close but no cigar. On a one to ten, he was an eight. Not that he didn't have a great voice. I can't explain, but it wasn't what I saw in Steven Tyler or Bon Scott. And more image than great songs. But I thought Punky Meadows was an amazing guitar player, and a great-looking sex symbol. This was the second Kiss that Neil Bogart was trying to put out there. Because they were heavily made-up—it wasn't a natural torn clothing kind of thing."

For the Rock & Roll Marathon tour, Angel ditched the all-whites and went out in typical rock 'n' roll stage wear. "At that time we were just tired of it," reflects Frank. "It wasn't something where we thought, okay, let's do something different. It was also because we had a couple of crew guys from each band working together, instead of each one of us having our own crew. So we had one crew for everybody. There were four bands and there wasn't a whole lot of time to do all the stuff that we did formerly with Angel costume-wise and getting ready and all that stuff. So the thought process was to scrap that and let's just go out and be a regular band and just play—like we approached everything, just this time without the costumes. And I guess a lot of people were let down by it. But it's no different, I guess, than Kiss unmasking and going out. I'm sure we would've gone back to the costumes had we gone out again, especially headlining. We would have gone back to building on the show. But that particular tour we decided to get rid of all the frills."

"For me it was one of the best tours," continues DiMino. "I had such a great time. That was four bands that were just kicking ass all night long. Steve Marriott and Bobby Tench, every night, we'd sing together. They would bring me up on stage, singing with them, you know, '30

Days in the Hole' and some other songs. Punky got sick one night and couldn't do the show and Steve brought me out and he made a big speech to the audience, how we wanted to do the show and no, we weren't able to. 'So what we're going to do,' he said, 'is we're going to bring out Frank and we're going to do some songs together.' That was early on in the tour and that progressed into me coming out almost every other night. And the three of us used to sit together in the bus after we were done singing on stage. So it was a great tour for me and all of us."

"Mother's Finest we knew—all those guys were great, Wizard (Jerry "Wiz" Seay, bass) and all those guys in the band, really. The only ones that we didn't know that well were Mahogany Rush, and that got off to a bit of a rocky start. But it's like anything else; once you start playing, everyone starts to understand and gets it, how you work to do what you do. Everyone starts to appreciate what each band does. That's the reason it worked: because all the bands worked together. So it was a great tour."

"David Krebs was a friend of mine," explains Punky, charting the connection that caused this tour. "That Bux album on Capitol, I did that with Jay Messina, so I had met Jack Douglas a long time before Angel when I was living in Boston. And so anyway so that broke up and we put Angel together and as I said earlier, David Krebs was one of the managers that I wanted to come and see us play, and then there's the story of him wanting me and Mickie to join the New York Dolls. So anyway, we turned into this band called Angel, David wanted to sign us, but no, the guys wanted to go out to California so that never happened. But Dave and I stayed close, we stayed friends. Every now and then we crossed paths on the road and we would talk. But we were now in California. We had fired our management company and everything else and things were kind of bleak for us at the time because Casablanca was folding, going broke. And so David called me up and said, 'Hey, I'm putting together this tour called Rock & Roll Marathon—do you guys want to do it?' 'Yes.' Because we wanted to play; we wanted to keep going."

"So we did the tour with David's blessings and that's when we decided to go out not in white, because we felt like we were being typecast. But it's one of the dumbest things we ever did, putting aside the all-whites. We made the biggest mistake in our lives. But David Krebs always said to me, 'You guys are a rock 'n' roll band.' He wanted to make us like Aerosmith. He wouldn't have put us in white. That was Casablanca, and our management team—with Kiss being in black, we were going to be in white. So we went on tour out of costume, in our rock 'n' roll clothes, and a lot of fans didn't like that. But we thought we were breaking the mould because we didn't want to be typecast. And people were starting to put down bands like Kiss. Remember, Kiss even came out of costume at one point. But it was a dumb mistake. We should have stayed with the all-whites."

"It's funny, because many years later after I was all done with the band, when I was living back here and I first got on Facebook and I started seeing pictures of us, Angel on stage all in white, then I realised how cool that was then. Before social media, I never really saw any of that. I'd be on tour and people would say, 'Hey, you guys were great.' But then I would go

to the next town and I'd forget that I would never see those people again or hear their praise ever again. When I got on social media and Facebook, I'd see, 'Man, I loved you guys. You guys were great' and 'You inspired me; you're the reason I play guitar.' And then I started seeing all these pictures of us they would post online and I thought, well, it really *did* look fucking cool. It was very magical. And then I would see pictures of us on the Rock & Roll Marathon tour and we looked like every other band. So I realised then how it was a mistake going out without the costumes. But I also then became a fan of Angel myself because I saw how cool we really did look before that."

"By that point I was just disenchanted and drained by the whole thing, "continues Meadows, "but like I say, later I became a fan myself. I could see why people loved it and why it had an impact on people. So when I did my solo thing, the video was Frank and I, and we did 'Lost and Lonely,' and I was dressed all in white, to promote the Angel thing. And even when we did the Punky and Frank tour, I dressed in all white too. And then of course, when we decided to put Angel back together, we said that we're going to have to be in white because it's just the coolest."

Recalls Felix, "We weren't working, we weren't in the studio. David gives us this opportunity to go on tour. What we thought we were going to do was get some songs together and go record again, right? Didn't happen. So that's the plan: go on tour, do our

COLLECTION OF R GALBRAITH

show, but what are we doing? We're sharing the stage with three other bands. And you can look at that lineup there and say, well, everybody has their own story. I could run them down for you. Humble Pie was obviously Steve Marriott, in my opinion, one of the founders of heavy blues rock, a great star, and I was thrilled to meet him and to play with him. 'Cause he actually sat in with us several times. So to me, that was the coolest part of the tour. Mahogany Rush, we had maybe played with Frank before. I have a high opinion of them all. Mother's Finest, great band, really great guys, terrific live act, kinda like moving the bar back and forth between funk and rock. I got to know the bass player pretty well on that tour and we had a lot of fun together."

"But the tour was very arduous, a lot of dates, pretty low budget. It couldn't have made much money because I know that we didn't make much money. We played venues that had been part of the faded glory of the heavy rock or the hard rock years. I don't think it was promoted right, or maybe promoted the only way it could be promoted. It's a marathon, it's four bands, but people weren't coming to see any one of them particularly. They were either coming to see all of them or they were just showing up because it was the only thing to do in town that night. We had some pretty good crowds in some towns. We headlined sometimes, other bands on the bill headlined other shows, but nobody had more than an hour on stage and it became tedious for everybody. Everybody drank too much and there were way too many drugs."

"Then it got kind of splintered after a while," says Frank, charting the end of Angel, which actually was more of a fade over two years of nuthin' much happenin'.

"Because when Neil sold his part of Casablanca to PolyGram, we were left with a lot of people we didn't know. We owed them one more album and we were already in the studio. In fact, we were working with David Paich from Toto. He was helping us put together some arrangements on a couple of tunes. You know, the Record Plant was home to us, actually. We knew everyone there and we were really comfortable—we were always going into the Record Plant to record. Whoever was there was engineer for us because we knew everyone there. So we kept doing what we normally did. We already had, by that time, five or six songs ready to go. And what happened was, at that point, everything was supposed to escalate. The production cost escalated. And also if we got a name producer, anything over three points they would pay."

"But what happened was, I had gotten pretty friendly with Jack Douglas. Jack was going to do an artist in Canada. I asked Jack if he would do the album. He said, 'At this point in time, I'm really kind of more comfortable with working with a singer-songwriter, and that's what I'm doing in Canada.' And I said, 'Jack, I think you would be great on this stuff we're doing now. And you would really help us out. I know that you know the stuff we all want to hear.' So I took my time talking to him, over the course of about two weeks. And finally he said, 'Okay, I'll do it. Let's just get the lawyers together and let's do it.' And I said okay, great. So our lawyers talked to his lawyer and that worked out fine. We figured everything out, and then we went to Casablanca and said this is who we want. And Casablanca said, 'Well, we're not going to pay that. We're definitely not going to pay that.' And I'm going to lawyers… this is already in the contract. So there was one of these fiascos that never should have been. And I felt that I was in the middle of this. Because I had pulled Jack away from this other project he was doing. I don't remember who it was. I took him away from that to get him to do our thing, and now the record company is backing off, saying if you're going to do an album, you don't need a name producer—it's too much money."

"But I said, 'This is not the deal. We want this producer and in the contract it's already stated that whenever we use a name producer…' and I said, 'Okay, let's split after that. After three points, let's split. Instead of you taking the whole thing, after four or five points, we'll take half and you take half.' So it got crazy and they just kept backing off. And then they wanted to give us less money for the production. So we ended up saying we want to get off this label. We were trying to get onto Boardwalk with Neil. It just never materialised."

Indeed, before Neil's death in 1982, he was very busy with this new label called Boardwalk for a couple of years, signing myriad artists, pumping out records and having a couple decent hits with Joan Jett & The Blackhearts plus Night Ranger, who were pretty much Angel 2.0—also similar to Angel were Boardwalk act 707.

"Then Neil got sick and then the whole thing went down," continues Frank. "So we were back and forth with PolyGram. And when things like that happen, you're sitting there and it's very frustrating. So what happened was, Felix ended up falling out of the picture. We got Rudy Sarzo to come in. And then Ozzy asked Rudy to do a tour with him, so Rudy kinda went his way. After that I went, you know, I've got this other thing going on. When you're stuck in that situation, and you're fighting to get done what is supposed to be simple and it's not happening, it gets really frustrating."

As to what direction the sixth Angel album might have taken, Frank says, "It was the same as *White Hot* and *Sinful*, but it probably would have been more like *White Hot*. Like I say, *Sinful* was, this is what we had, okay, we'll do this song, that song and we went in and did it. The *White Hot* album was us actually participating together; it was us really getting involved in it—that's what really would've happened again."

Chapter 8

Hiatus

"I was seeing my opportunities were not in going to rehearsals with Angel."

"Well, he thinks he was," chuckles Felix, asked if David Krebs now was the manager of Angel, at least by proxy, given shared involvement in the Rock & Roll Marathon. It's an answer typical of the band's affairs as 1980 blurred into 1981, and it's the type of answer you'd tend to get from all sorts of baby bands stumbling their way through the business just off the Sunset Strip, trying to make it in a demoralizing business.

"He was the guy that came in after Neil had sold Casablanca and David Joseph, our full-time manager, decided that he was leaving that role. He resigned. I can't speak for him. I know that after he left, I personally got a call from someone who said they had now purchased his interest in the existing management contract. Apparently somebody thought it was still in force. And David apparently had generated revenue from taking in partnerships."

Asked if Joseph went back to Australia, Felix says, "I think he did. We're friends with his daughter. But I don't want to say too many bad things about David. I don't have the details nor do I have a grudge. He was a very elegant man, a very intelligent man, and why he stopped being our manager was because I believe he saw that the liabilities were going to outweigh the advantages, and whatever personal financial burden he was carrying had become something he wanted to get away from. So he left."

"And so we had a meeting. We were without management and we were without a record company. Our contract had expired with Casablanca. We did not have a new contract. We were waiting for them to offer us a new contract. The numbers that were being discussed in the background were not good, and I think this is part of the reason Joseph left. He could see that his portion of reward for a new contract with Casablanca was not going to be good. Casablanca, having now become a property of Polygram, was only interested in the back catalogue. They did not want to sign us to a new multi-year lucrative recording contract. And if they were going to sign us, it was not going to be for the $250,000 signing bonus that we would have gotten with Casablanca, had it still been them."

"All of that tradition was gone," continues Robinson. "Whatever was going to happen was going to be far less lucrative. David was leaving. Neil was leaving. Neil had told us that he would make sure that we were taken care of, that the legacy was secure, that Polygram was going to go on to invest in the band and make us continue to increase our potential for success. And as Frank remembers it—and I don't fully remember it—those promises seemed genuine. But in fact, they never came around. They never happened. Am I going to say to you that Neil was making that up? No. I think Neil was a promoter. I think Neil would say what he felt was justified at the time. I think he might've had sincere desire behind what he said, but it never happened. This is before he got sick. This is when he was rolling in dough. I mean, Polygram paid him something like $50 million."

Asked about an accounting of record sales, Robinson says that, "I think they sold far more than what we were told. Given my understanding of how things had occurred in the Casablanca transition to Polygram, all the financial records were destroyed at some point. All the financial records from Casablanca had to be shipped to and received by Polygram. And I think there was some massive disaster that caused them to be destroyed. I mean, Larry Harris actually told me that, you know, that everything was destroyed and he never understood how that could have happened. So how many records did we sell? All I know is what my attorney at this point tells me. I have a very active involvement going on with a very good attorney who is poised to reclaim all of my songwriting credits and all of my publishing, and everything that needs to be fixed from all those years with Angel that has never been resolved. And I tried to get the rest of the guys to go back into a new operating agreement, but we haven't been able to come to terms on that. I hope that someday we can, because I think that if we did it right, we could probably get closer to fixing some of those problems as a band instead of individually, which is going to be much harder to do."

"Frank and Punky are touring, doing shows in nightclubs; I know they did a thing on a cruise ship recently. I'm not going to criticise what they're doing as they're able to make a little money. I'm happy for them. They had asked me to come and sit in. I did that twice; actually three times: I did a music video. And I felt like there was good reason to continue doing that, but I can't see a good reason at this point, because if it's not going to be as good as what Angel could've been, then I'm not going to be part of it."

Asked to backtrack to that final meeting about management, Felix says, "Here's kind of what happened. I'll give you a better answer on the Marathon tour at that point in time, when Casablanca had pretty much shut the door, not in our faces, but we could see that there was no reason to continue 

on pursuing a deal with Polygram. We had a meeting as the band. I remember that meeting very well. We had an outdoor barbecue and we all got together and talked about what to do. I don't know who it was that mentioned that David Krebs had been in touch and was interested in managing the band and had expressed an ability to get a new record contract. I remember that London Records had been mentioned. I'm sure there were other record companies mentioned. The other guys might remember better."

"We discussed this and should we go with David Krebs? And the culmination of that meeting as I recall was yes, we should go with David Krebs. This is a guy that has broken many great bands, is managing Aerosmith, has a lot of powerful relationships and that we should do this. He's got a tour for us. I remember we didn't know what the tour was going to be. Of course, as things progressed, they didn't progress that quick. Unfortunately we agreed to go on this Marathon tour."

"Now I'm going to change the topic a little bit back into a generic overall: what were musicians doing in general at that point? No one was doing that well. I'm not saying that Kiss wasn't selling records. They were. I'm not saying that The Police weren't selling records. They were. There were great bands making great records. But there were many other bands like Angel in-between record deals, that had incurred debt as we had with our prior record company. We weren't the ripest apple on the fruit stand. We took what was available to us. We took the manager with a great track record offering opportunities and we took the tour. Yes, there was also a depression in the economy. I don't know if you remember, but in 1980, '81, man, the record business was going downhill very quickly."

"Still, I know that we did have a chance to record a little bit," continues Robinson. "We were writing in hotel rooms. It was not fun, but we'd bang them out. At one point we went into a recording studio in Columbus, Georgia. We were on tour. We were in-between dates, between maybe like Little Rock and Atlanta, touring on our bus. David Krebs was managing the band. We had a different road manager at that point. He made arrangements for us to go into a small recording studio that was owned by The B52s. Punk rock was very strong at that point and there were these alternative rock bands, new wave bands. People weren't following heavy rock 'n' roll as much as we wanted them to."

Except in the UK! Angel weren't exactly Riot or Y&T at this point, but they were still very well regarded over there, and garnered some press. What I'm talking about is that we are now into the New Wave of British Heavy Metal, and along with the heavy British bands all over the place, fans there—and almost more importantly, the writers at Sounds and later Kerrang!—loved what those guys would call pomp rock more so than power pop, the term Punky seems to like. AOR, for adult-oriented rock was also (ill)-used, as was the term "wimphem," a sobriquet for light mayhem, essentially.

"Yeah, well, we could never tour Europe because we had this big show," shrugs Felix. "I was told it was too expensive to take it on the road. We'd never break even. We'd be subsidizing it if it had gone to Europe. Nonetheless, we went into this little studio in this little town. It possibly had been a garage at one time—I remember that it had garage doors that opened and closed. We dragged the gear out of the truck, put it in there, started recording the songs. We had four songs that we had polished up to the point where we could record them. We were fortunate to have with us on tour a real engineer; it happened to be a girl that I was living with at the time who was one of the head engineers at The Record Plant. She did a wonderful job of recording what she could do. I have a copy of all those recordings. It sounds good. I digitised it. I have all four songs and no one else has ever heard them."

As for the direction of these songs, Felix calls it "heavy rock, Angel rock. They're driving hard rock songs. One is kind of an arena rock ballad. The other three songs are heavier and I co-wrote two or three of them and most of one of them. And I kept the tape for years. It was reduced down, a dupe. The original recordings I think were given to Jim Allen, our tour manager. He might've given them to David. No one's ever been able to find them that I'm aware of. I'm the only guy that has a copy of the songs. I never gave a copy to anybody else and no one else in Angel has them that I'm aware of. And I'm just sitting on him. I don't know what to do with them."

But it's never taken any further. "Nope. We never recorded those songs in a real studio. We're all beat. We're tired. We'd had it. David is in touch, but everybody's wiped-out from that tour. We come back and we load our gear into a rehearsal studio. I think it was SIR in the Valley. I'm not sure exactly where. We're trying to rehearse three days a week but everybody gets busy with other things and life in general."

"I go into rehearsal with a band called Poco," continues Robinson. "I had rehearsed with them three or four times. Through their manager, it was suggested I could join the band. They were replacing their bass player. I don't know what the problem was. They had an album out at that point that was doing well. They needed to go on tour. I'm in Angel. I'm not really sure whether I want to leave Angel or not. It was just kind of playing around. They offer me the job. At one point at a rehearsal, their manager came over to me and said, 'You know, you can't join the band because you're still under contract to Polygram.' And maybe he talked to somebody and they said, 'No, we will not release Felix from his contract unless you pay us.' I think they wanted money."

Meanwhile, agrees Felix, things were not getting better with Angel. "No, and Sharon Osbourne called me and offered me the gig with Ozzy, getting ready to go on tour. Randy Rhoads was in the band at that point. I don't know who recommended me to Sharon. I might've asked her but I don't remember. I know that she wanted me to go with the band. And I remember sitting on the edge of my bed, talking in my bedroom on the phone at my house. And I said, 'Well, Sharon, you know, that might be something I'd be willing to do. I was hoping to join a band and be a partner.' 'Oh, well you can't join Ozzy's band. He doesn't have partners in his band—I'm the only partner.' And I said, 'Well, that's kind of tough. How much money will be involved here?' And she gave me a figure and I remember hearing the figure and thinking, you know, that's not enough money. I probably should have been better at negotiating. I should have asked her for more. I should have asked for a per diem which would have made the difference. I should have gone on tour with Ozzy. Rudy joined the band, so this is after Bob Daisley. Maybe this is when she had decided that he was going to leave. Maybe he didn't know it. All I know is she called me and offered me a job and we couldn't come to terms. And I said, 'Thank you very much' and she never called me back."

But back at Angel, the guys never really officially knocked it on its ear, so to speak. "No, we didn't—we don't do that. What we do is we go into rehearsal but we're not getting much done and there's a few arguments here and there about what we're going to do. The pressure is building because we don't have a record deal, we have no income, no money coming in, we can't draw any sort of a stipend. We were in-between royalty payments. We had an attorney that was getting involved, who Gregg had gotten involved with. We're having meetings with this attorney who is saying, 'I'm going to make you guys rich.' Well, we had heard this before. We were losing the spirit of making the band continue. Certainly journalists have written about how we broke up too early. We should have waited for MTV. We could have been huge. We had the songs, we had the look, but at that point we were a wasted commodity and as individuals we were tired of beating that drum."

"Also as individuals, we were finding opportunities elsewhere," continues Robinson. "I know I was and I know that Frank was. Frank was the first to leave, at some point during rehearsals. He said, 'Guys, I'm done. I've got other things I need to do.' And he was getting busy with the opportunity that Giorgio Moroder had presented him to be part of that soundtrack for *Flashdance*. He just felt that there was every reason not to keep banging that same old drum of we're going to get Angel back together, we're going to tour, we're going to make records, it's going to be fantastic. So Frank had an opportunity and said he had to leave and I think it was a week or two later that I said, 'Guys, you know…' I was seeing my opportunities were not in going to rehearsals with Angel. My opportunities were going to be to join another band. I had heard from Sharon, I had rehearsed with Poco. I liked playing with Poco—that was country rock. Talk about The Eagles. I mean, that was one step away from being in The Eagles. I love that kind of music. I wanted to play hit record music or I wanted to be in a very heavy metal band—it was one or the other for me. I just didn't want to go back into playing in club bands."

As for where Felix actually wound up, well… "What was next for me was a series of missed opportunities to be in great bands, so I got hooked up with various songwriters. One of them was Michael Japp who wrote with Kiss, mostly co-writing with Paul Stanley. He had contributed songs to some of the Kiss albums—brilliant songwriter. He's from Wales, which is where my family's from. Michael and I became very fast friends. His wife, Ciri, was our costumer designer for the last major tour. She had done those great white satin costumes from the *Sinful* tour and from part of the *White Hot* tour. He said, 'Felix, come and play with me.' We did some shows, played a few different locations in Los Angeles. That was a great band."

Japp also wrote a bit with The Babys plus did some work with John Waite as a solo artist as well as Matthew Fisher. He died in 2012.

"I came back to Angel a couple times," continues Felix. "Not Frank or Punky, but Gregg and Barry kept trying to keep Angel together. They struggled with that for another… I'm gonna say six months; it could have been a year. All I know is that a couple times I got a phone call, 'Felix, we got a great singer. You gotta come down. We can make this happen.' There was Fergie Frederiksen at one point—terrific singer. I know that they wanted me there because it would help them to call it Angel with a different singer. The vibe was, 'We got a record deal pending, as long as we can get some songs together.' But to me it was just pushing the same cart up a very steep hill. I might have rehearsed with them two or three times with Fergie in the band and Mötley Crüe was one door away. We were sharing the canteen and the rehearsals studio, which was a dump, a real dive out in the Valley. So we were hanging around those guys. They were coming into our rehearsal room, drunk on their ass. We were all socializing with them but I could see that they were just a real motley crew. And that's what the LA scene was moving toward: heavy-duty tattoos, heavy-duty piercings, that trashed rock 'n' roll relic look. But Angel was polished, a different world."

Punky's summary with respect to why Angel didn't break covers some of the same terrain, with Meadows expressing many of the same regrets.

"We didn't make any money in Angel," begins Punky, "but although we never got huge fame, just as important, I made a lot of people happy, and for me that means a lot. It's more important than anything else that people really remember us. Angel fans are really fierce; they just love the band. And to this day, if you're on Facebook, we have a lot of fan pages up there and it's always so vital. Every day people are posting pictures or saying things about the band, how much they love it."

There are many reasons the situation went south. But to reiterate, I really do believe that jealousy from other bands at the hype, plus the fact that the band had the show and the nice gear, kind of put them on the outs with various actors within the industry. I feel like some of this is lost on the guys, with Punky typically going to the explanation that they were just too good—which of course breeds a different kind of offence, one that we talked about before, that the guys just thought too much of themselves.

"Always the stories," sighs Punky. "Every time we'd get on a tour with a headliner, like say Aerosmith, we got thrown off. It was always like that. One time when we were playing with Roxy Music, there was no room on the stage whatsoever. They had all the equipment. And so I asked, 'Would you mind please moving that saxophone stand? Would you mind that?' And they said, 'Absolutely not.' And the reason was, we would open up and come on stage and the kids would just rush the stage and go crazy. And then of course we'd be done and the headliners always felt threatened by that."

"So we were forced to headline prematurely in places like the Midwest where we were much bigger, but we were playing smaller venues, like 3000-, 4000-, 5000-seater shows. We would sell those places out. But you know what was nice about that? We got to do our whole magic act. When we were opening up for other bands, we couldn't do that. But here's the thing: when we came out in all-white like that, that was an effect in itself. So even without the illusions and stuff, we still came out as an effect, right? Blew people away. And I've seen so many times where people said, 'You know, Angel came on and when Styx came on, I left halfway through their set.' They just wanted to see Angel, you know?"

Which is kind of interesting, because what that says is that the headliner could have felt that these fancy boys outsmarted them, did an end-around, sneaking an effect onto the stage when they were told no. And look at Gregg's keyboards. Who does this guy think he is? And what's with the hair?

And don't forget, other than perhaps Barry, these guys weren't bashful and self-effacing. Chuckles Punky, "The thing about Gregg was, Gregg had the gift of gab, and Gregg always wanted to be the leader. And that's why Gregg always got mad at me when I became pretty much the focal point of Angel. I wasn't trying to be. It had to just happen that way. And Frank Zappa decided to write a song about me and I kinda got all the press. Whenever they would do contests or whatever I would win the contest; you know, like a contest to go with your favourite Angel member to dinner. I would always win that contest. But Gregg was a really big personality; he's a real alpha male. And he was always trying to lead the way. He would manipulate everybody. He even told a lot of people that he was Jewish because the record company people were Jewish (laughs). He's that kind of a guy. Now don't get me wrong, he's very ambitious and he gets his way, so you have to give him credit for that."

But my point is that there were big egos across the band, not just with Gregg, again, something that might have rubbed people the wrong way.

"Yes there were," agrees Punky, no apologies. "You know, I think in the old days—everybody knows this—when you're younger like that, you're easily impressionable. I'm a very competitive person anyway, but I just think when you're younger like that, your heads fills up with shit. When you get older, you realise what you had and what you lost and you realise what you lost over really stupid things. You would have little arguments building into something bigger and it was just unnecessary. When you get older, you actually realise that it's about the music and not the egos. It's not, 'What can I get out of this?' It's about the music and doing what's best for the music."

With the same question to Punky about record sales that I asked Felix, he adds in the phantom sales for *White Hot* and figures that if everything was counted properly, *White Hot* would be gold-certified in America, adding, "We did get a gold record in Japan, but this of course is smaller, so it's not hard to do there. But *White Hot* was the biggest selling one."

Then Punky offers the same sort of play-by-play outlined by Felix, with a few notable differences, beginning with manager David Joseph. "We actually let him go. We were at our wit's end. Casablanca was folding. Casablanca just fell apart. Neil Bogart was the heart and soul of that business. But Neil Bogart got the… not the axe, but was up for misappropriation of funds or whatever it was. After the last meeting we had with Neil Bogart, where we sat down and we played our last record for him, which he loved, he smoked a joint and he said, 'Listen, you guys have lost a few bouts but you're gonna win the war.' And he said, 'I'm going to stick behind you guys.' He said he was going to write— because we were into Casablanca for $1.5M or something— he said he was going to write that off and he wasn't going to make us pay that back. And he said we were gonna make it no matter what."

"Neil was a cool guy, but like I said, he got the axe," continues Meadows. "And after that Casablanca was just run by a bunch of college kids; they didn't know what they were doing. I think Larry Harris tried to run it for a while, but he was a shmuck. We put our live album out and they didn't know how to promote. It was not working and we didn't know what to do afterwards. So we kind of blamed our manager, which again was a mistake. Young and stupid. So we got rid of him and we thought we'd get maybe David Krebs to manage us. The music business is all about politics. It really is not how great you are; it's all about who you know and luck. That's the game and that's what turned me off to the whole thing and why I actually left. I love music—I just despise the business."

As for the $1.5M owing—or not, if you buy the very real possibility that the amounts and types of revenues Angel might have been generating were not adequately shared with the band—that seems mired in the changeover to Polygram. Which, if Felix is to be believed, was rendered chaotic by the paper trail going poof when all the accounting was destroyed.

Asked if the band paid that money back, Meadows says, "No, because that was transferred to Polygram, or Polydor, whatever it was. We had a person looking at that for a while and then they said, no, you know, you still owe us that and this and that. But apparently we sold a lot more records than we were told. Stan Diamond, who is a big lawyer who actually managed David Bowie at one time, he was a lawyer for us when Gregg, Frank and Barry and I were making some demos and thinking of doing like a revamped Angel thing. Anyway, Stan was our lawyer and we saw a check coming in that he showed us for a million dollars that went right across our laps for record sales—he showed us a check for that. And it was like, 'Where the fuck did that come from?!' So I think obviously money was being held back from us. Again, the artists always get screwed and the lawyers and the managers, they get everything."

This makes it sound like a case of Angel going on offence. Faced with an apparent debt of $1.5M, the band was countering with, no, you owe *us* money.

Continues Punky, "So we had a guy trying to get us some money saying we think the guys are owed money and all that kind of stuff. You know, we can't prove it. You know what I mean? They say, no, you know, you guys still owe us, this and that. And you know, in those days, we gave away our publishing rights just like the Beatles did. We didn't know any better. We didn't have legal minds. We'd want to get on the road for Casablanca. We'd say, 'We need a hundred thousand dollars to get on the road, you know, to get the trucks, the buses and all that stuff to get started on the road, tour support.' And then they'd give us a hundred thousand dollars or whatever. I'm just making an amount up. And they'd say, 'Well, sign this here.' Meanwhile, you're signing away all your publishing rights. The manager would says,

'You need to sign this so we can get the money to go on the road.' You know, 'Don't worry, it's only 25% of whatever,' you know what I mean? So every tour you start doing that, and before you know it, you don't own any of your publishing. And your publishing is really your social security. For example, if somebody does 'Wild and Hot' and it's a big hit, well, I could live off of that in my retirement days. But because I don't own the publishing…"

But again, as had been conjectured by many analysts of the band's career, had the timing been different, there might have been enough money for everybody.

"If we would have had MTV it would have been a whole different story," reiterates Punky. "Angel had bad luck. Or if we could have just gotten one radio hit. 'Cause that would have done it. But back in those days they were playing more soft rock, like Fleetwood Mac; they weren't playing really heavy stuff. And Angel was a heavier band, even though at the end it was more power pop. But it still had big drums, big singing, big guitars, big bass but they were heavy pop songs. I'm proud of that, but I don't want to be wimpy at the same time either. But we just couldn't get a hit single. If we had gotten a hit single or if we had hung around until MTV hit, it could have been different. Because we were such an image band, a visual band, I think we would have broken because that's what broke all those bands overnight—TV liked Def Leppard and Quiet Riot and they were broken overnight. Back when we went out, you couldn't see a band unless you toured, unless you came to their town once a year or something. But when MTV came on, you saw them 24 hours, seven days a week over and over and over again. If you had a look and an image and a good sound, you were going to be big and they were going to break you."

When I asked Larry Harris from Casablanca why Angel never broke, he said, "Because their manager wasn't as good as Kiss' was, for one. Plus their stage shows screwed up too many times. I mean, things went wrong. It was almost a circus of errors, I guess. There's a part in *Spinal Tap* where they get stuck in these eggs; well, they took that from Angel getting stuck in the stuff that they were using previous to that. And Angel songs just weren't as accessible as Kiss'. They weren't 'Rock and roll all night and party every day.' It wasn't that fun rock 'n' roll. It was more melodic than maybe it should have been at that point."

"We could never get a good even FM hit out of them," said Larry, speaking with Sam Dunn. "They just didn't write hit records as well as Kiss did. There are a lot of bands trying to make it in that area because of what had happened before, but everybody can't make it. Record companies, there's kind of a saying  in the business, you throw ten albums up against the wall and you hope one sticks. Even though somebody might be good—and I think The Godz were good and I think Starz were good—well, Billy Squier made it. And he had the same manager as Starz and Kiss, but Starz didn't make it. Why? They just didn't write the right songs. They just didn't write songs at that point in time that the public was willing to accept. Sometimes it's timing, sometimes it's luck. I mean, we had a band called Trigger we had to ignore because there was just too much on our plate when their album came out. And that happens with every record company—it's just the luck of the draw, really."

Bill Aucoin, manager of Kiss and Starz, doesn't quite know why Angel didn't break as big as Kiss. He's just sure something somewhere had gone adrift. "I was more of a consultant to Casablanca than I was to the band," muses Bill. "Because Angel never really happened. They kind of almost happened. It was like Kiss was the dark side and Angel was the white side. And Neil thought, hey, if I can do it once with Kiss, we can do it again with Angel. And yet it never quite came together. But you know, Punky Meadows was a great

　　　　　　　　　　　　　　　　Martin Popoff

guitar player. I suppose it never had the depth that Kiss had. We had Kiss covered from every angle and I don't think Angel quite had that."

We've heard about where Felix nearly ended up after Angel, but what about Punky?

"Well, when Ace left, Kiss had a cattle call in the local musician paper in LA," explains Meadows. "I wasn't really that aware, because Gregg and I, we were putting kind of a revamped Angel together, with Fergie Frederiksen and Ricky Phillips from The Babys, who is in Styx now. And we were working with Andy Johns and we were getting ready to shop that. Barry Levine was the photographer for Casablanca and us. He did all of Kiss' pictures, and Angel. Barry Levine was a good friend; we all became really good friends with Barry Levine and his brother Al Levine. And I was at home in the Hollywood Hills, and Barry calls me up from The Record Plant—I think it was The Record Plant—a studio, and he says, 'Hey, Punky, Kiss, they're auditioning guitarists,' and he said, 'I mentioned your name to Gene and Paul, and Gene said, "What a great idea!"' And so, I said, 'Well, that sounds cool, Barry.' 'So let me have Gene call you.'"

"Ten minutes later, Gene calls me up on the phone, 'Hey, Punky, we're auditioning guitarists. Ace is gone, and we're looking to replace him as a guitarist. We think you would be a great fit. Why don't you go ahead and learn any side of the live album? It doesn't matter. Learn one side of the record and come on down to SIR Studios and we'll rehearse.' And so I said, okay, that's cool. So I went down to SIR Studios, I walked in and they were playing 'Communication Breakdown.' It was just Paul and Gene and Eric Carr was playing drums, then. I plugged up and we played four or five songs and it sounded really good, really great. We finished playing and we sat down on the stage there, on the drum riser, and Gene said, 'Well, let's talk business, man; you've got the gig.'"

"And I said, 'Okay, that sounds great, but I'm doing a deal with… I'm with Gregg right now, and we're shopping a deal.' Well, as soon as I said that, I guess I insulted him for some reason. He just got up and said, 'Come on, Paul, let's go.' And they just... they both walked out, out of the rehearsal. And left me there with Eric. So I sat there, and I talked to Eric for about half an hour. We talked and shot the shit for a little while. And so I go home and Barry Levine calls me up on the phone, and he goes, 'Punky, what did you do?!' I say, what do you mean? He says, 'Gene and Paul came back to the studio with their jaws down on the floor.' Gene said, 'No one has ever turned down Kiss.' And I said, 'Well, I didn't turn them down. I just didn't say yes right away.' And I told them I was working with Gregg. But it turns out Gene was just so insulted by the fact that I didn't jump on it right away. I mean, I didn't have a chance to say yes or no. I just said I was working with Gregg. Gregg and I had been together for a long time and I didn't want to say, okay, fuck Gregg. But I guess I insulted Gene so bad. And then Barry said, 'They were going to offer you $160,000 a year plus points.' At that time I didn't have... I was pretty broke, so that kind of struck a chord. But, you know, things happen."

"I thought they were a good band," muses Ace Frehley, the axe legend that Punky almost replaced, on why Angel never wound up where Kiss were. "Angel pretty much was Neil Bogart's brainchild, and I think they were the antithesis of Kiss. We dressed all in black; Angel dressed all in white. But I think their biggest flaw was the fact that they weren't great songwriters and they never had a really major hit, like Kiss. I think that's why they died out. But the concept and the idea was great. I love the fact that their logo, if you turned it upside-down, it reads the same thing. I'm surprised I didn't design that myself, because I love doing logos. I did the Kiss logo and I did some other logos. We were friends, and I remember, in Las Vegas, I bumped into Gregg Giuffria, and he reminded me, he goes, 'Ace, do you remember the night we stole a car in Detroit?' I didn't remember (laughs). I'm just going, 'Yeah, that was great.' But I guess me and him got loaded and we stole a car, you know, went for a joy ride and just ditched it somewhere. That's gotta go in my second book (laughs)."

Ace agrees that Casablanca wasn't the problem, and were in fact behind Angel all the way. "For sure. Neil Bogart was a bundle of energy and ideas. And he wasn't afraid to take chances. And he was definitely a visionary. With Kiss, he wasn't even sure that the makeup was right. We actually got a call from Neil the day that we were shooting the album cover, 'Are you guys sure you want to wear the makeup?' And we said, 'Yep.' And he said, 'Okay, I'm just checking.' But he was a visionary and he didn't mind taking chances—you know, he signed Donna Summer. It's a shame we lost Neil so young, to cancer. He'd still be cranking out great hits, you know? Prior to getting involved with Kiss and Angel, when he was with Buddah Records, he was responsible for a lot of the bubblegum hits—he had a good ear for music."

"Uh, I don't remember that one," chuckles Frank, asked about the panic in Detroit. "We did do a lot of crazy stuff, typical things, wrecking hotels and stuff. But those Kiss guys were really good friends and really helped us along in the beginning. It kind of fractured after that, but Ace was always great. He's always great to be around, always great to talk to him."

Like Punky, Frank agrees with this idea that some of their fellow bands thought they were too big for their white tights, qualifying with, "Definitely when we first came out. At that time there weren't a whole lot of bands that were doing costumes and having a logo, like our big George logo back then. No one would let us use it. It was different back then, with the competitiveness. We had big guys on the crew, and they would stand next to the power center. Headliners would shut the power off on us back then if we went over our limit. Someone would either turn the lights on really quick or shut the power off. It was a different animal back in the '70s. Thank God, but I think now it's all calmed down and changed and everyone's kind of appreciating each other instead of being competitive so much. But it definitely was dog-eat-dog back then."

But would Frank agree to the idea that all the physical trappings and the sort of red carpet treatment afforded the band by the label was accompanied by egos just as outsized?

"Yeah, probably, probably not," is DiMino's curious response, somewhere between a vacillation and a disagreement. "You know, I think maybe that's the reality of it. I certainly can't agree with it, but I can't imagine that anyone else… I'm sure there were a lot of other people that did the same thing and kind of rubbed people the wrong way. But once it came to the fact that we were on the same label as Kiss and knew the guys in Kiss and that Neil's trying to push another band like Kiss, that's probably where all that started. But I don't feel that way about the egos. We've always stayed in touch with each other, even after the band broke up, and I don't think that was a problem with us. We were always really, really concerned with the music that we were doing, with the music we were writing and the music we were recording. That was always first and foremost. So no, I don't think that got in the way."

Back to Casablanca, Frank emphasises that, "Neil was great; he was exceptional working with the bands, and ideas, and what he wanted to do. But the thing is, the people he had working around him… I don't know what happened there. When Neil and Joyce got married, they got married at Neil's house, and we all went to the house, to the ceremony, to the reception and all that. And we went to the premiere of *Thank God It's Friday*, so we were all kind of supporting each other. Our whole thing was that we wanted to concentrate on the band, and what we had to do, and leave the rest of the stuff up to the manager and the record company, which was probably a mistake. But Neil was not the kind of guy who… he was easily accessible; you could always go there and talk to him, and we would have great meetings with him. When we told him what we wanted and our ideas, he was always very gracious, a really nice guy. He said a number of times, 'Sorry I haven't really taken care of you guys the way I'm supposed to. I haven't put the time and effort into you guys, because there is so much other stuff going on.' From our point of view, it's not really what we wanted to hear, but it's better than not hearing anything at all and being brushed aside—and I felt he was being honest as well."

At one point, as was alluded to, Rudy Sarzo almost joined Angel, plus we've heard about Ricky Phillips. But as Punky says, no one could match up to Felix, who was so good that his abilities caused tension in the band, with certain members feeling threatened by his skills.

"Felix Robinson is a great fucking bass player," reiterates Meadows. "Felix can play anything. Rudy Sarzo and I, we became friends. We started hanging out since before Quiet Riot. He told me that he used to get in the shows backstage. He would say he was me! 'Cause he got his hair cut like me and stuff like that. So he would tell stories like that. But Rudy and I hung out for awhile. One summer out in LA, he was living with his girlfriend Rose in an apartment and we would go to the Rainbow and Roxy together. The reason a lot of people didn't like Felix is because Felix is a great singer. He's also a really good keyboard player and he's actually a pretty good guitar player too. And he's a great bass player. He's really multitalented. We got Rudy in the band and he was in Angel for a little while. And I remember showing him the songs, thinking to myself, wow, he's just not Felix. You would show Felix a song and he would come up with all these amazing bass lines. Felix always impressed me."

Asked if anybody in the band felt directly threatened by Felix, Punky says, "Everybody was! Because Felix and I would come down… as I mentioned, I would go into a rehearsal studio early and Felix would be at the piano, singing 'Georgia' like Ray Charles, playing the piano like that and shit. And I'd say, damn, that's fucking awesome shit, man. That's why I wanted Felix in my solo thing, because Felix was such a great bass player and a good singer, a great musician. So everybody was a little intimidated by Felix at one point. That's just the way that goes."

As it happened, we didn't hear from Punky in the '80s, despite, again, the blindingly obvious fact that on paper he was made for the hair metal era. But then again, was he? He clearly demonstrates disdain for what happened with hard rock in the '80s, oscillating back to a glorification of the music from an earlier era.

"In the '60s and the '70s, it was so diversified. You had The Byrds, Hendrix, The Doors—everybody sounded different. And in the '70s it was the same way—everybody sounded different. Styx didn't sound like Queen. Queen didn't sound like Kiss. Angel didn't sound like Aerosmith, Cheap Trick, so-and-so. But unfortunately what happened in the '80s, all those bands started sounding the same. Everybody was tapping on the fingerboard. Everybody was having the same kind of anthemic rock 'n' roll things. 'I'm a jackhammer baby. Come and get me.' That kind of shit. It got redundant and that's why the pendulum swung in the '90s. Especially when you saw like Michael Angelo Batio, when he had the two guitar necks he's playing, it became a parody, it became a joke, it became funny. It was no longer about feeling. It was about all these guys that graduated from GIT showing you all this music theory. You could play all over the place, but rock 'n' roll came from the streets, man. We came from the blues—you had to have feeling. If you couldn't play the blues, they didn't care. They didn't give a shit. If you couldn't play the blues, you were no good—you had to be able to play."

We heard a little more from Frank DiMino in the '80s but not much. In 1989, he appeared on the Paul Raymond Project's six-track EP called *Under the Rising Sun*. But his main credit is singing a bit on the *Flashdance* soundtrack album!

As background and as discussed, Angel put together an all-in disco song called "20th Century Foxes" at what was to be the close of their original run. Explains DiMino, "We did that one while we were on the road, recorded that at The Record Plant in New York, and that's how I developed my

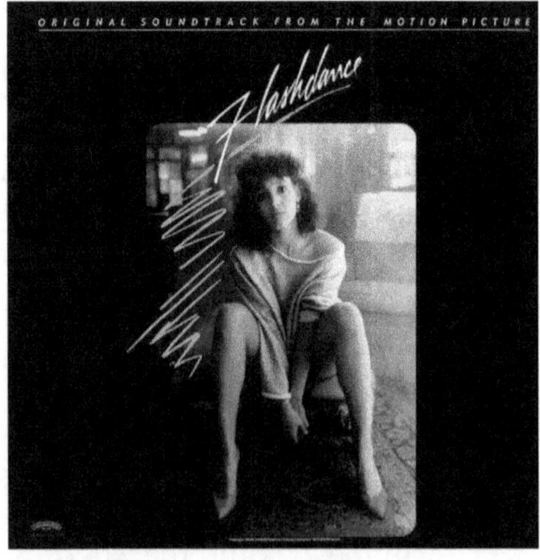

relationship with Giorgio Moroder. After the band split up, that's how I ended up doing all that studio work for

Flashdance. I also did the backgrounds to a couple of Sparks albums. I did some of the stuff for *Metropolis*. So whatever Giorgio was doing, I did."

On *Flashdance*, Frank was part of an act that didn't really exist called Cycle V; they have one song on there, called "Seduce Me Tonight." "It was just all studio musicians and Giorgio came up with the name. At the time I said, 'Giorgio, I believe that's the name of a dog food.' If you remember, there was a Cycle one, two, three and four. He said, 'Oh, no one will ever relate it to the dog food.' I said, 'Since it's not a band that I'm not going anywhere with, that's fine. Whatever you want to use.'"

Flashdance, issued in 1983, went six times platinum in the US and sold 20 million copies worldwide.

Meanwhile, the following year, Gregg Giuffria produced (and arranged) a band called White Sister. He is credited as a co-writer on a song called "Love Don't Make It Right" and he plays on two tracks, "Walk Away" and "Whips," the latter of which is credited to Punky Meadows, Fergie Frederiksen and Ricky Phillips. Also in 1984, Gregg issued the self-titled album by his band Giuffria, which reached No.26 on the Billboard charts but failed to reach gold certification.

"The local scene can help as well as choke," mused Gregg at the time, speaking with Katherine Turman for the LA Times. "There's an onslaught of signings, but only so many can emerge out of the heap." He tells Katherine that with Angel, "it took six semis to move and had 35 people on the crew. We didn't concentrate on the music. I do thank that whole thing for making me see that it all starts in the groove—it's got to be in the record. That helped me to formulate my attitude on putting this band together. The music had to come first." Gregg describes Giuffria as, "cinematic rock-orchestrated heavy rock 'n' roll. It's a band. I speak up a lot, but it's not egotistical. I want good music, no matter what I have to do to make the music right. I play 11 keyboards, I sing backup, I produce the band and I write most of the songs with Dave (David Glen Eisley), so if I had to sing, I'd shoot myself. I knew exactly what I was looking for in a singer."

With respect to the acquisition of guitarist Craig Goldy, Gregg saw him playing with Rough Cutt and said, "I asked him to join right there on the spot. And he packed up his guitar and came with me that night. That's where it

helped being in Angel. I had some credentials, some credibility. We put the group together last January, did the demo in March, signed with MCA-distributed Camel Records in May and recorded the album during the summer. We did the video, released the album in November, and I was going to retire in December."

As it happened, Gregg didn't hang up his hair brush, because a second Giuffria album followed in 1986 called *Silk + Steel*, before Gregg moved a few of the parts around and remerged with House of Lords. A self-titled debut was released on Simmons Records, with the production duties

handled by Gregg, Andy Johns and Gene Simmons. *Sahara* followed in 1992 before Gregg left the band and became wildly successful as a gaming technology entrepreneur in Las Vegas. In 1992, House of Lords issued *Demons Down*, but that year also produced the first proper Angel hits package. Issued under the Casablanca Records brand, *An Anthology* featured 20 tracks crammed onto one very full compact disc.

Net it out then, and it's really only Gregg that had any sort of profile in the '80s—and right where we thought he should be, in the thick of the hair metal explosion with not one but two bands. Back to Felix Robinson, well, he almost got there, through an association with White Lion, but first, there's a little more of an examination into the wilderness years and what could have been.

And what could have been, as we've discussed, is Angel making it in the '80s, but what we haven't addressed, really, is how a band from the '70s participating with the new bands might have been viewed. To be sure, Kiss, Aerosmith and Alice Cooper managed, but Angel would have been more akin to a case study like Y&T, or Krokus.

"These are bands that have what I call a semi-national following," muses Robinson. "And I can just go on with the names one after the other. They had multiple album releases and a somewhat loyal following. So they did a lot of live shows and almost nobody made any real money. It was just keeping the band alive. And there were thousands of other newer bands playing in clubs at that time, playing the songs and style that we all originated. So it was a whole new culture of rock 'n' roll then. It was like plankton, a biosphere. And in this, Angel fell apart although there were attempts to get things together. Subsequent to that, I did move to New York and yes, I joined White Lion and it was not joining a band. It was coming down to a rehearsal, with three guys who wanted to put a band together. I'll say this right now. If it hadn't been for me, there would not have been a White Lion. All they had were a couple of hooks, a couple of song ideas and a lot of guitar solos. And I had been through the mill with arranging songs and coming into bands that needed

songs to be completed. They didn't know how to do it. I took
those songs and I forced them to make three- and four-
minute songs. I arranged every song that the band had. I quit
after the first album and they took that album and released it
too late because it was not very well recorded. It was a good
album. I thought the songs were good. There were two songs
that I co-wrote that we had recorded for that album that went
on to be tunes on their next two albums, which were very big
records."

"They did have
quite a bit of success
after I left the band,
and some of the songs
were pretty good. They
co-wrote those tunes
and they had people
come to help them
write those songs and
they did a much better
job of getting songs
written and working
with producers and
engineers. And they did
some cover songs, which were actually pretty big. I was in
conflict with them from that point forward. I had to sue them
to collect money that was owed to me. The lawsuit went on,
and they pretend that I was never in the band and that pissed
me off. I'm still in litigation with them, but I'll give them their
due. They had much better success than Angel ever did. So
good for them. I wish they would have collected the money
that was earned, because like with Angel, they ended up
owing far more money than they ever made."

"It was at that point that I went into legitimate
business and started a career in the audio visual industry,
which I went ahead and did and had success with that. I was
vice president of one of the largest companies in the industry.
I had a great time and recently considered going back into
business and that may be happening for me very soon."

As I write this, Felix is 67 and looking happy and healthy, as can be seen in a recent picture taken of him with Dave Ellefson from Megadeth.

"We did a bass show together. He's been a good friend for the last few years. He actually got me revitalised in a way. He made me feel good about having done what I'd done and about doing what I can do. I'm producing other bands now. I've been in the studio for the last two years. I'm pursuing that as an additional musical endeavour. I'm still playing. If I get an opportunity to go on tour I will do it and I'll be ready. I'm not too old to go and do whatever I can do. I don't know that those guys want me on stage with them because I'm frankly, you know, I'm not a side-man."

Chapter 9

Fallen Angel and
Old Habits Die Hard

"Melody and rhythm will always live on."

The path toward the fully resplendent and resurrected Angel band we got in 2019 began with solo albums from Punky and Frank, both within months of each other in 2016. First there was *Fallen Angel* from Meadows, issued on Main Man Records on May 20th, a record of tough, tight melodic metal laden with drama and some considerably heavy moments.

For a band, Punky had along with him his main songwriting partner Danny Farrow (a.k.a. Danny Annielo), who also serves as second guitarist. On vocals there's Chandler Mogel, on drums, Bob Pantella, and on keyboards, Charlie Calv. Angel mate Felix Robinson makes his return as well, playing bass on all tracks.

"It's a hard rock album but I wanted to do an album that would be a fun album too," Punky told me in 2016. Indeed it is, with Chandler bringing a Dennis DeYoung sense of flair to the proceedings, on songs full up with spirit, evoking, sensibly, Styx, but also Survivor, Loverboy and Night Ranger, even Queen.

"I didn't want it to be so serious. I want people to enjoy this album, have fun with it. So even the heavy tunes have anthemic choruses and hooks to them, and verses are hooky too. I like a really good song. I don't want to hear a heavy riff and then into the stratosphere. I want songs with good riffs and choruses. So even the heavy songs are very commercial-oriented, which I like. I see nothing wrong with being commercial. I like to sing along with the radio and sing along with songs myself. So there are heavy songs, there are power pop songs, there are a couple ballads too. It's very diversified."

"A lot of bands, you listen to the album, the songs all kind of sound the same, but it's just a slightly different chorus," laughs Meadows. "This record is so diverse, you'll have a power pop song that is almost like a heavy Beatles song, yet it's heavy but still pop. It might be something that you might hear in the '60s but it's still current for today's sound—and heavy. So that's really cool. And then we have heavy, heavy songs that are just really guitar-oriented, heavy riffs. But like I say, even those songs are very, very commercial and singable. You have songs you want to sing along with it and hear again. But the songs are all well written; Danny Farrow is my partner and we wrote all the songs together and produced the album together and we came up with the concept for the album cover and everything else too. He's my best friend and partner and he's a great songwriter in his own right. So together we have a really good chemistry. I'm very happy with this record."

It's almost as if you hear the entire history of American music across this record, but tilted to the Midwest and the East Coast. In particular there's this Midwest rock sound—add to the above cited bands, Shooting Star, Kansas, .38 Special—exemplified by the likes of "Straight Shooter," "Breathless and Jaded," "Lost and Lonely," "Home Wrecker," "I Wanna Be Your Drug," "Searchin'," "Something Strange" and "Shake Shake," which is most of the album! Elsewhere there's some molten riffery and some southern rock balladry, even one called "Shadow Man" that sounds like punchy Foreigner.

"I hate to use the word eclectic," says keyboardist on the record Charlie Calv (soon to be in Angel), asked about the contours of the album. "But he just wanted to do a bit of everything, show people that he likes pop stuff, he likes heavy stuff, show that he was a country guitar player—he did that on 'Leavin' Tonight.' He was very happy with it. Those were mainly his songs. He did write some stuff with Danny. It was fun doing that for him. It was kind of his first thing coming back out of retirement and I know he's very proud of it. He really likes that record and I think it's got some great stuff."

Continues Calv, "The first thing I heard when I got asked if I would be interested in the project was 'The Price You Pay,' and that was an awesome song. I thought the riff was great, I thought Chandler really nailed the vocals on that one and Punky was playing really well. I thought 'Straight Shooter" was a really good track. We did that album quick; I think that was keyboards in one-and-a-half days. Really, actually, I'd just gotten the gig, and Danny was kind of, 'Okay, we're gonna record the keyboards in two weeks. Here's 17 songs.' I was like, holy shit, are you kidding me? So I kind of got thrown into the fire on that one. And it was like, him and Punky came to the studio, and that was the first time I'd met Danny and Punky. So it was a little nerve-racking, trying to track 16 songs or whatever. I'm trying to come up with parts, and you've got Punky Meadows sitting behind you."

As for an assessment of Punky as a player, Charlie goes, "Let me tell you, man, this guy… I can't say enough. He's a legend, man, and he's such an awesome player. And besides being an iconic figure, when I say figure, just the image, it's like, who didn't want to have hair like Punky Meadows back in 1978 and '79? That's what everyone wanted to look like. So that's what I always had in my head. And then you go in the studio with the guy, and you say, 'Holy shit, this guy can fuckin' play!' He does a lot of finger-picking, not using a guitar pick, which gives him a very unique tone, and a very unique sound that comes out of an amp. It's one of those things you hear about guitar players—is it the gear or is it them? And I can definitely tell you it's him. Because when we tour, he doesn't always travel with his rig. We're using rental gear or whatever, and no matter what he plugs into, when he starts playing, it sounds like Punky Meadows."

"I'm kind of putting all my influences into the record," continues Punky, lining up nicely with Charlie's framing, "to where I aim to please a lot of people, not just one genre of people. I just love music, and to me, melody and rhythm will always live on. The trouble with a lot of bands, especially metal bands today, there's not a lot of melody going on, so that's why they tend to stay underground. In the '70s, there was so much great songwriting; that's where all the pioneering was really happening."

As for getting the band together, Punky explains that, "Felix lives in New York and everybody else is in Jersey. I'm in Charlotte, North Carolina, so I'm flying up there, and I was there for three weeks, just doing the final mixes. I stayed at a hotel up there, and we'd all get together and record. I did some of the guitar tracks down here in Charlotte, but basic tracks up in New Jersey, so I was flying back and forth."

"There's a lot of great guitar stuff on the record as well," adds Punky. Which is to be expected, of course, but it's certainly not the first thing one thinks of across this expanse of bright, optimistic songs. *Fallen Angel* is very much about peerless, punchy production applied to ruthlessly catchy, melodic songs played full band, full volume. "I don't want to sound conceited, but I'm very proud of the guitar work that is on here, and I'm proud of the songwriting. I have a killer singer in Chandler Mogel—he delivers the goods—and Charlie is a really great keyboard player, and then there's Felix, and Bobby from Monster Magnet is playing drums, and he's great too."

Mission accomplished, through what was unarguably a triumphant return, but the next step seemed blindingly obvious: that we would see the return of Angel. In fact a trial run was soon to come, in a 2017 single version of "Lost and Lonely," teaming Punky and Felix with Frank (this was also included as one of two bonus tracks on a special edition of the album, which also came autographed and with a Punky Meadows pick).

"There's talk about that," Meadows told me at the time. "I don't know if Gregg would ever want to do it or not. Everybody keeps giving us offers. I had a guy the other day, Peter Kalish… actually Felix was out in California, and he had dinner with Peter Kalish, who is managing Frank right now. And Peter Kalish offered to do some things for me too. He actually asked me to come out and play on Frank's next video. But we've had offers in the past, to go to Japan, and put Angel together, and they would pay us a lot of money, but I turned that stuff down back then because I was done with the music business. I washed my hands of it. I started my own business and I was very successful, happy and the whole thing. I just didn't want anything to do with music anymore."

"Once I left LA, I mean, I love music, but I hate the music business, you know what I mean? So I never went on board with that. But anyway, Felix was talking to Peter Kalish out in California a couple weeks ago, I guess, and Peter said if Angel would get back together, if he could get us gigs for $75,000 a night, would we do it? Now, I don't know, that sounds a little… maybe he has more faith in it than I do (laughs). But he said he knows people, promoters, that would literally want the band to do that, and play, and I guess do Las Vegas for eight nights or something like that."

Offering a little more about Gregg's career situation alluded to last chapter, Punky said that, "He got together with his brother, Clay—Clay used to be Gregg's roadie— and apparently Gregg and Clay started this slot machine thing, and I guess it's a chip or something. Every time a slot machine is pulled down, you hear a song play, you get a royalty. So yeah, he made a lot of money doing that and that's a great thing. And I talked to Gregg, I guess, six months ago, when I was doing this album. I said, 'Would you like to play on the record?' He said, 'I would love to.' But he was telling me that he had cancer at one point, and after a while he just said, 'I don't want to do music anymore.' He didn't say it to me. I don't know, he said he has his own studio there and that he plays music all the time. But people have said Gregg doesn't want to do it again. So I never asked again, followed up. I never pushed him. The next time we talked, we just talked about old times and his family and stuff like that. So I don't know if he would want to do it again or not."

Meanwhile, across the country, Frank was delivering his own record, issued on Frontiers July 3rd, 2016 in Europe and July 10th in North America. *Old Habits Die Hard* reflected how Frank was a little more tapped into what the hard rock and metal community was doing, built up through years of staying visible and sociable. The result was the picking of co-conspirators who were comparatively known quantities, and an album that was a little more street. In essence, *Old Habits Die Hard* was reflective of hard rock history from the '70s and '80s, whereas Punky's album was reflective of Angel's history from *White Hot* to *Sinful*.

"I'm not sure what style it fits into," laughed Frank, when I spoke to him at the time, myself pleasantly confused about trying to put the record in a tidy box. "When I first started it, at one time I was going to use some old material that I had, that I mounted up from the past. But the more I thought about it, I thought, you know, this is not a band, it's a solo project, and it's something new. So let's have a new, fresh approach to it. So I just decided to write all new stuff for it. My main and front concern was the songs. So without having to worry about writing for a band or a certain kind of style, I just went ahead and wrote songs—I just wanted to make sure they were good songs. And the style just came about. When I started writing with Oz (Fox, guitarist, Stryper), and then with Jeff (LaBansky, guitarist, The Lawyers), we talked about what kind of style we should be going to and my feeling was, let's just not worry about that. Let's just write some songs and choose the ones we think are the best and that's what we did."

As for what Oz brought to the table, Frank says that, "Oz and I have been playing together for a while now, and we were first in a band called Playground, and along with that we put together our own thing called Vinyl Tattoo, which we still do. We do some Angel stuff, we do some Stryper stuff, and then we also do a bunch of songs we like (laughs)—some Zeppelin, Beatles, there's some Dio in there, Rainbow, Deep Purple, all kinds of stuff. Whatever we like and kind of grew up with."

Frank's Zeppelin influence really comes through on the record, as does that of the blues boom in particular, but then again, filtered through '80s metal, of a hair variety but also from what you would call American power metal, evident on songs like "Rockin' in the City," "Mad as Hell" and "The Quest." Of note, power ballad "Even Now" finds Frank writing once more with Barry Brandt.

"Yeah, I'm drawing from my roots," muses Frank. "Basically my main roots are Beatles and Zeppelin. So there's that, which kind of dilutes down a little bit, because of the stuff I've done in the past. So it's not, I don't think, too reminiscent of Zeppelin or Beatles, although it's part of what I grew up on."

"I love Bad Company and Whitesnake, yeah, yeah," answers Frank, when I suggest those bands as a comparative as well. "It's funny, we do that stuff with Vinyl Tattoo. We do Bad Company, we do Whitesnake, some Deep Purple, so it's all that combined."

As for a production philosophy, DiMino says that, "I talked to Paul (Crook – producer) about it. My main concern was to have the same guys do the bed tracks. I wanted the same drummer, bass player and kind of keyboard player. And what he brought up to me—and brought to the table—were the guys in Meat Loaf," meaning, John Miceli on drums, Danny Miranda on bass, Justin Avery on keyboards and Paul

Crook himself, on guitar. Danny is also currently in Blue Öyster Cult and Jon is ex-BÖC. Crook has also played with Anthrax, Glenn Hughes and Sebastian Bach, plus starred in the Queen musical *We Will Rock You*.

Explains Frank, "I knew John for a while, and I felt that it's exactly what I want to do. I didn't want to feel disconnected. I didn't want it to feel like, oh, this guy did this song and I sang with you guys doing that song. What I wanted to do was keep some continuity. And the thing with Danny Miranda, I've known Danny for a while. We played for a while out here (again Las Vegas is Frank's base), jamming with each other, and sat in on open mics and stuff. And I know them way back from *We Will Rock You*; they were here for that *We Will Rock You* musical out here. And what happened was, with the guitar players, I felt that, okay, I've got Paul, I've got Oz, and I've got my friend Jeff. So those guys can split up and do some solos between them or whatever, and maybe one or two of them will do the bed tracks with John and Danny and we will be good to go."

"But what happened was, this guest guitar player thing started out, and it really kind of happened organically. It wasn't something that I wanted to do, or I was looking to do. It just kind of happened. Pat Thrall was going to be involved in the production at the beginning, but maybe he had some other obligations he had to do. But he had said, 'I would love to play on a couple of tracks; if you have some you want my playing on, I will definitely do that.' So with that in mind, we kept some stuff open for him to do. I didn't know exactly what songs yet, because we hadn't really finished anything yet, but we kept Pat in mind. Also I called up Punky and Punky said, 'Yeah, I'd love to play on a track.' So I sent him 'Never Again.'"

Indeed "Never Again" is a highlight of the record. Heavy, occasionally boogie and always sturdy of melody, the track was placed first on the album, and at 5:00, it's the second longest song on the album. The quality of the song augured well for future collaboration between the two Angel legends.

"And from that point on it kind of grew," continues DiMino. "I had Rickey Medlocke, who, when we did 'Tears Will Fall,' my main thought was, we need a good slide guitar on this thing. And so I said to Paul, 'Maybe between you and Oz you can put some slides on there.' And Rickey is a really good friend of Ken Ciancimino, who is the executive producer, and Ken said, 'Well, why don't we just call Rickey? I'm sure he'd love to do it.' And that is someone who *really* plays slide. So he said he'd love to do it, we sent him the track and all this just happened as we went along. It was really a lot of fun."

Also on board are Jeff Duncan from Armored Saint and Eddie Ojeda from Twisted Sister, but as Frank says, there's definitely a continuity to the album—it sounds like a single band of seasoned veterans playing top-shelf traditional hard rock and heavy metal balancing tropes from the '70s with those of the '80s, filtered through the production craft of the 2000s.

Adds Frank, "No matter what I asked Paul to do, he was always, 'Okay, let's try it and see what it sounds like.' It was never, 'Oh no, that's not going to sound right. Let's do something else.' That was important for me, that relationship and that trust."

As he told me at the time, 2016, "Paul and I have already started working on some new material for the next one. I have a two-album deal, so I'll be working on the next album. But yes, my approach with the solo album was not to do Angel kind of stuff—because I didn't have the other four guys there. So my approach was much different. My thought process was more in the Steve Marriott, Paul Rodgers, kind of Stevie Winwood vein. As I mentioned, that last tour we did with Angel and Humble Pie, when Humble Pie would come on, Marriott would call me up on stage and I sang songs with them. And then after we were done with the show, Marriott and myself and Bobby Tench, the three of us would sing together all night long. So it was a lot of fun and a big learning process. It was a huge learning curve, because I had two guys that sang a little bit differently. Listening and learning is always something that you've got to be open to. I'm always open to listening to new music, especially stuff that excites me."

In the Beginning **and** Risen

"This has been the best year
of my life, man."

Flash forward—way forward—to late 1999, and lo and behold, here comes a new Angel album, called *In the Beginning*.

Unfortunately the record was Angel "in name only." To be sure, there would be sufficient connections to the past in terms of personnel to legitimise using the name, along with, on the cover, both the face-with-wings logo and the upside-down logo, but the music enclosed didn't bear much resemblance to the material on the first five albums.

First, however, we look at how the reconstituted Angel band came to be. As Frank told me in April 2000, at which point he was living in Boston and not Las Vegas, "When I first moved back to Boston to take care of my mom, I was already in the process of trying to lay down the tracks that Barry and I already had, the songs we had written. Before I came back to Boston, we were using a guitar player from out in Los Angeles. We went through a lot of guitar players there and we were using this bass player Leo (Borrero), who eventually ended up on the album. This was about four years ago. We laid down two or three tracks, then we changed guitar players, we did some rehearsals, laid down a few more tracks, then we went out and did a gig in Las Vegas. Someone offered us a gig and I thought, well, you know, if it's enough money for us to get down there… and I thought it would be good for the band to get out and play live rather than just be in the studio."

"So we did that gig, came back, and we had a problem with this guitar player. The first guitar player was Scott Richards. The second guitar player I was just talking about—we actually used some of his tracks—his name was David DellaRosa. David had a couple of CDs of his own, but nothing big. Then we went to a friend of ours, who Barry and I had known from DC; this guy was a good guitar player, but he never really played with a lot of bands. And we kind of like coached him along, brought him along, and he finally put his mind to it. Because he was always doing other things. I had already moved back here to Boston and now I was commuting back and forth from Boston to Los Angeles, which is kind of crazy (laughs). So anyway, we got a warehouse and we laid down all the tracks, the rest of the stuff we had—that's when we had about 12 more songs."

The other problem with *In the Beginning* would be the somewhat jarring variation between songs production- and arrangement-wise. As Frank explained to me just before the physical product came out, "What we did was, we put the CD out on the Internet, and close enough to the

sound we wanted. So now we're going down to Florida, where we have a chance to remix the stuff. And if this guy wants it for a movie, for example, now I can remix the stuff a little bit more. I've got some time and a little bit of movement so that I can use the studio to go in and remix if need be, maybe get a few of the songs I'm not exactly happy with, get them closer to where I want them."

Again, because the songs were recorded with so many different players and over time and in different studios, there's a fair bit of difference between tracks, most notably, this fairly demarcated mix of acoustic songs and electric songs.

Continuing on with hammering down who is actually in Angel at this juncture, Frank says that, "At this point we have Gordon Gebert on keyboards and Randy Gregg on bass. Gordon did that *Kiss & Tell* book; I thought that was pretty funny. And Randy Gregg was in a band called Garlic. But another thing

that happened with this thing was, there was another Kiss convention, and I thought, you know, I don't really want to do these unless there's a reason to do it. So I thought, well, we have the CD, and we're putting it out of the Internet; maybe what we'll do is a release thing at this Kiss convention. It was in Swansea. It was supposed be one of the bigger ones, so I thought, let me put something together and it'll make sense. So we'll put the band together, we'll play and everything, and get it going that way."

"So I asked the guys to come down to Boston. I had a rehearsal place over here. They came down here and I wasn't sure it was going to work. It's one of those things. Even though you hear them play on a CD, before you see them and meet them and stuff, it's a whole different thing. You don't know until you start to play if it's going to work. But once we started, it just felt right. The guitar player I used for that is a guitar player that I've known from out here, who I had been doing local things around here with, just to keep myself working and in shape. Because I just like singing. So I have like a little thing going on here and I thought I would use this guitar player so I don't have to worry about... the guitar players are the hardest piece of the puzzle."

Enter Steve Blaze, of Lillian Axe and Near Life Experience distinction, if not exactly fame.

"Right, well, what happened was, after we did the think in Swansea, and after Barry and I felt comfortable enough with Gordon and Randy, I thought, okay, these two guys, they are the guys—we want these guys. Now let's focus back on guitar. So we went down to New York and we set up an audition, but people that they knew and that we knew… nothing was happening. And I thought, we'll have to do an open call. So we did one of those things. And then I think Steve came in through Gordon. He flew in. He wanted to come to the audition. And when he played with us, the first time he played, it went really well, amazing. All these other guitar players who came down, they wanted to do the audition and play with the band and stuff, and a lot of them didn't even take the time to learn the songs. So you're coming in for an audition, and I'm like hey, what are you thinking? You're not going to come in here and expect us to waste time teaching you the songs. You can't do that. The way we did it was—and we told them too—you have only this much time slotted for you, this much time slotted for the next guy. That's just the way we had to do it. So the last thing I expected was a guy to say, 'Well, I kind of know that song; what are the chords?' I don't want to hear that."

"So when Steve came in, it was like really nice. He knew all the stuff and so we focused on the songs. And then we were able to arrange a couple of things. Because he knew the stuff, we were actually able to rehearse with him. So what we did was, he stayed, and as we were doing other auditions, in-between a few, we had him come back down and rehearse with us again. So I mean, we felt really good with him. We were supposed to, at that point, do a European tour that kind of fell through. When we were going to do the European tour, we asked Steve to do it with us he because it felt good, and I didn't want to delay the tour. I said, 'Let's do this. If you have the time, and you're able to it, let's do the tour and we will take it one step at a time.' So that's how that whole thing started. And now I've kept in touch with him, and I'm just waiting for something to happen again so we can go out. I know that he is doing his thing, and I'm not going to hold up his thing he's doing for this."

At this point Frank took my address and a week or so later I received a copy of *In the Beginning* in the mail. However, Frank voiced his qualification—maybe even call it a warning—about what I was about to hear.

"The next thing I have to do is after we do this remix, we'll see if we can get a deal from a major label. I don't wanna have to go running and chasing anyone. It doesn't have to be a major, but I want to make sure I don't have to be chasing people to get money, or to be fighting with anyone—I don't want to do that. You didn't hear the thing that Richie and I did, did you? There was one of those tribute CDs. Cheap Trick (this was called *Stiff Competition*, and Frank and Richie Ranno from Starz are featured on a version of 'On Top of the World'). You've got to hear the new stuff. It's not really different, but it's more in a… Barry and I get into open tuning. So it's a little bit more Zeppelin-like. But I say that only because we do a lot more A tuning and stuff like that. So it sounds like us, but it's different. A lot of fans will go 'This is not really Angel.' What can I say? We are Angel and this is what it is (laughs). Like I say, what else would it be, *Sinful* 2000? I don't know. At the end of the day we did what we wanted to do. We did what we would like to do."

Fortunately for the fans, Executive Producer of *In the Beginning*, Danny Stanton, under the umbrella of his company Collier Entertainment (Danny is one of the great unsung movers and shakers for a multitude of classic rock and hair metal bands over the years), created a booklet for the CD issue of the album that is professional and packed with information. There are a pile of pictures, along with lyrics for every song and with writing, performance and studio credits split up by song. There are also introductory liner notes by Frank and Barry working as a team, plus a short essay from radio personality Gail Flug.

Even more fortunate for the most dedicated of fans, explains DiMino, "What I did was, for Angel fans, we put their names in with a special thanks. We gave them like a cut-off date. If they put their names in on the web site, we said that we would put their names on the album. So we did this on the CD. There were so many names, that the writing had to be so small. At one point I thought, I don't even think we can read it. You have to get a magnifying glass to read it."

Into the first track on *In the Beginning*, and the caution we've talked about is justified. "The Crow" is essentially acoustic guitar (with a bit of distantly mixed slide), plus bass, Bonham-esque drums, and vocals from Frank that sound more like low-crooning Robert Plant than anything previously heard from Angel. Felix Robinson guests on bass, while guitars are handled by Richard Marcello. Second track, "The Rain Song," is more of the same, Zeppelin-esque, very much like "Over the Hills and Far Away," just as Bonham-esque from the bottom, and even more Jimmy Page-like on the guitars.

"Hero" doesn't sound like old Angel either, but more like funky hair metal. Again, Frank's voice sounds huskier than it did on the old stuff. Punky guests on this one, providing the guitar solo.

Next it's "So I'll Say Goodbye," where Frank really leans into this idea of singing like Robert Plant, atop a dark and bluesy ballad that sounds like a cross between "Since I've Been Loving You," "Babe I'm Gonna Leave You" and Thin Lizzy's "Still in Love with You." Once Barry crashes in, the arrangement evokes images of a blend between the two Bonham band albums, *The Disregard of Timekeeping* and *Mad Hatter*. Then we're onto "Long Gone," which sounds like… Led Zeppelin, but this time, something that might have fit on *Presence* or *In Through the Out Door*, or perhaps the first Robert Plant album or Jimmy's *Outrider* solo album. It's a big and booming blues, slow-moving, very John Paul on the bass (played by Felix), with Frank vamping and phrasing like… you know who. Guesting on bar-room piano is Danny Peyronnel of Heavy Metal Kids and UFO fame.

Almost humourously at this point, our next selection, "In the Wake of the Storm (The Millenium Y2K)" is a hybrid of "So I'll Say Goodbye" and the early more acoustic tracks on the album. There's the straight line to Jimmy Page playing folk, on top of drums played like Bonzo and recorded like Bonzo. There's also distantly mixed slide.

"Set Me Free" is an elegant ballad, not particularly of the Zep camp, although Punky plays acoustic very much like Robbie Blunt on *Pictures at Eleven* and *The Principle of Moments*. But these are not Zeppelin-eque melodies, and the production is a completely different kettle of fish, with Barry sounding quite processed and '80s-like. There's a searing power ballad-esque guitar solo from Punky, over chord changes that recall Meadows favourite Queen. Felix plays the bass but curiously it's Frank who is credited with keyboards, which are prominent, resembling a string arrangement.

"The Greatest Love of All" is the most Led Zeppelin-like song on the entire record, again sounding like a *Presence* or *In Through the Out Door* out-take, once more with Frank playing along, playing Robert and Barry playing along, playing Bonzo. Credit-wise, we're back to the core band on this 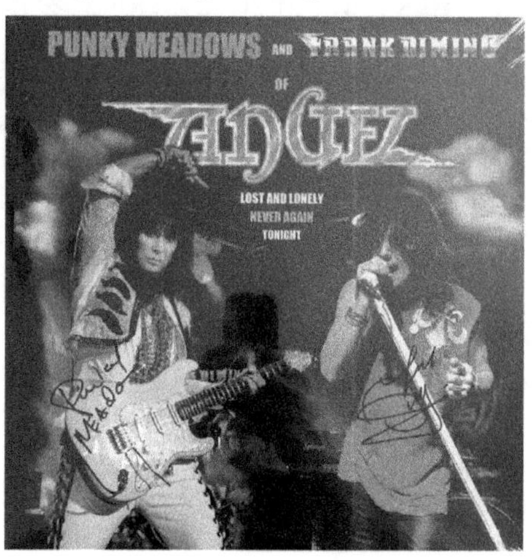 one, namely Frank, Richard Marcello on guitars, Leo Borrero on bass and Barry on drums. The biggest divergence from the core band would be the fact that Felix plays quite a bit of bass on the record. Still, the idea of this being the core band is underscored by much of the writing being attributed to the Frank, Richard and Barry threesome.

"Shangra La" is almost as Zeppelin-like as the song before it, and again tilted toward the latter incarnation of the band, into Robert solo and then past that, into Jason Bonham's fine two records as part of the Bonham band. Core band performance and writing on this one, as is the case with closing number "Trapped in Paradise," which is exactly, precisely, more of the same! And when I say more of the same, fortunately, it's really good stuff, solid material, like pretty much all that came before. Alas, however, it sounds nothing like Angel, and thus our earlier assertion: Angel in name only.

I wondered what Frank would say about this strange chapter in Angel history (and in our Angel book) 20 years down the line.

"It's funny," muses DiMino, now in 2020, "I was just thinking about that, because I was reading some comments. Some people just hate that album—some people love that album. *In the Beginning* was basically Barry and I, some things we had written. But when we put it together, it wasn't as a part of being the next Angel album because Angel had already been done. So we were moving on and we thought, well, we'll figure out something as we go. Unless we put a band together, we were never, ever thinking about calling it an Angel album."

"Until it got to the point of a record deal," continues Frank. "Getting a record deal was much easier using the name Angel than anything else. So we ended up talking to Punky and Felix and they said, 'Yeah, go ahead, use the name; it's okay with us.' And that's when I asked them to play on a couple of the songs. We still really didn't have a band. We had bits and pieces of people that we were writing with and people we were going to go in the studio with for certain songs. And that's how we ended up approaching it. We used Richard Marcello, who was a friend of ours, all of us, Punky and Barry and myself from back in Washington, DC, in Maryland. But we had known Richard for years."

Not sure why—maybe he hadn't played the damn thing in years!—but the comparisons to Led Zeppelin kinda go over Frank's head. "The other thing about that album," DiMino told me, "is a lot of people, for some reason, think that it's like a Led Zeppelin kind of album. And I have no idea where that came from. I kind of remember someone asking me and I might've said that, you know, I think there's an A tuning song on that one. It might've been 'The Crow' or 'The Rain Song,' I think, that has an A tuning sound to it. And I thought, sure, kind of a Zeppelin thing. But that album is by no means… I don't understand it. We did take a lot of Barry's drumbeats and moved songs around, because Barry always wanted to get a certain kind of drum beat, you know, even for the Angel albums. So with that album, when we recorded it, he said, 'Look, it's just the two of us.' So I said, 'Get the drums the way you want them and we'll build the stuff around that.' So we did a lot of that kind of thing on *In the Beginning*."

The record remained a low-key release, but what's almost important is that Angel became a touring identity again, although, oddly, with none of the guys on the record being part of the fold, other than Frank and Barry. Steve Blaze played with the band from 2000 through 2008. Gordon G. G. Gebert played keys from 1999 to 2002, after which Michael T. Ross took over, through 2008. Randy Gregg was the band's bassist from 1999 through to 2008. Entering the set list from the new record were "Hero," "So I'll Say Goodbye," "Shangra La" and "Trapped in Paradise."

The next time I spoke to Frank was in September 2007, and intriguingly, at that point, it sounded like a new Angel album with the current touring lineup was just around the corner. "Right now we're just finishing up writing stuff for a new CD. We've got pretty much all the material intact now—it's just a matter of recording it. I think that should be happening within the next couple of months. We're still working with a couple

of different record companies right now. I don't know exactly which direction we're going in, but I'm not worried about that right now. What I'm concentrating on is getting all the material together in the right way to get it down on tape. There are more keyboards on this one. So I think it's more like maybe the first and second album. Right now we have Michael T. Ross on keyboards, and Barry and myself, and Steve Blaze—I wrote some stuff with Steve—and Randy Gregg, bass player. We have guys who are spread out all across the country, so we have to figure out when everyone is available; that's always kind of a problem right now."

"I'm also trying to see if I can get some dates together in Europe as well," continued Frank. "It seems that Europe at this point is the place for us to be, because they still have all the festivals and stuff. Just a few years ago we had to do the Bang Your Head festival with Alice Cooper and UFO and people we hadn't seen in awhile. I mean, I did a lot of stuff with Paul Raymond; Paul and I worked together on a lot of different projects and I hadn't seen him for a while. It was nice to see  him again, and other people I hadn't seen in a while. So it's a little more conducive now. We've done Sweden Rock; maybe three or four years ago (June 9th, 2001; Bang Your Head on June 26th, 2004). It's time for us to go back there too."

And the *next* time I talked with Frank was in 2016, at which point he and Punky had their solo projects talked about in the last chapter. A record with Angel was still a very real possibility, given how in touch everybody was.

"Yes, well, Punky lives in North Carolina, and he just sent me a track today, so I'll be in the studio tomorrow putting some vocals on the track he sent me," explained

DiMino. "Which will be a lot of fun. And he's playing with Felix. He and Felix are together, so that will be interesting. And Barry is out in LA, and Barry and I are always in touch. In fact, he'll probably be coming here in a couple weeks. He wanted to write some stuff together. So I'll probably have some new material for the next album. He got sick when I started to work on the first solo album; I believe it was kidney stones. That's why he wasn't so heavily involved in it. But hopefully he will be more involved in the next one. Plus Gregg is around. Maybe he'd be involved; who knows?"

As well, Frank seemed to be fully ensconced in the business and thus the most ready of all the guys to be the catalyst for an Angel reunion. "Sure, I play—and I teach. With Vinyl Tattoo, it's Oz and I, and Scotty Coogan is on drums; he's out there with Ace Frehley now. Let's see, we have Jeff Duncan from Armored Saint. There's a lot of guys out here that are part of the scene so it's becoming a pretty good scene, actually. We always play Danny Koker's place (Count Vamp'd; this is Danny from Counting Cars); he always has great bands there, and he has his own band there, Count's 77, with Stoney Curtis. And yes, I still teach. Every time I'm teaching someone, I remember something (laughs). So it keeps me on top of things. I'm always on my toes. Because I'm teaching, I want to make sure that I'm listening to my own advice. When I tell them to do something, I want to make sure that I'm following my own advice."

To be sure, keeping a hand in the game—and staying sociable in one of the most sociable cities in the world, Las Vegas—could only be an asset in terms of someone flag shipping an Angel reunion. As well, Frank and Punky each putting out excellent solo albums couldn't hurt, especially for Punky, in terms of bringing back that confidence level. Additionally, product makes touring more viable, more purposeful, and indeed playing shows together represented another rung on the ladder—another riser on the stairwell, so to speak—toward what would become *Risen*.

"Yes, for sure," agrees Frank. "I think what happened was that we started out as Punky Meadows and Frank DiMino, and I was doing my solo stuff and he was doing his solo stuff and he asked me, 'So what do you think about doing a couple of dates?' Because the singer was not going to be able to do some dates and this and that. I said, 'Yeah, sure. I'd be more than happy to do a couple of dates. What do you want to do?' 'Maybe do some old Angel stuff and a couple of things off of your solo album, my solo album.' So I said, 'Okay, let's see what we can put together. So we put some shows together and it was a perfect situation. The guys that we got weren't from his original solo band, which was good, except for Charlie (Calv) and of course, Danny (Farrow). But we just had so much fun doing it, we decided to keep going with it (laughs). And then eventually we changed it to the reformation of the band and the successful writing and the album itself, *Risen*."

"I think Danny is really kind of the catalyst of the whole thing," reflects Calv, on how these two records and these duo shows brought about the resurrection of Angel.

"First and foremost, getting Punky out of retirement. You know what I mean? Punky was pretty much done with the music business. No one had heard about him. It was one of those MIA, 'What ever happened to Punky Meadows?' stories. And Danny kind of got him back up playing. As you probably are well aware, the music business is not fun (laughs). Punky really became very disheartened after everything fell apart and he moved back East and just wanted out. So Danny got him back out and made him feel comfortable in just playing music, trying to have fun and not worrying about the business, and letting him know that people still like Angel and still want to hear them play. So he's a big part of that, and a big part of getting Frank involved too. There are a lot of moving parts. The other guys are still alive, and obviously, everyone was approached—I'm talking about the original lineup. Danny kind of helped with orchestrating all that; if he didn't spearhead that, it would never have happened."

Asked about the construction of what would be Frank's and Punky's first album together as a team in 40 years, Frank explains that, "Personality-wise, *Risen* was a case of re-establishing ourselves. As far as working with Danny, it was the first time I was writing with Danny. So that was the beginning of a great experience for me. Always when you start writing with someone new, you wonder, is this gonna work or not? But between the three of us, it started out really good and it ended up even better. But the whole recording process was such a blur for me. I was on the East Coast doing the vocals and staying in a hotel there. I did all the vocals in like two weeks. I didn't really have any days off. It was pounding every single day on a different song and then doing backgrounds and trying different ideas. A lot of the songs, we didn't have the luxury of playing out a whole lot of them, like we used to do with Angel. There were a few, but a lot of those songs were straight studio creations. We were adding background as we were going along as I finished the vocal. So there was an awful lot of singing and like I say, it was a blur."

"We did do a couple of rehearsals for it," chuckles Charlie, adding to the story of the record's assemblage. "We did the first bit of it in New Jersey, because we live here, meaning myself, Billy (Orrico, drums) and Danny. The three of us live here. Steve (E. Ojane), the bass player, is in Delaware, Punky's in North Carolina and Frank is out in Las Vegas. So some of the writing was done remotely. Myself, Billy and Steve didn't really get involved in the writing. But there was a lot of writing done ahead of time. Punky and Frank did fly in a couple of times and we did do a couple rehearsals with the band, just to get an idea of what was going on. But for the most part it was done remotely. And I know the drums and the bass… I wasn't there, I don't know if they tracked them together, but they were all done in the same studio. And I believe Punky tracked the bulk of his guitars down in North Carolina in a studio down near him."

"I have a home studio," continues Calv, "so all the keyboards… Punky, Frank and Danny came to my place, and we just kind of blocked out this very long week, and I think we did it in three days of ten-, 12-hour days, which is kind of crazy, because I was kind of engineering and playing and trying to absorb all these thoughts being thrown at me at the same time. And then Frank flew back out later and we did the bulk of the vocals here in New Jersey. And I think towards the end, just because of the studio time, Frank went back, and I think Oz Fox finished the last two songs at his studio out in Vegas. And then it was mixed back out here."

Asked for some additional detail about Angel's spiffy new rhythm section, Charlie explains that, "Billy is from New Jersey. Steve is originally from upstate New York, currently living in Delaware. Billy, I would run into from time to time over the years. He's a fellow New Jersey musician and awesome player. I mean, I've got to tell you, they couldn't have picked a better guy to take the place of Barry Brandt. Besides being a huge Barry Brandt fan, when we go to play live, he really nails that stuff. Frank has made a couple comments: 'I can't imagine how the guy picks up on the stuff that Barry used to do.' And Frank could be intimidating. Not in a bad way, but you don't know what the guy's thinking. Even with me, the first time I got in a room with him, he's got the glasses that are tinted and you can't see his eyes. So the first time we do 'The Fortune,' he's five feet away from me, just like staring at me while I'm doing it. Does he think I suck? Does he like it? And no expression, I can't see his eyes, and it was so nerve-racking."

"But yeah, Billy is awesome. And Steve kind of came in… Danny or Punky knew him from something, and asked him to come out. And actually Billy and Steve did a show. Because the guys that we had for the solo band could not make one of the things we had on the schedule. So both Billy and Steve actually filled in. And then from there, when Frank and Punky decided to go out and test some waters and play some Angel stuff, I was asked to come aboard to do that. It's just a great band; they're great guys to hang with. No one wants to put up with BS from anybody. It's, 'Go out and play.' You want guys that get along as well and they're both awesome guys. I love hanging with them."

Asked about jobs outside of music, Charlie explains that, "Punky doesn't do anything but play music as far as I know. He's pretty much retired. Frank does his vocal lessons and I'm not sure what else. Danny is a very talented sculptor. He does a lot of art sculpting. For me, it's kind of cool, because he does all the old *Planet of the Apes* figures and the Marvel stuff. He's kind of the guy who does the original sculpture from which they do the mass manufacturing, which is an interesting gig. Steve, I'm not sure, to be honest with you, what his day gig is. Billy has been in the business, mainly as an audio post editor. He does a lot of film work, with HBO, Netflix. You'll see his name running in the credits of a lot of different films. And myself, I'm a part owner of a record company called Deko Entertainment. That's kind of my main thing; it's what I do by day, and play by night."

"That's the million-dollar question," reflects Charlie, asked why Angel's drummer is Billy and not Barry. "I don't know. I've met Barry. Barry is the only one who has never kind of come out and sat in at one point in time with Punky and Frank or the new band or whatever. I know Frank and him are still very close. I know health-wise, he's probably not doing the best, but I don't know what kind of conditions he has. But I think it's more of just, he doesn't want to do the small-scale tours. And I can understand from his perspective. It's tough being a drummer and going out and playing two hours and giving it your all and not having the big crews to take care of your stuff like it was in the '70s."

"I love Barry; he's my brother," says Frank. "He's really a humble guy and a gentle soul. He's a great drummer. Like I said, he's like my brother, but he couldn't deal with not having his kit to use at every show. When we played back then it was easy, but these days, if you can't play on someone else's kit… some of these places, some of these festivals, the drums are brought down by the companies and stuff. So yeah, it's very difficult. He gets really frustrated with that stuff really quick."

Which prompted the question: was there something unique or out of the ordinary about his kit? "No, not really. Funny, Barry and I first met, I think, in 1970. He was playing a marching band bass drum. It was ten inches deep. He always felt that he could hear his foot better that way. So after that it was always difficult getting him to… he finally did change it. He gave that kit to his brother and he went with those Ludwigs for a long time. And then when we he and I went out when we reformed and went out to do those things in Europe, he got a DW kit, which is a huge kit. And I remember the guy from DW saying, 'You know, everyone's getting smaller kits. What are you doing?!' He said, 'I don't want a small kit!'"

As Punky says, it's worked out great with Billy. "Yes, we wanted to get somebody to play live with Angel that was like Barry and Billy fit to a T because Billy loves Barry's playing, and Barry is one of his idols. It's great that we found these guys like Charlie and Bill. They were both big Angel fans and so is Steve. I met Steve when I did my opening at BB King's for my solo album. Steve did a meet-and-greet to  meet me. I could see him in line. We had a long line, a lot of meet-and-greets, and he was smiling like 'There's Punky' and all that."

"So he walked up to me and we were talking and he said, 'Yeah, man, I saw you guys live.' And I said, 'You're too young. You didn't see any of this.' And he goes, 'No, no, I really did.' And I said, 'Damn, you look really good then.' Then he goes, 'Well, I'm a singer in a band, but I'm really a bass player.' I said, 'Really? Awesome.' So then later on, when we needed a bass player after Felix left, because he had some heart problems, surgery and stuff, we had Keith Robert, who's a radio disc jockey in New York, play with us for the West Coast gigs. We told Steve to send us a video of him playing. He sent that in and he was good. So we thought he'd be perfect, 'cause he looks great, he fits in, kind of got the blond hair like Gregg and he's a really good bass player. So we said, 'Dude, you're in the Angel band.'"

"So he—and then all these guys—were so happy. I remember we were playing over in Europe, in England, and man, we finished the show and Billy looked at me and he goes, 'You know, this has been the best year of my life, man.' I was really happy for that, because that's the thing about these guys in this band: there are no egos. Everybody gets along, we all love each other, there's no fragile egos. Nobody is like, 'What about me?' No, it's a team."

As for Punky's recollection with respect to how the record was assembled, he says that, "We wrote the songs first. I write a bunch of songs and then Danny writes songs too, and then Danny and I get together and work on them. Sometimes I'll have a completely finished song, other people too, sometimes we have to help each other, like put a bridge in. Then we bring Frank in and he puts his lyrics to it. Melody-wise, usually we have a hook line that's already kind of mapped-out. Then we go into rehearsal with the guys and we show them the songs, pre-production kind of thing. Billy and Steve, that's really the basic tracks; you want to make sure that the bass and drums are playing together. But first I went in and did a single scratch guitar for all the songs. Then we took that scratch guitar and went into the studio and Billy played the drums along to my scratch guitar—which is really odd, because in the old days, everybody would get in the studio together. But it's done differently now. I played my scratch guitar to a click track and then Billy would put his headphones on and he'd play the drums. Billy's a great fucking drummer, man. I noticed how great Billy was when we did 'The Tower.' And it's funny because that's when I realised how great Barry was too (laughs). But Billy's got the power down just like Barry. And when I watched him play on the video screen and he was playing and I heard it coming back, I went, 'Holy shit, that's some serious fucking drum shit going on right there.'"

"But anyways," continues Meadows, "we did the drums to the scratch track and then Steve came in and did his bass parts to the drums and the scratch track. We did all that in New Jersey. Then I came back down to North Carolina here and went in a studio down here because all my gear is here and I have a really good studio for guitars at hand. Danny came down here too. So we went and did all the guitars down here in North Carolina. Then I went back up with Danny, back up to Jersey, and we got all the keyboards done with Charlie in his home studio. Then Frank came back up from Las Vegas and we did all the vocals. After that, Frank went back home and Danny and I mixed the album and that was it. And then of course we had to master it too. We had Glen Sheck master—he's great. I mean, he did my album for free for the first thing, 'cause he loved Angel so much. And then he only charged not very much to master our record."

Mastered record in hand, here comes *Risen*, opening with "Angel Theme (Prelude)," a fitting tribute to all that came before, followed by spirited rocker "Under the Gun," hard-hitting but more of a Frank solo-type song… until the song's gorgeous chorus, laden with melody and underscored by angelic keys from Charlie.

"'Under the Gun' was one of Danny's and mine," notes Punky. "Danny is my partner; he's the one that got me out of retirement. Danny flew down here to where I live in Charlotte and we got together for four days and threw our songwriting ideas around together, and 'Under the Gun' was the one that we wrote down here. I like songs that are singable. Because of my love of melody, I've always loved the Beatles and Paul McCartney and John Lennon. It's all about melody to me. Melody and rhythm always live on. Everything else is just frosting on the cake. So all the songs on *Rising*, whether it be the heaviest stuff or not, have great hook lines and melodies that you can sing along with. With me it's hook line first, generally, then verses and all the rest."

"Shot of Your Love" is even more "singable" than the one before it, dependable "Louie Louie" chords placed on a great AOR groove, and then, after a shotgun crack, blessed with an effortlessly enjoyable vocal melody come chorus time, with Frank strengthened by support harmonies.

"Slow Down" has Billy hitting the cowbell on a great party rocker, recalling the most bar-room rocking material from *White Hot* and *Sinful*, and back to *On Earth*, actually. There's a bunch of great chord changes too, and a novel structure with that stop/start an' chuckle from Frank.

Says Meadows, "When I did that crazy beginning to 'Slow Down,' I was thinking of 'Broken Dreams' from our first album, you know, with that frantic, crazy progression? 'Slow Down,' of course, *is* kind of a progressive song, because there's a lot of pieces and parts to it. But even that has a single hook line, you know? 'Slow Down' is something to sing along with that you remember. I'm the kind of guy that likes bubblegum music. Whenever I hear 'Sugar Sugar' by The Archies, I roll the windows down and sing along with it. I love that kind of stuff."

Late in the sequence, there's a bluesy solo from Punky, and this after a brief barrage of drum licks from Billy. "I'm really a blues player," reiterates Punky, plainly demonstrated here. "I cut my teeth on the English blues players, and even Gary Moore and David Gilmour. David Gilmour can play one note and you can't wait to fucking hear what he's going to do next as opposed to something like a thousand notes. To me, that's all just a lesson in manual dexterity. When you hear a guy playing a hundred miles an hour and tapping on all the frets and stuff, well, that's impressive. But when I hear David Gilmour or Stevie Ray Vaughan play, I'm inspired. I always say 'Don't impress me—inspire me.' Little kids playing all that stuff on the internet—it just bores the shit out of me. All you're doing is copying. Whereas a guy like David

Gilmour plays from the heart and soul and it just goes right through me and means so much more."

Next is "Over My Head," which begins one way and then Frank starts singing, and we're into another elegant rocker bridging all of Angel's longitudes, latitudes and solitudes, one fresh part to the next and then back 'round again.

But then we're onto the record's 7:08 showstopper, "1975," which opens with a traditional Angel keyboard solo, now at the hands of Charlie Calv. "I was kind of left to my own devices to come up with that intro part, which I thought was very cool," says Calv. "Personally, for me—and this has nothing to do with ego—I would have loved to hear more keyboards on the album. We actually recorded a lot more keyboards than made the final mixes. But I'm just happy to be doing it, so I'll keep my mouth shut (laughs). But no, I thought '1975' came out really cool. It was one of the first ones I heard that was finished, or close to being finished, and I thought the lyrics were great and really tipped the hat to 1975, when the band started and everything that was going on. Fans like it because they can relate to it. It's a nice lengthy song, with the big keyboard intro that Angel are known for on their earlier records. Not to compare to 'The Fortune,' but it's sort of similar, where you have that one-and-a-half-, two-minute keys lead-up to the song itself. It's a good epic piece with a really distinct Angel vibe to it."

Seems like a good time to ask Charlie about the shoes he was now filling in Angel, those of Gregg Giuffria. "First, he's one of my all-time favourite keyboard players," begins Calv. "People ask me my top four, and it's Keith Emerson, Rick Wakeman, Jon Lord and Gregg Giuffria. And all for slightly different reasons. Gregg I love because… I'm an Angel fan, but I'm a little bit younger; I'm the youngest guy in the band currently, so I never got to see Angel in the heyday. Some of my older friends had the records, but I kind of discovered Gregg first. My friend brought over the first Giuffria record, and I thought, wow, this is awesome. I loved what he did, plus what he did with Angel as well on *Sinful* and *White Hot*, kind of lush strings and the big pads and the orchestrations. Then I got the Angel record, *The Anthology*, and then went back to the catalogue."

"What I found the most interesting and most difficult was trying to wrap my head around his solos. Because they're very erratic, and I don't mean this in a bad way, but kind of all over the place. Like, what the fuck was he thinking? Where was he going with this? (laughs). Some of them were very difficult to learn and come close to, because there really wasn't a thought-out methodology behind it. One thing I thought was interesting, a lot of these things that I thought were like overtones or harmonies going on, when I actually sat and talked to Gregg a couple years ago, I kind of asked him that question. And I found out what he used to do back in the day was, because on the old analog synths, you have the two oscillators to work with, he would choose one, like a third or a fifth, of the main tone that he was using, so he would always get that weird kind of third and fifth happening. But yeah, I could never figure out if it was double-tracked or what he was doing."

Specifically on the topic of Gregg and his gear, Charlie says that, "There's the Memorymoog, and if you look at Gregg's set-up and Emerson's set-up, they're pretty close. I know that they had become friends as well. Gregg really kind of pioneered—as Keith did and Rick Wakeman did—the whole Moog thing when it came out. Plus the Arp that was used on the first record, specifically on 'The Tower.' There were guys experimenting with all these cool keyboard sounds no one had ever used before, and that's where some of the erratic-ness comes from. They were kind of

experimenting and learning these new instruments. They'd
used the Mellotron which had been around for a bit, but as
far as the analog synths, that was all being invented at the
same time that Angel got together."

"When we did '1975,' I said to Charlie, 'I want you
to write a keyboard intro like "The Fortune,"' remembers
Punky. "I said, 'Here's the chords. It's going to be in E Minor
and you can use E Minor and G. And at the very last note,
I want you to hit a B flat major chord, 'cause we're going to
do a big swell into that.' And I said, 'Think of "The Fortune"
and do that.' So he wrote this piece and he played it, sent it
to me and I said, 'That's going to sound great. That's fucking
awesome. That's perfect.'"

"The reason we hired Charlie," continues Meadows,
"was because when I was doing my solo album, we were
looking for keyboard players and we were gonna use the
keyboard player that was in Bebe Buell's band because they
already knew him. And he was supposed to be a really good
keyboard player. Well, Chandler, the singer in my Punky
Meadows thing says, 'There's this keyboard player named
Charlie. He would like to audition.' And he said, 'He's a big
Angel fan. He knows every Angel song and every keyboard
part that Gregg played.' We thought, well, that's a no-
brainer—let's hear him. So we heard him play and we said,
'You're in, dude.' He knew fuckin' everything."

Comments Punky, on the mournful, almost "Hotel
California"-like solo section to "1975," "When I write songs,

if you'll notice, a lot of times I will write a whole different chord progression for my guitar solo so it becomes a song within a song, right? In '1975,' which is a great song, that guitar solo piece is a whole different chord progression than the rest of the song. I like to write pieces in songs. If I write a bridge, I always write like a little intro into the bridge, a piece and then the bridge. I don't just go from the verse into the bridge. I'll write up a little bit of an instrumental lead-in to the bridge."

And hence the "Hotel California" chord progression under the heavy blues solo. And this added onto the very odd "My Sweet Lord" melody to the pre-chorus, where there are backing croons paired with a whispered "1975." When the true chorus arrives, for the first time at the four-minute mark, the clouds part for a truly memorable Beatles-esque and even Byrds-y thing. When this is reprised after the solo for the big concluding piece, Frank layers on a ton of impassioned vocals. Finally everything goes quiet for a little Queen-like flourish to close the book on this song that is the beating heart of the *Risen* album.

"That's a really kick-ass heavy song, with a lot of guitar shredding going on," says Punky about the next number, "We Were the Wild." "I love to do that kind of stuff too." Indeed this is the second most heavy metal song on the album, with a sophisticated riff, punchy rhythms from the engine room and power metal singing from Frank. Again, not particularly Angel-like, but then again, deft demonstration that an old dog can learn new tricks.

"I.O.U." sounds very much like a New England ballad, or Angel from the *Sinful* era, in both cases, the writers channelling their love of the easy listening pop they heard as kids on AM radio in the '60s.

"I wrote 'I.O.U.' and I love that song," explains Meadows, "but a lot of people think that you guys are heavy metal band—that's just some schmaltzy love song. No, I've always loved ballads. The Beatles wrote the most beautiful ballads ever and that song is a beautiful ballad song. The concept of the song is 'I owe you.' You know, that I took this girl for granted, but please take my I.O.U., you know, please let me make it up to you. I would do anything for you if you take my I.O.U. It says in there, 'When you saw that red dress in the window, I should have bought it for you.' Those are clever lyrics and I'm very proud of that song. It's the kind of song that chokes you up. And I tell men, I say, 'Listen dude, if you're ever having a fight with your girlfriend and you want to make her feel better and tell how much you love her, play her "I.O.U."'

"But sure, I had one critic say, 'Man, the song "I.O.U.," that's just a schmaltzy love song. Dude, what is wrong with you? I want stuff to fucking headbang to.' I don't bang my head all day long. I have a lot more dimensions to me than that. What's wrong with you? Are you just a bonehead, man? Wake up, man. You know what I mean? There's a lot of beautiful stuff out there. Listen to it. Please don't feel so boxed in that you can't appreciate something. I'm going to tell you something: sometimes the most delicate and sensitive things are the hardest things to do. When I'm trying to play a simple little acoustic part, I stumble over that for a long time because it's delicate and it can be the hardest thing to do. So don't gloss over stuff like that."

"I remember talking to Danny once. We were writing a song and thinking it was probably a little too heartbreak-y or something. Once again, you're putting the girl down or whatever. Maybe we should write a song that is more uplifting. And I said I think I'm gonna do that. It's hard to do that because a lot of songs that are so inspirational are songs that kind of make you sad, maybe. I don't know why. It must be the blues in being an artist. It's like the clown: the happy clown is really a sad, depressed person when he's not being a clown!"

Next is "(Punky's Couch Blues) Locked, Cocked and Ready to Rock," which is a swaggering and egregious hair metal rocker right outta 1989, expensive-sounding big-shot producer production values included. Punky indeed performs a brief blues intro, plus there's an involved solo section later played over a double-time rhythm.

Explains Meadows, "Blues, country, rockabilly, Elvis… rock 'n' roll is about blues and rock and country mixed together. I wanted to do 'Punky's Couch Blues' because every night when I sit down and watch TV, I have my guitar and my recorder. The first thing I do is I just play some really fun, cool blues licks. That's what I go to right away. And so I thought it was really cool to do something like that, where I'm just playing some not really super-distorted blues, not really high-octane, just cool blues riffs. I thought I would do that and play those little blues riffs. And then, bang, to the high-octane thing. But yeah, playing in house bands, late teens, early 20s, if you couldn't really play the blues and B.B. King you weren't nothing. And so I really became a blues player more than anything else. So 'Punky's Couch Blues' is just kinda tipping my hat off to those blues cats."

Barely past half-way, track ten on the record is "Turn Around," an unassuming power popster that leads perfectly into the relaxed '70s rock chording of "Desire," which sounds like melodic Kiss. Points out Punky, "On 'Desire,' there's a little bridge where there's almost like a chorus. I really wrote that as like something from *American Bandstand* where they'd be dancing. It goes, 'Hey honey, honey, I got a little money, let's go out and light up the town.' Well, I took that from like, 'Hey, sugar, sugar,' that kind of thing. I love that shit, but yet the song 'Desire' is a rock song, although it's a really basic rock 'n' roll song. Then it goes into that little bridge thing that was extra, to be kind of a second chorus at the end. So yeah, it has that *American Bandstand* dancing and *Soul Train* thing going on. So if we ever did a video, I would have an *American Bandstand* thing going on and maybe The Archies in the background. But it's fucking great. Then I go, okay, I've got a lot of really good power pop songs. Now I gotta get some heavy songs in here too. It's like a stew."

Indeed, past this gorgeous gem of a song, or at least the hand-clapped Archies part of which Punky speaks—one of the most endearing passages on the record frankly—we're next into the most technical and progressive heavy metal song on the album. "Our Revolution" is smartly assembled and bitingly performed, with Billy driving the thing home—note his rhythms under the solo section. In any event, "Our Revolution" adds to the panoramic variety across *Risen…* so much style, so much substance.

Notes Charlie, a big part of this one despite its heft, "Personally, I like 'Our Revolution.' I thought it was heavier for Angel, but I think when the chorus kicks in, I love the keyboard melody on that, and I love what Frank did with it. And I really like the rocking-ness of it."

Then at three snaps of Billy's snare drum and some arch-garage rock guitar tones, we're immersed in the '60s pop of "Tell Me Why," where Angel channel The Kinks, The Shondells and The Small Faces en route to Piper, Billy Squier solo and Cheap Trick.

"On the flipside, I thought 'Tell Me Why' was a cool bubblegum poppy kind of tune that came out great," says Charlie, appreciative of the versatility of the band. But again, this is Punky's domain, with Meadows remarking that "'Tell Me Why' is just total pure pop bliss. It's Beatles, but it's a power pop song. And actually that song got voted No.3 on one of the big websites looking at the Top 200 songs of 2019. When I was growing up, it was all about the early Beatles stuff like 'All My Loving.' Those guys had diminished chords and stuff in those songs and I couldn't figure out how to finger it. I used to think that stuff sounded so simple, but you have no idea. It's what I call sophisticated simplicity. You have no idea how hard it is to write a song like that."

"'Tell Me Why' is a song about lying and cheating, right?" continues Meadows. "Yet the song sounds really up and poppy. It's a funny thing. My inspiration for that song was 'Tell Me Why' by the Beatles. 'Tell me why you cried and why you lied to me.' And John Lennon goes, "I gave you everything I had.' To me that song sound uplifting, but it's about lying and cheating. I thought that was fucking cool. It has a really poppy positive kind of major-y feel. I don't know why that is. That's in a lot of rock songs though, when you really get down to it. Even from the '50s and '60s, they're all about a bluesy hard time. Listen to The Animals: 'In this dirty old part of the city, where the sun refused to shine.' And they have kind of sad titles. There's an old saying: the reason you sing the blues is to get rid of the blues. The guy sings about how this girl broke his heart, and then he says, 'But if you won't love me, your sister Regina will' (laughs). A lot of rock songs are written as sad commentary. Fleetwood Mac: basically that's all about broken hearts, jealousy and cheating, yet they sound uplifting. And that's all over this *Risen* album and why I like it so much."

"Don't Want You to Go" is the second of a trio of songs late in the sequence that is pure pop confection, classic late '70s Angel crossed with Queen but mostly a deep understanding of '60s pop and into the likes of The Raspberries and Big Star. On top of the exacting hard pop playing, Frank puts on a vocal clinic for the ages, oddly not showing his age but somehow not sounding particularly like young Frank either. Maybe it's his phrasing, the articulation or the efficiency of the amount of air he's pushing now (being essentially a professor of the voice at this point), but it's sounding like a Frank renewed on top of music that sounds modern as well, certainly with respect to production values.

Then we're onto the third of this almost conceptual pop suite at the end of *Risen*. "Stand Up" is more of the same plush and lush pop sweetness, a little bit Cars, a little bit The Knack, but arranged like hair metal. Says Punky, "That could be a hit single. Heavy rock stations or the power pop stations, every song on that album… unfortunately, like Danny says, there's so many songs on the album, a lot of the songs get lost in the end. Because there's some great songs like 'Stand Up;' that's a beautiful song. It's a song about not letting people put you down, people that are bullied. Don't let people bully you. And yes, it's another super-melodic one."

Adds Charlie, "'Stand Up' definitely had a *Sinful* vibe to it. I like the way the keyboards came out on that; pretty much everything we tracked for that song was used in the final mixes."

Risen closes with "My Sanctuary," a curious number mostly heavy metal but somewhat proggy. First thing that comes to mind—and then spreads to the consideration of so many other tracks on the album—is Charlie's comment about the dearth of keyboards on the album, or alternately, the way they are used. With this song, they are somewhat incidental, and what really stands out is the near clinical hair metal production and arrangement of the thing. In other words, missing in terms of *Risen* really sounding like vintage Angel is that analog blend between guitars and keys, and indeed, reverb, echo and bottom end on the drums.

In any event, the album *really* closes (a long time after it began) with a new recording of "The Tower," kind of neither here nor there, sort of underscoring the idea that this record has been afforded all the digital efficiency of the modern era. Says Charlie, "I personally think we did a really good job on the remake, or the recording, of 'The Tower.' We kept it true to the original, but we added a little bit of stuff, a flair, kind of how we'd been doing it in the live set, with a different perspective. The keyboard solo's a bit different, but I think all of the main elements of Gregg's parts are there. I think the album is a great representation of Angel overall. It covers elements from the first album, all the way through *Sinful*. There's a lot of songs on it. We kind of tried to cover all eras of the band."

It's a good point Charlie makes. To a man (in white), the guys now seem kind of shocked how many songs are on the album. But what Charlie implies, it kind of took that many to cover all these facets of the band, and literally "cover" as well, addressing the "Angel Theme" again plus reimagining "The Tower." In this writer's opinion, the heavy stuff is too removed from the heavy persona of the original band, but the pleasant surprise is how brave and fresh the pop stuff sounds. It's like the guys, no doubt led by the personal force of nature that is Punky Meadows in his 70s, have further and fantastically validated the risky directions of *White Hot* and *Sinful*. That tranche of songs at the end of the record—"Tell Me Why," "Don't Want You to Go," "Stand Up"—no reformed band of rockers would dare to do something like that, and no one could pull it off with such skill and grace as Angel does right here.

"They should have broke big, but I think they didn't stick around long enough," continues Charlie, reflecting on the legacy of this band of which he was now integral. "I believe that if they didn't break up, they would've made it towards '81, '82; they would've exploded. They were vying for the MTV generation. It's an interesting band. You go out and tour and it's cool, because these people show up. There are these diehard fans. But the problem is, Angel never had that song on the radio that was like Blue Öyster Cult, where you're always going to hear '(Don't Fear) The Reaper.' With Foghat, you're gonna hear 'Slow Ride.' Even a band like Head East, you're gonna hear their tune. All those bands had that one song that made it to the radio and Angel never had that. And I thought they had the tunes. I thought 'Don't Leave Me Lonely' would've been a great radio hit back when the record came out, and it never happened for them. Although if it had happened, I never would've got hired (laughs)."

Adds Punky, in summary with respect to the album, "My guitar sounds better than ever and also my playing has changed a lot too. The songwriting is great and Frank did a great job—the guys killed it. But yes, there's a lot of songs on that album. It's funny because we were talking about the next album and were saying we should probably only have 12 songs at the most. But I've already written a bunch. So has Danny and Frank and we have thrown things around together too. So our next album's probably going to be a double album too because it's hard to throw things out. I have a surprise for the next album that's going to be really cool. I want to do a cover tune but it's not a rock song. I'm going to talk the guys into it."

Raising the stakes, Punky swears that, "In fact, when I work out, the only albums I listen to are *Risen* and my solo album, not because it's me but because I fucking love the albums! They're so much fun to listen to. My guitar sounds crazy. I get chills every time I hear a song. So when I'm out in my workout room, I blast that fucking thing on my stereo and I pump the weights like crazy. But I have to say that these guys who love the early Angel stuff, like Danny, they did open my eyes and ears up to those records. I do hear it now and I'm a lot more affectionate about it. I can hear why people like it, even though maybe I wasn't as crazy about it."

"But I read an article where Ritchie Blackmore said the same thing. He said that when he would do a Deep Purple album, he would never listen to it again because he was never happy with his performance. And that's Ritchie

Blackmore! He was sounding great; everybody loves him. So I guess that's just the way guitarists are. Unless you have your total freedom to do it the way you want, I think a lot of times you're kind of displeased with the whole thing. But if you go back with open ears and an open mind and listen to what your fans are saying about it, then you kind of can see the light of day."

"But *Risen* is an Angel record of today," continues Meadows. "It sounds great, it's a great album, but the songwriting is diversified because I never saw Angel as a one-trick pony. A lot of bands, with the first song, you've heard pretty much the whole album, like AC/DC, although I love AC/DC. From our first album, which was very proggy, with 'The Tower' and *Helluva Band* with 'The Fortune' and those kinds of songs, it was a sign of the times. With *On Earth* we became a little more commercial sounding and the songs weren't as progressive. That was a sign of the times too. Angel was always growing and I was always growing as a songwriter too. I grew up playing in bar bands where I would be in one club for three years straight as a house band and we would play everything. I've never been the kind of guy who just liked one type of music, and you hear that on *Risen*."

Agrees Frank, "With Angel, we started out as a progressive band, but we have always had melodies and we always worked hard on melodies. The progressive stuff to the pop, the heavy pop stuff, even to the hard stuff, there was always a lot of melody going on. So that was a tradition that we kept going on this last album."

Then, January into February of 2020, the coronavirus pandemic hit. Wide swaths of human endeavour were barely affected, other industries went through temporary and partial shutdowns. But rock 'n' roll? Packing people into sweaty clubs was at the very top of the list of things that seemed suicidal. The concert industry was annihilated.

"Unfortunately, 2020 would've been the big *Risen* tour," says Charlie. "We were scheduled for Japan, come back to North America, then do the UK and Australia and Europe. And all that got cancelled. We were doing some West Coast shows, you know, the Angel tour in 2019 before the record came out, and we were playing stuff from the back catalogue, but I think we started introducing stuff from the new record when we played Vegas and Los Angeles. Then we came back and did a couple shows in the Northeast. We had the whole 2020 thing planned out, but the only thing we got to do was the Rock Legends Cruise. We literally just got back right before everything hit and then everything was cancelled. Now we're looking maybe at 2021, and we're probably going to do a new record before we even get a chance to go back out and tour again."

Despite the business known as Angel having 90% of their identity taken away from them through the death of live performance, believe it or not, there's optimism.

"We have new management now," explains Punky, eternally hopeful. "Ron Rainey Management is big. We just did that Rock Legends Cruise back in February with all those big bands, UFO and stuff, and I ran into Ron Rainey. He used to manage Gregg and I for a very short period of time out in LA. And we were out on the boat and he goes, 'Punky, it's me, Ron Rainey.' And I go, 'Ron, how are you doing?' I said, 'Hey man, you thought of doing management?' And he goes, 'Well, no, but, you know, I might be interested.' So we talked and he came to all three of our shows we played and he was blown away. I gotta say, we blew everybody away on that fucking cruise. People walked away talking about Angel more than anybody else. Angel was always like that. When we get on stage, we just knock the dick in the dirt, you know? That's what we do."

"But Ron really dug it. He signed us up and it turns out Ron owns a booking agency. He has the live side, he owns that booking and he owns the Rock Cruise thing and he has his own record company. So he's big. So now we have a big agency behind this too. So we're going to be big, or at least one of the bigger and better things. But in the meantime, what he's done is he's trademarked our logos for us finally. So we own the upside-down logo; Frank and I own that, and Danny, we have three of us, we have a partnership. And he got the partnership together for us too. So even though we can't play, there's a lot of things going on behind the scenes here. So he's got our trademark, both with the logo with the angel wings and the face and also the upside-down logo. He's got the partnership and we have a new bank account and stuff. The new booking agent is going to get us a lot more shows and stuff worldwide. Things are clicking in the background. Plus he just put up a new merch store which is going pretty well."

And as Punky alluded to, it's full steam ahead on a second reunion album. "It's funny, people always say, 'Is this a good song for Angel?' And I always say, 'I never wrote a song for Angel.' I wrote a song because it's something I wrote. I gave it to Angel and I thought Angel would record it. Well, when Frank sings it and I play my guitar and the rest of the band is there, it's going to sound like Angel no matter what. You know, all

my guitar parts on *Risen* I did in probably three days, because once I get in the studio, I get so into it and so inspired and have so much fun that I just have a blast. And Danny is really my biggest fan. I gotta tell you. When I get in there and start playing my guitar, I'll play a solo and I'll stop and he goes, 'Why did you fucking stop?' I say, because I'm like, I can do it better. He goes, 'Dude, that was fucking great. Don't stop next time!' But because I'm thinking I can do it better, I stop and start again. But then he plays it back and I'll say, 'Well, that does sound pretty cool, actually, now that you say it.' So yeah, I can't wait to get started on the next album."

"Less songs is one thing that has been talked about," chuckles Charlie. "For two reasons: obviously Angel hasn't put out a record in so many years, and 17 songs is a lot to digest. But fans have been waiting 35 years. Let's get them a double album. But I think some of the feedback that we've gotten, not that the songs are bad, but it may have been a stronger album if we saved some for the next one. So I think it will be a shorter record. Then again I can't say that, because when these guys start writing, there's so many songs flying around. I haven't heard anything yet. I know Danny and Billy just got together the other night to start working on some drum patterns for a couple of new tunes."

"You know, from my perspective, *Risen* was done kind of quick. We kind of got the deal, people have been waiting 35 years, and all of a sudden we're trying to get everything done in a short time period and I think the album suffered a little bit. So I think this time around we should just spend some more time on it and kind of let everyone do their thing, bring their contribution to the table. I know Punky and Frank and Danny have their vision, and Punky is really into producing these records. He really has vision, when he comes in, for the overall song. I'm talking keyboard parts and drums and all that. Which is cool. He's got a lot of great ideas and he's a wonderful person to work with. Because when he writes the song, it's not, 'Hey, I got some chords.' He really has the whole thing in his head, the melody line, some of the lyrics, keyboard parts, bass parts, drum parts. And I figure everyone's a bit more comfortable now, so I think everybody will have a bit more ability to add a bit of their individual style to the next record."

"I don't think we have to worry about changes—I think we just write," reflects the wise man at the microphone, the Heaven-sent voice of Angel since the beginning, Frank DiMino. "It's the approach I took with the solo album as well. We just start writing and see where it takes us. I don't think there's any kind of philosophy that we're following, other than adherence to melody and our heavy tradition, although not really heavy metal. I don't know, Martin, we'll just keep moving forward. I try not to think about why things didn't turn out the first time. It's hard to figure that stuff out. We just went ahead and did what we were doing. We wrote and recorded and didn't pay attention to that stuff. You kind of think that the rest will take care of itself. But it doesn't always work out that way and I don't know why. People who listened to the band and knew the band liked the songs, liked the material, and if you went to see us live, we were a tight band with a pretty high-energy show. But now, as long as that feeling is there, and everything's positive and you feel good about going out with the guys that you're playing with… I mean, I feel great going out with these guys. I don't feel like, 'Oh, this guy's gonna do this tonight or that.' There's just none of that. And at this stage of our lives, that's pretty important because there's not that much time left (laughs). Those things that weren't that important back then are really important to us now."

Discography

A few points on format, I've included a notes section for anything I thought was interesting that needed to be said about the record at hand, such as personnel changes. Singles I've kept simple, theming it toward the home territory of the US. Compilations, no song timings for sake of reducing redundancy.

What else? Quote marks around songs only in Notes section. Spelling and punctuation of song titles, plus timings and order of the names in the credits as per actual release, US issue as priority. I've noted side 1/side 2 designations for all releases from the LP age, which basically ends in 1990, when the CD age is ushered in for real. Credits on live albums and compilations added only for songs not previously credited.

A. Official Studio and Live Albums

Angel

October 27, 1975; Casablanca, NBLP 7021

Produced by Derek Lawrence and Big Jim Sullivan

Side 1: 1. The Tower (Giuffria, Meadows, DiMino) 6:52; 2. Long Time (Giuffria, Meadows, DiMino) 7:00; 3. Rock & Rollers (Giuffria, Meadows, DiMino) 3:57

Side 2: 1. Broken Dreams (Meadows, DiMino) 5:13; 2. Mariner (Giuffria, DiMino, Lawrence, Sullivan) 4:19; 3. Sunday Morning (Giuffria, DiMino) 4:15; 4. On & On (Giuffria, DiMino, Meadows, Jones) 4:22; 5. Angel (Theme) (Giuffria, Brandt) 1:38

Notes: Initial Angel lineup: Frank DiMino – vocals; Punky Meadows – guitars; Gregg Giuffria – keyboards; Mickie Jones – bass and Barry Brandt – drums. Black-and-white inner sleeve. Definitive reissue is on Rock Candy from 2012, which features liner notes by Dave Reynolds and 24 BIT audio remastering (albeit no bonus tracks).

Helluva Band

July 1976. Casablanca, NBLP 7028

Produced by Derek Lawrence and Big Jim Sullivan

Side 1: 1. Feelin' Right (Giuffria, Meadows, DiMino) 4:41; 2. The Fortune (Giuffria, Meadows, DiMino) 8:37; 3. Anyway You Want It (Meadows, DiMino) 2:42; 4. Dr. Ice (Giuffria, Meadows, DiMino, Lawrence, Sullivan) 5:15

Side 2: 1. Mirrors (Giuffria, Meadows, DiMino) 4:24; 2. Feelings (Giuffria, Meadows, DiMino) 5:40; 3. Pressure Point (Meadows, DiMino, Jones, Brandt) 5:22; 4. Chicken Soup (Giuffria, Meadows, DiMino) 4:43; 5. Angel Theme (Giuffria, Brandt) 3:30

Notes: Definitive reissue is on Rock Candy from 2012, which features liner notes by Dave Reynolds and 24 BIT audio remastering (albeit no bonus tracks).

On Earth as It Is in Heaven

March 1977, Casablanca, NBLP 7043

Produced by Eddie Kramer

Side 1: 1. Can You Feel It (Meadows, Giuffria, DiMino) 4:41; 2. She's a Mover (Meadows, Giuffria, DiMino) 3:37; 3. Big Boy (Let's Do It Again) (Meadows, Giuffria, DiMino) 3:54; 4. Telephone Exchange (Meadows, Giuffria, DiMino) 4:13; 5. White Lightning (Meadows, Morman) 4:45

Side 2: 1. On the Rocks (Meadows, Giuffria, DiMino) 3:39; 2. You're Not Fooling Me (Meadows, Giuffria, DiMino) 3:59; 3. That Magic Touch (Meadows, Giuffria, DiMino) 3:29; 4. Cast the First Stone (Meadows, Giuffria, DiMino) 4:37; 5. Just a Dream (Meadows, Giuffria, DiMino) 5:16

Notes: Includes two-panel colour poster. Definitive reissue is on Rock Candy from 2012, which features liner notes by Dave Reynolds, 24 BIT audio remastering and use of the clearer, punchier Japanese mix (albeit no bonus tracks).

White Hot

January 3, 1978, Casablanca, NBLP 7085

Produced by Eddie Leonetti

Side 1: 1. Don't Leave Me Lonely (Brandt, DiMino) 3:56; 2. Ain't Gonna Eat Out My Heart Anymore (Sawyer, Burton) 2:44; 3. Hold Me, Squeeze Me (Meadows, Giuffria, DiMino) 3:48; 4. Over and Over (Meadows, Giuffria, DiMino) 3:59; 5. Under Suspicion (Meadows, Giuffria, DiMino, Robinson, Brandt) 4:40

Side 2: 1. Got Love if You Want It (Meadows, Giuffria, DiMino) 4:23; 2. Stick Like Glue (Meadows, Giuffria, DiMino) 2:38; 3. Flying with Broken Wings (Without You) (Meadows, Giuffria, DiMino) 3:32; 4. You Could Lose Me (Meadows, Giuffria, DiMino) 4:56; 5. The Winter Song (Meadows, Giuffria, DiMino) 3:46

Notes: Felix Robinson replaces Mickie Jones on bass. Includes colour inner sleeve. Definitive reissue is on Rock Candy from 2012, which features liner notes by Dave Reynolds, 24 BIT audio remastering and two bonus tracks, "Better Days" (Meadows, Giuffria, DiMino) and "The Winter Song" variant "The Christmas Song" (Meadows, Giuffria, DiMino).

Sinful

January 1979, Casablanca, NBLP 7127

Produced by Eddie Leonetti

Side 1: 1. Don't Take Your Love (Giuffria, DiMino) 3:31; 2. L.A. Lady (Meadows) 3:47; 3. Just Can't Take It (Meadows, DiMino) 3:43; 4. You Can't Buy Love (Brandt, DiMino) 3:37; 5. Bad Time (Giuffria, DiMino) 3:41

Side 2: 1. Waited a Long Time (Brandt, DiMino) 3:31; 2. I'll Bring the Whole World to Your Door (Meadows, DiMino, Leonetti) 2:52; 3. I'll Never Fall in Love Again (Giuffria) 3:34; 4. Wild and Hot (Meadows) 2:57; 5. Lovers Live On (Meadows, Robinson) 2:57

Notes: Includes colour inner sleeve with lyrics. Definitive issue is the digitally remastered CD from 2013 featuring liner notes by Neil Daniels (albeit no bonus tracks).

Live Without a Net

February 1980, Casablanca, NBLP-2-7203

Produced by Eddie Leonetti

Side 1: 1. The Tower 4:58; 2. Can You Feel It 4:10; 3. Don't Leave Me Only 3:55; 4. Telephone Exchange 4:20; 5. Ain't Gonna Eat Out My Heart Anymore 3:08

Side 2: 1. Over and Over 4:07; 2. Anyway You Want It 3:28; 3. On the Rocks 9:12; 4. Wild and Hot 2:44

Side 3: 1. All the Young Dudes (Bowie) 4:10; 2. Rock & Rollers 8:15; 3. White Lightning 8:35

Side 4: 1. Hold Me, Squeeze Me 3:40; 2. Got Love if You Want It 3:28; 3. Feelin' Right 6:05; 4. 20th Century Foxes (Giuffria, DiMino) 4:25

Notes: Double live album in gatefold sleeve. Generic Casablanca inner sleeves. Three slight differences from the studio albums with respect to song titling. Definitive reissue is the digitally remastered double CD from 2006 featuring liner notes by Alan Robinson.

In the Beginning

1999, Coallier Entertainment, no catalogue number

Produced by Frank DiMino, Barry Brandt, Richard Marcello

1. The Crow (Marcello, Brandt, DiMino) 4:52; 2. The RainSong (Marcello, Brandt, DiMino) 4:49; 3. Hero (Richards, Brandt, DiMino) 4:06; 4. So I'll Say Goodbye (Marcello, Brandt, DiMino) 5:51; 5. Long Gone (Marcello, Brandt, DiMino) 3:42; 6. In the Wake of the Storm (The Millennium Y2K) (Marcello, Brandt, DiMino) 4:45; 7. Set Me Free (DiMino) 4:33; 8. The Greatest Love of All (Marcello, Brandt, DiMino) 5:16; 9. Shangra La (Marcello, Brandt, DiMino) 4:16; 10. Trapped in Paradise (Marcello, Brandt, DiMino) 4:43

Notes: Core band lineup: Frank DiMino – vocals; Richard Marcello – guitars, keyboards; Leo Borrero – bass and Barry Brandt – drums. Bass on "The Crow" Felix Robinson. Guitars on "Hero" David DellaRosa and Punky Meadows. Bass on "Long Gone" Felix Robinson and keyboards on "Long Gone" Danny Peyronnel. Bass on "In the Wake of the Storm (The Millennium Y2K)" Felix Robinson. Guitars on "Set Me Free" Punky Meadows and bass on "Set Me Free" Felix Robinson.

Risen

October 4, 2019, Cleopatra, CLO1494

Produced by Punky Meadows, Danny Farrow

1. Angel Theme (Prelude) (Giuffria, Brandt) 0:32; 2. Under the Gun 3:18; 3. Shot of Your Love 3:03; 4. Slow Down 5:42; 5. Over My Head 4:20; 6. 1975 (intro by Calv) 7:08; 7. We Were the Wild 4:27; 8. I.O.U. 4:51; 9. (Punky's Couch Blues) Locked, Cocked and Ready to Rock 5:17; 10. Turn Around 4:55; 11. Desire 5:19; 12. Our Revolution 4:18; 13. Tell Me Why 3:22; 14. Don't Want You to Go 3:43; 15. Stand Up 4:05; 16. My Sanctuary 3:08; 17. Tower (Re-Recorded) (Giuffria, Meadows, DiMino) 7:06

Notes: Band lineup: Frank DiMino – vocals; Punky Meadows – guitars; Danny Farrow – guitars; Charlie Calv – keyboards; Steve E. Ojane – bass; Billy Orrico – drums. All songs written by Meadows, DiMino, Farrow unless otherwise specified above.

B. Selected Compilations

The Anthology

Notes: 20-track compilation issued by Casablanca in 1992, includes liner notes by Kerrang!'s Dave Reynolds, plus, for rarities, "The Christmas Song," as well as the band's non-LP cover of Left Banke's "Walk Away Renee" (Brown, Calilli, Sansone) and "20th Century Foxes" (DiMino, Giuffria).

The Collection

Notes: Official UK compilation issued by Connoisseur Collection/Universal in 2000 featuring 13 tracks.

The Casablanca Years

Notes: 2018 box set issued by Caroline International/Universal that includes all the albums of the original run plus a disc of rarities, consisting mostly of mono mixes and single edits, but all the known non-LP tracks, including the songs from *The Anthology* as well as "Better Days."

C. Selected Singles

"Rock & Rollers"/"Mariner"

"That Magic Touch"/"Big Boy (Let's Do It Again)" "Don't Leave Me Lonely"/"Stick Like Glue"

"The Winter Song"/"Can You Feel It"

"Flying with Broken Wings (Without You)"/"Under Suspicion"

"Don't Take Your Love"/"Bad Time"

"20th Century Foxes"/"Can You Feel It (live)"

D. Selected Solo Projects and Miscellaneous (in chronological order)

Angel - *Radio Concert*

Notes: Double LP promo-only sampler album, issued by Casablanca in 1978. Despite the title, this features 13 tracks culled from Angel's four studio albums as of 1978, in order: "The Tower," "Can You Feel It," "On the Rocks," "Don't Leave Me Lonely," "Telephone Exchange," "Over and Over," "Hold Me, Squeeze Me," "Got Love if You Want It," "Ain't Gonna Eat Out My Heart Anymore," "Anyway You Want It," "Rock & Rollers," "Feelin' Right" and "White Lightning."

Foxes

Notes: Double LP soundtrack album issued February 1980 by Casablanca. Includes two non-LP Angel songs, "20th Century Foxes" (DiMino, Giuffria) and Virginia" (Meadows).

Giuffria - *Giuffria*

Notes: Debut album issued in 1984 on MCA. Band named after Gregg Giuffria, who provides keyboards and backing vocals and co-writes every song with lead vocalist David Glen Eisley (guitarist Craig Goldy is also credited on three tracks). That band is rounded out by Chuck Wright on bass and Alan Krigger on drums. Production is by Andy Johns, Gregg and Angel connection Lee DeCarlo, acting as associate producer.

Giuffria – *Silk + Steel*

Notes: Second and last Giuffria album, issued in May 1986 on MCA. Craig Goldy has been replaced by Lanny Cordola on guitar and Chuck Wright has been replaced by David Sikes on bass. Except for the Mink DeVille cover, Gregg is listed as co-writer on every track, along with David Glen Eisley. Guitarist Lanny Cordola co-writes on two songs. Production is by Pat Glasser, Gregg and David Glen Eisley.

DiMino – *Old Habits Die Hard*

Notes: Frank's 11-track solo album from July 3rd, 2015, issued on Frontiers. Production is by Paul Crook. DiMino works with a number of guest stars, including John Micelli, Danny Miranda, Justin Avery, Oz Fox, Jeff Labansky, Eddie Ojeda, Rickey Medlocke, Pat Thrall, Jeff Duncan, Punky Meadows and Barry Brandt.

Punky Meadows – *Fallen Angel*

Notes: Punky's 15-track solo album from May 20th, 2016, issued on Main Man Records. Production is by Punky Meadows and Danny Farrow Anniello. Band lineup is: Chandler Mogel – vocals; Punky Meadows – guitars; Danny Farrow – guitars; Charlie Calv – keyboards; Felix Robinson – bass and Bob Pantella – drums.

Interviews with the Author

Aucoin, Bill. July 10, 2000.

Calv, Charlie. September 11, 2020.

DiMino, Frank. April 28, 2000.

DiMino, Frank. September 13, 2007.

DiMino, Frank. February 19, 2016.

DiMino, Frank. September 18, 2020.

Frehley, Ace. September 4, 2020.

Harris, Larry. 2009.

Hill, Bob. May 7, 2008.

Jones, Mickie. January 17, 2008.

Krebs, David. November 28, 2012.

Lawrence, Derek. 2010.

Meadows, Punky. March 16, 2016.

Meadows, Punky. September 14, 2020.

Moore, Eric. July 21, 1999.

Prince, Michael. July 11, 2000.

Robinson, Felix. August 16, 2020.

Romeo, Roger. August 25, 2007.

Additional Citations

American Music Press. Angel: The Heavenly Band with Down-to-Earth Problems by Devorah Ostrov and Billy Rowe. 1993.
Billboard. Helluva Band record review. June 5, 1976.
Billboard. Angel/Piper concert review by Roman Kozak. July 2, 1977.
Billboard. White Hot record review. January 21, 1978.
Casablanca Records. White Hot record bio. 1978.
Casablanca Records. Sinful record bio. 1978.
Circus. Angel—Hard Rock Messengers by Jeff Burger. Issue No.129. March 23, 1976.
Circus. Earth Angels by Michael Gross. Issue No.152. March 31, 1977.
Circus. The Balloon that Never Broke by Kris Nicholson. Issue No.153. April 14, 1977.
Circus. Angel's Earthly Roots by Max Thaler. Issue No.179. April 13, 1978.
Circus. White Hot record review by John Swenson. Issue No.179. April 13, 1978.
Circus. All This and Heaven Too by Daisann McLane. Issue No.184. June 22, 1978.
Classic Rock. Down to Earth: How Angel Fell from Grace by Ken Sharp. October 27, 2016.

Creem. Angel: More Sheep in Godzilla's Clothing? by Air-Wreck Genheimer. March, 1977.

Dunn, Sam. Interview with Larry Harris. 2009.

Green Bay Press-Gazette. Rocking Angel Has 'em Smokin' by Warren Gerds. March 16, 1977.

Hit Parader. Angel: the props don't interfere by Deane Zimmerman. No.164. March 1978.

Hit Parader Annual. On the Wings of a Pure White Angel by Richard Robinson. Winter 1977-78.

Kerrang!. Hungry for Heaven by Dave Reynolds.

Kingsport Times-News. Angel concert promises solid rock show by Mike Clark. July 31, 1976.

Kingsport Times-News. Keyboardist for Angel glad to be back in South by Bill Gupton. April 15, 1978

Legendary Rock Interviews. ANGEL bassist Felix Robinson gives an extremely in-depth interview on his days in the band and beyond by John Parks. August 10, 2011.

Legendary Rock Interviews. ANGEL Vocalist Frank DiMino talks NEW reissues, reunion possibilities and new business by John Parks. September 24, 2012.

Los Angeles Times, The. Angel—Paint the Group White by Dennis Hunt. April 30, 1978.

Los Angeles Times, The. Giuffria: An Ex-Angel's Band on a Rapid Ascent by Katherine Turman. January 30, 1985.

Morning Call, The. Hard rock pleases 4000 as summer series opens by Jonna Bartges. July 2, 1976.

Record Mirror. White Hot record review by Robin Smith. March 18, 1978.

Record Mirror. Live Without a Net record review by Malcolm Dome. March 1, 1980.

Record World. Angel record review. November 29, 1975.

Record World. On Earth as It Is in Heaven record review. March 5, 1977.

Rock. Angel: Climbing Toward Heaven by Timothy Green Beckley. September 1977.

Rock. Angel: Climbing Toward Heaven by Timothy Green Beckley. September 1977.

San Antonio Express. It pays to be pretty by Ben King Jr. May 15, 1977.

St. Louis Post-Dispatch. Angel Performs at Fox Theater by John S. Cullinane. July 23, 1976.

St. Louis Post-Dispatch. Eddie Money Band, Angel at Kiel Auditorium by John S. Cullinane. March 23, 1979.

St. Louis Post-Dispatch. Instruments Stolen from Rock Group. July 26, 1976.

Tucson Citizen. Styx predictable and deadly dull, but Angel soars by Chuck Graham. February 15, 1979.

Acknowledgements

The author would like to acknowledge Alexandre Hebert for his dedicated fandom and kind patronage in helping make this book a reality.

Huge Angel fan for many years, Alex's favourite song from the band is "The Fortune," which he calls: "a true mark of excellence from the consummate traffickers of epic pomp, an opulent, stately saga of grandeur and majesty intertwined with a sombre, haunting, "chanson-de-geste' allegory, a chilling classical dirge laden with hauteur and disdainful arrogance from an aristocrat in the midst of the French revolution, noblesse oblige in the face of tragic destiny, stark genius in both Gothic form and feudal nature, a crown jewel from the progressive rock magnum opus, a solitary exemplar of towering and magnificent art for the ages."

As well, I've named this book *The Fortune: On the Rocks with Angel* in Alex's honour.

Also I'd like to thank my buddy Kevin Julie for his fine research work concerning the Angel press archive. The graphic design and layout of this book is by Eduardo Rodriguez, who can be reached at eduardobwbk@gmail.com. Pleasure working with the guy—he's done about 50 for me now. As well, special thanks to Agustin Garcia de Paredes who applied his eagle eye to a copy edit of this thing.

About the Author

At approximately 7900 (with over 7000 appearing in his books), Martin has unofficially written more record reviews than anybody in the history of music writing across all genres. Additionally, Martin has penned approximately 90 books on hard rock, heavy metal, classic rock and record collecting. He was Editor-In-Chief of the now retired
Brave Words & Bloody Knuckles, Canada's foremost metal publication for 14 years, and has also contributed to Revolver, Guitar World, Goldmine, Record Collector, bravewords.com, lollipop.com and hardradio.com, with many record label band bios and liner notes to his credit as well.
Additionally, Martin has been a regular contractor to Banger Films, having worked for two years as researcher on the award-winning documentary *Rush: Beyond the Lighted Stage*, on the writing and research team for the 11-episode Metal Evolution
and on the ten-episode Rock Icons, both for VH1 Classic. Additionally, Martin is the writer of the original metal genre chart used in *Metal: A Headbanger's Journey* and throughout the Metal Evolution episodes. Martin currently resides in Toronto and can be reached through martinp@inforamp.net or www.martinpopoff.com.

Martin Popoff – A Complete Bibliography

2020: The Fortune: On the Rocks with Angel, Van Halen: A Visual Biography, Limelight: Rush in the '80s, Thin Lizzy: A Visual Biography, Empire of the Clouds: Iron Maiden in the 2000s, Blue Öyster Cult: A Visual Biography, Anthem: Rush in the '70s, Denim and Leather: Saxon's First Ten Years, Black Funeral: Into the Coven with Mercyful Fate.

2019: Satisfaction: 10 Albums That Changed My Life, Holy Smoke: Iron Maiden in the '90s, Sensitive to Light: The Rainbow Story, Where Eagles Dare: Iron Maiden in the '80s, Aces High: The Top 250 Heavy Metal Songs of the '80s, Judas Priest: Turbo 'til Now, Born Again! Black Sabbath in the Eighties and Nineties.

2018: Riff Raff: The Top 250 Heavy Metal Songs of the '70s, Lettin' Go: UFO in the '80s and '90s, Queen: Album by Album, Unchained: A Van Halen User Manual, Iron Maiden: Album by Album, Sabotage! Black Sabbath in the Seventies, Welcome to My Nightmare: 50 Years of Alice Cooper, Judas Priest: Decade of Domination, Popoff Archive – 6: American Power Metal, Popoff Archive – 5: European Power Metal, The Clash: All the Albums, All the Songs.

2017: Led Zeppelin: All the Albums, All the Songs, AC/DC: Album by Album, Lights Out: Surviving the '70s with UFO, Tornado of Souls: Thrash's Titanic Clash, Caught in a Mosh: The Golden Era of Thrash, Rush: Album by Album, Beer Drinkers and Hell Raisers: The Rise of Motörhead, Metal Collector: Gathered Tales from Headbangers, Hit the Lights: The Birth of Thrash, Popoff Archive – 4: Classic Rock, Popoff Archive – 3: Hair Metal.

2016: Popoff Archive – 2: Progressive Rock, Popoff Archive - 1: Doom Metal, Rock the Nation: Montrose, Gamma and Ronnie Redefined, Punk Tees: The Punk Revolution in 125 T-Shirts, Metal Heart: Aiming High with Accept, Ramones at 40, Time and a Word: The Yes Story.

2015: Kickstart My Heart: A Mötley Crüe Day-by-Day, This Means War: The Sunset Years of the NWOBHM, Wheels of Steel: The Explosive Early Years of the NWOBHM, Swords and Tequila: Riot's Classic First Decade, Who Invented Heavy Metal?, Sail Away: Whitesnake's Fantastic Voyage.

2014: Live Magnetic Air: The Unlikely Saga of the Superlative Max Webster, Steal Away the Night: An Ozzy Osbourne Day-by-Day, The Big Book of Hair Metal, Sweating Bullets: The Deth and Rebirth of Megadeth, Smokin' Valves: A Headbanger's Guide to 900 NWOBHM Records.

2013: The Art of Metal (co-edit with Malcolm Dome), 2 Minutes to Midnight: An Iron Maiden Day-by-Day, Metallica: The Complete Illustrated History, Rush: The Illustrated History, Ye Olde Metal: 1979, Scorpions: Top of the Bill - updated and reissued as Wind of Change: The Scorpions Story in 2016.

2012: Epic Ted Nugent, Fade To Black: Hard Rock Cover Art of the Vinyl Age, It's Getting Dangerous: Thin Lizzy 81-12, We Will Be Strong: Thin Lizzy 76-81, Fighting My Way Back: Thin Lizzy 69-76, The Deep Purple Royal Family: Chain of Events '80 – '11, The Deep Purple Royal Family: Chain of Events Through '79 - reissued as The Deep Purple Family Year by Year books.

2011: Black Sabbath FAQ, The Collector's Guide to Heavy Metal: Volume 4: The '00s (co-authored with David Perri).

2010: Goldmine Standard Catalog of American Records 1948 1991, 7th Edition.

2009: Goldmine Record Album Price Guide, 6th Edition, Goldmine 45 RPM Price Guide, 7th Edition, A Castle Full of Rascals: Deep Purple '83 – '09, Worlds Away: Voivod and the Art of Michel Langevin, Ye Olde Metal: 1978.

2008: Gettin' Tighter: Deep Purple '68 – '76, All Access: The Art of the Backstage Pass, Ye Olde Metal: 1977, Ye Olde Metal: 1976

2007: Judas Priest: Heavy Metal Painkillers, Ye Olde Metal: 1973 to 1975, The Collector's Guide to Heavy Metal: Volume 3: The Nineties, Ye Olde Metal: 1968 to 1972

2006: Run for Cover: The Art of Derek Riggs, Black Sabbath: Doom Let Loose, Dio: Light Beyond the Black

2005: The Collector's Guide to Heavy Metal: Volume 2: The Eighties, Rainbow: English Castle Magic, UFO: Shoot Out the Lights, The New Wave of British Heavy Metal Singles

2004: Blue Öyster Cult: Secrets Revealed! – update and reissue 2009); updated and reissued as Agents of Fortune: The Blue Öyster Cult Story 2016, Contents Under Pressure: 30 Years of Rush at Home & Away, The Top 500 Heavy Metal Albums of All Time

2003: The Collector's Guide to Heavy Metal: Volume 1: The Seventies, The Top 500 Heavy Metal Songs of All Time

2001: Southern Rock Review

2000: Heavy Metal: 20th Century Rock and Roll, The Goldmine Price Guide to Heavy Metal Records

1997: The Collector's Guide to Heavy Metal

1993: Riff Kills Man! 25 Years of Recorded Hard Rock & Heavy Metal

See martinpopoff.com for complete details and ordering information.

www.ingramcontent.com/pod-product-compliance
Lightning Source LLC
Chambersburg PA
CBHW051546030726
47592CB00001B/152